THE SOCIALIST ECONOMY

A Study of
Organizational Alternatives

Benjamin N. Ward

UNIVERSITY OF CALIFORNIA, BERKELEY

RANDOM HOUSE
New York

THE SOCIALIST ECONOMY

A Study of
Organizational Alternatives

Acknowledgments

Robert Blum, Howard Sherman and Stanley Wellisz read an earlier draft of the entire manuscript and each is responsible for substantial improvements in that document. Andrzej Brzeski, Gregory Grossman, Paul Ivory, Roy Radner and Oliver Williamson offered a number of helpful comments on various parts of the manuscript. Platforms for initial presentation of parts of the study were offered by the American Economic Review in September, 1958 (Chapter 8), the University of Chicago's economics seminar in November, 1962 (Chapter 5), and the Faculty Seminar on Communist Society, Berkeley, in October, 1965 (Chapter 7). The Institute of Business and Economic Research, Berkeley, and Mrs. Eileen Grampp of the Center for Slavic Studies, Berkeley, provided clerical and administrative assistance. To these individuals and organizations I offer sincere thanks—without in any way committing them to the final product.

Contents

Part 1

Introduction

CHAPTER ONE

Economic Comparison

The comparison of properties of whole societies taken as units has occupied a position in the social sciences rather like that of cosmology in the natural sciences. Though no one would deny that the questions asked in these fields are of deep interest, there is a strong feeling that answers cannot be found by scientific methodology. Until a better understanding of the relevant phenomena is available many would be willing to leave the one field in the hands of the philosophers, the other in the hands of utopian novelists.

One major objection to attempting broad comparisons of economic systems is that it requires a degree of oversimplification—particularly through aggregation of variables—that is excessive, so that one can have little confidence in the meaning and stability of any conclusions that may be derived. For example, one kind of aggregation is based on the assumption that social units are like "black boxes" whose internal complexities are ignored, and the unit is described in terms of observable relations between inputs and outputs. If one makes the black boxes too large, internal interactions may dominate any such observed relations so that the latter have no predictive or explanatory value.

This is true enough—but it may not be relevant. An instance of this kind of aggregation is the typical model of income theory in which each broad sector is treated as a black box. Many economists are prepared to work confidently with some of the results derived from such models, even though the boxes are very large. Parts of this theory are much better founded than, say, any parts of a theory of urban growth, even though the boxes in this case constitute a much smaller share of population or gross national product than do the sectors of most income models. The point is that a priori judgments about the stability of aggregates cannot be formed simply on the basis of their size, so there is no bar in principle to the use of broad aggregates in comparative economics.

A second objection to the comparison of economic systems is that the number of observations is sharply restricted and far less likely to be substantially increased over time than is the case in other fields. Partly this is a matter of the small number of large-scale social units in existence. If national economies are the units of study, the number of such units has probably never exceeded one hundred in this century, though there are rather more members of the United Nations. If industrial economies are the units, there are perhaps a third of that number today. And of course if one is interested in organizational comparisons the numbers falling under each rubric of the classification are even fewer. Partly the problem is that units classified under a single rubric differ strikingly among themselves. The historical conditions under which they acquired their present form may have altered the way in which organizations function, just as diffusion, interaction with neighbors, and internal dynamics may drastically alter the outputs of an organization. In empirical comparisons much of the information available must be "sacrificed" in the attempt to control these divergencies. Related to this is the fact that social structures do not stand still so as to permit long-run observation. Observations on the American economy of the nineteen-twenties and nineteen-thirties have already outlived their usefulness in estimating many properties of the current economy.

This problem, too, is not unique to comparative economics, though admittedly it is a factor reducing confidence in the validity of probably all comparative propositions. Whether one looks at the household, the enterprise, the industry, or the economic sector, the problems of unaccounted-for structural change and limited observation are likely to arise. But technological change and international differences are no respecters of unit size, nor are there apparent limits to the kinds of change that can occur. That is, the limitation on observations is a matter of degree rather than kind with respect to other economic problems. Whether or not the degree is excessive should be judged in the individual case.

Another objection stems from the unique structure of many societies, resulting from the particular mix of resources, technology, properties of the population, etc. An important question is: What will be the effects of each of several different forms of economic organization on this particular kind of society? The problem is that only one of these forms can be observed at a time; another can be observed only by dispensing with further observation of the first. This difficulty is especially likely to occur in comparative economics.

Again the problem is one of degree rather than kind. Our example has a structure similar to that of the uncertainty principle in physics and to that of the identification problem in econometrics. It does not imply that one can learn nothing about unobserved social states, or even that one can only learn a little.

None of these drawbacks is disabling, and against them may be placed a measure of the importance of the results. Piecemeal social engineering is not the only feasible engine of change. Thoroughgoing economic reorganization is the most spectacular instrument of economic control; it is widely advocated as an instrument and rather widely practiced. Therefore even a little information, if it can be used to prevent a few of the grossest errors, may be of very great value.[1]

Models of socialist economic organization are likely to play a role in understanding economic activity similar to that which the models of competition and monopoly have played. The usual level of abstraction at which such models are constructed generally precludes serious testing of the hypotheses which are formally generated by the models. Rather they serve as sensitizers, in that they make economists aware in some systematic way of the problems that alternative organizations are likely to face. Out of this awareness it may be possible to generate lower-level hypotheses with some empirical content.[2]

Most models of this kind, including those in the present study, have some sort of casual empirical referent. In a sense, they may be construed as observations because of this. But it is a very weak sense, perhaps no stronger than the sense in which observations of human behavior in laboratory situations are interpreted as observations of the "real" world of marketplace activity. Nonetheless they do serve this dual role, on the one hand generating hypotheses, and on the other serving as structural analogs, as models of the real world in the literal sense.

Defining Terms

"Socialism," "centralization," "external effects," and "institutional equilibrium" are defined here in a manner useful for present purposes and broadly consistent with much previous usage. These definitions are certainly not the best ones for all

---

[1] Studies in fields as speculative and uncertain as comparative economics may tend to be undervalued in the profession. For there is a kind of hierarchy among researchers in which the highest status tends to be accorded practitioners in fields whose results appear to be the most precise. Though there are good reasons for this—for example, that the more precise and developed fields make sterner demands on the technical competence of practitioners—this hierarchy does not necessarily reflect the relative social importance of the output of the fields.

[2] Such as the propositions relating performance to oligopoly structure developed by Joe S. Bain in his *Barriers to New Competition* (Cambridge: Harvard University Press, 1956).

other uses, but they are convenient here, and hopefully will serve to minimize ambiguity in later chapters.

"Socialism" or "socialist organization" implies two things: (1) social ownership of the means of production in industry and trade, and (2) state control of the rates and directions of economic change. The latter is probably the only property on which nearly all socialists could agree, but the concern in this study will be only with organizational forms that satisfy both requirements.

"Centralization" and "decentralization" are not quite so easily dealt with. Two more or less distinct notions are commonly implied by these terms. The first relates the degree of centralization to the range of choice of a participant. Thus an organization has become more decentralized, with respect to choice, if the range of alternatives open to subordinates has increased. The second notion relates the degree of centralization to authority, to the control which can be exercised over subordinates. Thus an organization has become more centralized, with respect to authority, if there is an increase in the range of alternatives the authorities can impose on subordinates.

These distinctions provide a basis for comparison in only a few cases. To take an example, the shift from branch to regional industrial control in the Soviet Union in 1957 may have increased centralization in both respects in many enterprises, in the sense that the regional authorities were able to maintain closer contact with the enterprises, thus restricting the admissible deviations from plan targets. On the other hand, decentralization may have increased in the sense that the regional authorities were often less informed on the specific problems of various industries so that enterprise managers had their feasible alternatives increased. On balance the managers' choice sets neither expanded nor contracted; they merely changed by adding some alternatives and deleting others. If this was in fact true, it is not possible to say that in general choice-centralization increased or decreased.

Frequently the two kinds of centralization described above

coincide, as in the first part of the last example. But the difference can be important. For example, consider the Liberman type of proposal which would reduce the number of targets an enterprise is expected to fulfill. Since several bills of goods will typically fulfill the less detailed targets, while only one bill would fulfill the more detailed targets, one might say that decentralization has increased with respect to choice—assuming for the moment that only alternatives that fulfill the plan are considered by the manager. But the choice set of the leadership need not have been altered by this change. The leaders still have the same range of alternatives that can be imposed on the managers, for example the alternative of returning to the previous set of targets. So with respect to the leadership there has been no decentralization of authority.[3]

The definition of socialism given above seems to imply a socialist preference for authority-centralized organization. More will be said on this question later.

"External effects" has been traditionally defined as a divergence between private and social marginal costs or benefits. It has implicitly had a rather specific organizational component. In the static, perfect-knowledge, independent-technology environment, we know from Walras that the efficiency of competitive capitalism cannot be improved upon. Insert broad interdependence among enterprise and household decision units, and the same line of argument leads to the conclusion that efficient central planning cannot be improved upon and is superior to competitive capitalism. The reason for this is that economists have been unable to find any market-like partitioning of such an economy, the interest-oriented interactions of whose participants would lead to pareto optimality in the outcomes. The existence of external effects means that the behavior of some people influences the welfare of others, in ways not controlled

---

[3] Authority-based decentralization could have occurred if, for example, an effective constitutional change eliminated the previous alternative from the leadership's choice set.

by the market. If the "welfare of others" is valued by the society, that is, if its level affects the level of the social welfare function, then some group, more centralized in both senses than are any participants within the competitive model, may have to be the unit of decision if social welfare is to be maximized. Such is the organizational implication of external effects.

This has proved to be a most useful concept, suggesting as it does the choice-decentralizability of certain economies by use of the price system without any reduction in efficiency. The concept has a similar connotation when used in connection with socialist economies. However, when a variety of socialist alternatives is under consideration, a somewhat different and more general concept of externalities seems more appropriate—one which does not tie the concept exclusively to the consequences of using a price system. First, two more definitions. An *economic environment* is described by certain data relevant to the achievement of some optimal economic state, such as the tastes of participants and the available technology. An *organization* is described by certain data relevant to the grouping of participants into decision units, such as the choice sets and the criteria of these units. External effects occur when an equilibrium of the organization and environment, if it exists, is not pareto optimal with respect to the environment.

A couple of examples will illustrate some of the implications of this definition. As before, external effects do not occur for competitive capitalism operating in the classical environment. However, consider an environment in which tastes are strongly interdependent. External effects are now present with respect to competitive capitalism. However, under perfect knowledge, an authority-centralized socialist organization is pareto optimal—no externalities exist. Thus, in this definition, the presence or absence of externalities is not a fixed property of environments but depends both on the environment and the organization.

Even strongly authority-centralized socialist organizations are likely to contain elements of choice-decentralization because of the limited decision-making capacity of the leadership. Well-known schemes of organization, based on integration of the price system into the decision processes, are likely to play a central role in such decentralization. But other bases for choice-decentralization may be found.

Essentially, alternative forms of organization have been defined as different ways of grouping the participants into decision units. This implies that human interactions are being restricted in systematic ways, which in turn entails external effects, unless the restrictions have no effect on outcomes. For example, suppose that an environment contains several wholly autarkic sectors. An organization of each of these sectors into an independent decision unit in which there was no provision for communication or exchange between sectors would not entail external effects. The environment can be decomposed into several wholly independent subenvironments.

This situation is rare in economics. More common is a situation in which an organization can be designed such that systematic limitation of the information provided and transmitted by each decision unit need not destroy pareto optimality. This will be called *separability*, and is a necessary condition for most kinds of economically interesting choice-decentralization. The extreme case of competitive capitalism, in which relatively small firms and households are the decision units, makes use of separability—the information that is needed by each unit, for example, being its own tastes or technology and other prices.[4] Much of the discussion in this study will be concerned with the separability

[4] L. Hurwicz in his "Conditions for Economic Efficiency of Centralized and Decentralized Structures," in Gregory Grossman, ed., *Value and Plan* (Berkeley: University of California Press, 1960), pp. 162–75, has defined informational decentralization in terms of the properties of the information system used by the organization. Though his approach is most revealing, the terminology adopted here has seemed more useful in dealing with somewhat different types of organization in a much less precise way. For example, the Malinvaud planning scheme, described in Chap. Three below, can be used in a separable organization and produces a pareto optimal plan, but appears not to be informationally decentralized in Hurwicz' sense, since nonoperational messages occur during the plan-making process ("vector A_{37} is my preferred technology") and after ("unit x is directed to produce y units").

of various kinds of organizations which are to some extent choice-decentralized.

"Organization" and "institution" will be used interchangeably in this study. We will be dealing only with organizations that are going concerns, in which decision patterns have become institutionalized, and we will be concerned with effective decision making in organizations, not with the formalities of tables of organization; or rather our concern is with models, with stylized descriptions, which purport to show effective decision making.

Institutional or *organizational equilibrium* occurs when the environment is such that a given pattern of decisions, once achieved, will tend to persist without inducing significant changes in intra- or interdecision-unit behavior. Institutional or *organizational stability* occurs when a deviation from an equilibrium decision pattern creates pressures to return to the equilibrium pattern.

This last pair of definitions is somewhat less precise than those which preceded them. This is in part a result of the very incomplete descriptions of organizations which will be provided in this study and in part a result of the relatively limited development of organization theory to date. Again examples of possible usage will suggest the purposes which these concepts are designed to serve.

In a given classical environment, competitive capitalism has a number of organizational equilibria which differ from one another, with respect to the allocation of goods, depending on the initial distribution of wealth among participants. However, some competitive equilibria in the traditional sense may not be organizational equilibria. For example, wealth may be so sufficiently concentrated at the competitive equilibrium that a few participants may buy out a competitive industry and convert it into a monopoly. Or a few participants may possess the political influence to induce the government to grant them a patent of monopoly. In both cases the competitive equilibrium does not persist, even given that it is achieved. A competitive equilibrium which is also an organizational equilibrium may be stable with respect to technological changes which are consistent with the classical assumptions, but it will not be stable with respect to technological changes which create increasing returns to scale over the range of demand for a good. A competitive equilibrium which is stable[5] with respect to some range of environmental changes may not be organizationally stable if windfalls during the adjustment process offer the opportunity to change the market structure.

The descriptions of economic organization and behavior that follow are unfortunately less precise and less well developed than the analytic descriptions of competitive capitalist markets. As a result the above terms will often be used in a somewhat looser sense than the examples just given may suggest. But the spirit of these definitions has proved useful in distinguishing among certain types of behavior and an attempt has been made to use the terms in ways that are roughly consistent with these definitions.

Statement of Purpose

In the chapters that follow, a variety of socialist forms of economic organization are discussed. Three themes are emphasized: (1) the viability and effectiveness of the classical soviet organization; (2) the effectiveness of several relatively centralized and decentralized (in the sense of choice, primarily) organizations which are possible alternatives to the soviet form; and (3) the role of an organization like the Communist Party in economic decision making. Concern is restricted to the planning and control of production.

The aim is to relate aspects of socialist organization to economic behavior. The paradigm for establishing such relations is the socialist controversy, in which similar aims found expression; hence the survey of some writings from that controversy

---

[5] Stable in the sense that the economy converges to equilibrium by a series of price adjustments whose magnitude depends only on the level of excess demand.

in the next chapter. An attempt has been made to adopt a similar level of abstraction for each organizational analysis, so as to make some sense of comparisons. However, the level of precision and power of the models could not be made similar because of the differing states of development of various relevant areas of knowledge. For this reason intermodel comparisons are incomplete and in places inconclusive. A summary statement of the main conclusions appears in the last chapter.

CHAPTER TWO

The
Socialist Controversy

Can a socialist society find some method of organizing the allocation of resources which will permit the economy to function with a tolerable degree of efficiency? This question has been debated for some sixty years now, and constitutes the heart of what is known as the "socialist controversy." Today many, perhaps most, economists would consider it established that the appropriate answer is "yes." However, it is worthwhile to look over the ground briefly once again. In the first place, a "yes" based on the obvious fact that one socialist economy has been functioning for almost fifty challenging years, while a number of others have survived for twenty years is not an answer to the question posed by the controversy. For the soviet type of economic organization bears a somewhat distant resemblance to the conceptions of most protagonists in the socialist controversy. Then, too, many would agree with Abram Bergson that in comparison with American capitalism "Soviet socialism is the less efficient system."[1]

In the second place, the controversy is interesting from the point of view of recent developments in economic analysis.

[1] Abram Bergson, *The Economics of Soviet Planning* (New Haven: Yale University Press, 1964), p. 341.

Things can now be said that were not said by participants to the controversy and which can add something to it. There is a variety of conceivable forms of socialist economy whose efficiency and desirability may be contrasted. The answer may not be "yes" for every one of these. Indeed, it is fair to say that the question as posed remains an open one. In a sense, the present work can be considered to be another contribution to the controversy, beginning with a survey in this chapter of the main points made by some of the major participants. The aim here is not to present a history of the controversy, but rather to describe the participants' thinking and then to get an idea as to what was and what was not established, and what problems remain. Criticisms of capitalism, and capitalist-socialist comparisons will be ignored except where they are expressed within the framework of the controversy and contribute to an understanding of the participants' view of socialism.

The authors' empirical reference has played an important, but largely indirect, role in the controversy. Of course the views of those writing before 1917 could not have been conditioned by experience. Instead, they approached the problems of socialism at the same level of abstraction and within the same framework in which problems of capitalist resource allocation were being discussed. It was generally assumed that tastes and technology could be described by the same kinds of functions as under capitalism; Barone, for example, never questions in his paper the independence of both tastes and technology among families and firms. Nor is any attempt made to be more specific about the shapes of the functions; indeed, discussion of this point is largely avoided.

After 1917 there are only the vaguest references to the Soviet Union in most of the discussion.[2] In Mises and Hayek there is

---

[2] Maurice Dobb, whose *Russian Economic Development Since the Revolution* (New York: Dutton), appeared in 1928, is a major exception. However, his use of Marxian language puts him somewhat outside the main line of the controversy. He is included here because his criticisms of the participants are readily translatable into the language of the controversy and are fundamental.

some mention of the war communist period[3] as evidence that without money and prices an economy could not function, but very little beyond this. It is striking that almost all the authors turn naturally to capitalist rather than socialist experience to support their positions. However, the term "socialist economy" obviously does have some empirical referent and, however indirectly, aspects of the Soviet experience are at least implicit in the discussions of many participants. Rather than attempt to ferret out these connections it will suffice to state the problem in a manner typical of the discussion, and then relate some of the arguments and results to this version.

Consider an economy consisting of a number of families and a number of firms. Each family has a consistent pattern of preferences, and each firm is capable of transforming goods in a given pattern of alternative ways. The state by some process has arrived at a set of goals for society, goals which can be expressed, at least in part, in terms of the amounts of goods provided by society to each family. Having nationalized the means of production, the state wants to find the best allocation of resources in terms of this criterion, accepting as a constraint that nationalization means at the very least that there is no market, in the ordinary sense, for producer goods.[4]

It is hard to find any loading of the ideological dice in this formulation of the problem faced by a socialist economy. All that is really being said is that material welfare counts in socialism and that the state assumes the responsibility for prescribing the way in which it counts and the means for realizing it. Some socialists might argue that this does not get at the heart of socialism, which is really a matter of establishing brotherly

---

[3] Hayek especially refers to an early study of Soviet planning during the war communism period by B. Brutzkus, *Economic Planning in Soviet Russia* (London: Routledge, 1935). A German translation had appeared in 1928 but the original Russian edition dates from 1922.

[4] Because our primary concern in this chapter is the general framework of the problem, we shall make no attempt to state formally the conditions under which the various assertions are valid. The main lines of argument without details will serve.

attitudes in the populace. Others might argue that the material aspect of the problem is relatively trivial because of the much greater efficiency of socialism than capitalism. The first of these arguments lies outside the socialist controversy proper, though an aspect of it is treated in Chapter Five below. As for the second, today at any rate, with socialism finding most of its new adherents in low per capita income regions, the problem of scarcity is less likely to be denigrated.

Unfortunately it is hard to come to any comparative conclusions with this version of the problem. Wieser, who as early as 1889 argued that the problem of scarcity and the problem of relative valuation of alternatives derivative from it were equally problems of capitalism and of socialism, was content to state the issue in a way which emphasized the similarities.[5]

But merely to pose the problem in this way was more than nothing. Socialists had tended to mistrust the rise of marginalist economics as apologetics of capitalism, a reaction which reflected in considerable measure the uses to which the new methods of analysis were being put in the period before World War I. This resistance was combined with the socialists' heavy reliance on vaguely conceived institutional reorganizations to resolve economic problems, that is, on a rather utopian view of life under socialism. The English Fabians and the German revisionists represented major reactions to both these tendencies. Under their influence, many socialists came to realize that the question of the feasibility of socialism was of interest, and that scarcity was a problem socialist economists would have to take seriously. Even so, socialists did not attempt to provide an economics of socialism during this period.[6] The discussion seems to be a sort of parallel play, with socialists analyzing the defects of capitalism

---

[5] F. von Wieser, *Der Natürliche Werth* (Vienna: Hölder, 1889), pp. 59–66. Wieser's contribution is discussed in Carl Landauer's *European Socialism* (Berkeley: University of California Press, 1959), Vol. 2, pp. 1623–25.

[6] A survey of Marxian writings on the subject can be found in the Appendix to Oskar Lange's *On the Economic Theory of Socialism* (Philadelphia: Lippincott, 1938).

and antisocialists analyzing the common role that scarcity assertedly must play in all societies.

Barone

It is in this context that Barone's "Ministry of Production" paper appeared in 1908, and was a significant step forward.[7] In this first application to the socialist problem of the formal general equilibrium analysis developed by Walras and Pareto, Barone attempts to show that the form of the imputation rules for a socialist and capitalist society are the same, though the bills of goods produced would probably be rather different.

Barone assumes without comment that the technologies and preferences of individual decision units are mutually independent, and takes them as given. To avoid metaphysical argument about the subjectivism of utility theory, he starts with demand relations instead of deriving these from individual or family preference systems. He also considers both fixed and variable technical coefficients of production. By assuming market allocation of labor and consumer goods, he limits the socialist-capitalist contrast to the treatment of producer goods. His problem then is to contrast the competitive capitalist outcome with that achieved by the kind of socialism in which a Ministry of Production, which owns the society's capital goods, must operate so as to provide a maximum collective welfare in some sense.

Working within this framework Barone comes up with three general conclusions. The first of these is a characterization of the role of imputed prices in determining a pareto optimum. Suppose the Ministry has found a bill of outputs which just uses up the supply of productive services. It then can find one from among a number of possible sets of imputed prices which will cause the participants to demand just this bill of outputs. Taking this set as a starting point, the Ministry "will then make adjustments in

---

[7] An English version forms the Appendix of F. A. Hayek, ed., *Collectivist Economic Planning* (London: Routledge, 1935).

such a way as to attain the end of the maximum collective welfare."[8] The exact adjustment procedure it will follow is not described.[9] The optimal position will have the property that, if the equilibrium equivalents (imputed prices) are used to value goods and services, it will be true that no feasible reallocation of resources by an individual decision unit[10] can increase the welfare of some without reducing that of others.

This showed, in a more explicit way than had been done previously, that prices are not conceptually bound to the institution of the market. It also said something about the optimum which might be practically useful; namely, that there would be no tendency for participants to make any further adjustments once it was reached. Finally, it suggested that the trial-and-error process by which markets appear to seek an equilibrium could also be tried by the Ministry of Production for the same purpose.

Barone, like Walras before him, devoted considerable attention to the capital market and the determination of the interest rate. In static stock-flow relationships there is little to distinguish capital goods markets from other markets under capitalism; and the same applies to studying the allocation of these goods under Baronean socialism. The main purpose of his discussion is apparently to offer an imputational theory of interest to contrast with Marx's institutional one. The two theories are contradictory since Marx argued that interest would disappear along with capitalism.[11] Barone's approach is the familiar balancing of time preference and productivity.

As a second conclusion, Barone provides a partial explication

[8] *Ibid.*, p. 270.

[9] In a later discussion of equation solving (*ibid.*, pp. 287–88) he states that a direct solution of the relevant set of equations would not be impossible. See below, pp. 21–22.

[10] That is, a reallocation which does not violate the budget constraint or the given demand relations and technology.

[11] Such is the implication of the following passage: "It is indeed only the separation of capitalists into money-capitalists and industrial-capitalists that transforms a portion of the profit into interest, that generally creates the category of interest; and it is only the competition between these two kinds of capitalists which creates the rate of interest." *Capital* (Moscow: Foreign Languages Publishing House, 1962), Vol. III, p. 363.

of the phrase "maximum welfare for the people" or "maximum collective welfare." One of the properties of the optimum assertedly is the following: No movement away from the collective maximum can, even with compensation, improve the welfare of all, as measured by the total money value of the goods the participants obtain at the fixed, imputed prices of that maximum. However, that is not the whole story since there are a large number of these optimal points, representing alternative allocations of the social dividend.[12] The dividend is generated from the imputed return to productive services controlled by the Ministry. He recognizes that the allocation of the dividend cannot be wholly arbitrary, since it must not affect the equilibrium conditions of individual adjustment, if efficiency in allocation is to be achieved.[13] Barone recognizes also that the limitations on choice of allocations of the social dividend put the Ministry in the position of having in effect to choose among points each of which is pareto optimal.[14] He thus comes very close to stating the problem for the collectivist regime in the form used in the new welfare economics.[15]

Finally, Barone offers some very brief remarks on the practical difficulties faced by the Ministry of Production. He brings up the problem of solving "millions of equations" but seems to feel that this problem of magnitude is not completely insoluble. A considerable cost is entailed in making the calculations but, apparently by linearizing relationships, he thinks that it could be done. Since earlier in the paper he talked about a kind of trial-and-error

---

[12] Barone is not clear as to the differences among pareto-optimal points. But see footnote 15 below.

[13] Hayek, *op. cit.*, p. 257. He is cryptic on this point, however.

[14] *Ibid.*, pp. 285–86.

[15] For an evaluation of Barone's contribution to welfare economics, see Paul A. Samuelson, *Foundations of Economic Analysis* (Cambridge: Harvard University Press, 1947), pp. 214–17. On the role of moral values in Barone's welfare economics the following passage and its context should be decisive: "If it is considered desirable to benefit some at the expense of others, it is much better ... to make direct transfers from the latter to the former...." Hayek, *op. cit.*, p. 257. Thus values play an important role in determining the optimum by means of collective decisions about the social dividend.

approach to finding the optimum, it is not at all clear what he conceives this aspect of the Ministry's work to entail.[16]

Equally enigmatic are his brief comments on organizational aspects of the problem. He points out that profits vary from firm to firm under capitalism because of the differing degrees of competence and amounts of knowledge and experience possessed by businessmen. These he calls "economic conditions" of the problem.[17] In another place he suggests that these economic conditions, and especially the need to experiment with alternative technical conditions as a substitute for the trial-and-error aspects of market adjustments, raise insoluble problems of calculation for the Ministry of Production.[18] This appears to be the first recognition among participants to the controversy that variations in human responses to a given set of stimuli can affect economic outcomes and should be taken into account.

Taylor and Lange

For about twenty years Barone's paper remained the best survey of the allocation problem under socialism. There was a brief and retrogressive diversion around 1920, evolved in response to the war communism period in Russia, which is worth a comment because it continues to crop up from time to time. This had to do with the possibility of establishing a "natural" socialist economy, or one in which money and pricing are completely absent. Its proponents, notably Otto Neurath and Nikolai Bukharin, seemed to feel that prices were inevitably tied to markets and capitalist exploitation, and possibly also to the Marxian commodity fetishism.[19] In terms of the controversy, this would leave the socialist state with no alternative to the

[16] See especially Hayek, *op. cit.*, pp. 270ff.

[17] *Ibid.*, p. 252. Limitations on input adjustment by the producer are also included under "economic conditions."

[18] *Ibid.*, pp. 287–89.

[19] For references and discussion see Landauer, *op. cit.*, pp. 1635ff.; Ronald L. Meek, *Studies in the Labour Theory of Value* (London: Lawrence and Wishart, 1956), pp. 263ff.

direct solution of those millions of equations. Mises may well have had the natural economy in mind when he asserted that socialism was "impossible."[20] With present knowledge such a socialist society obviously could be feasible only with a highly ascetic standard of consumption.

In 1928 Fred Taylor suggested that the calculation problem could be simplified by applying the same rules for adjustment to socialist factories as Walrasian economists attributed to competitive capitalist ones.[21] The Ministry would fix prices arbitrarily at the start of the process. Firms would then calculate the output rates which would equate price and marginal cost at these prices, and report resulting outputs and inputs back to the Ministry. The latter would then calculate aggregate excess demand for each product, raise price wherever this was positive, and lower it for all goods with excess supply. This was a relatively simple job for the Ministry and put no heavier burdens on firms than did capitalist markets.

Oskar Lange in his famous essay[22] appears to have added only details to the arguments as presented by Barone and Taylor. He is thinking of the same environment as Barone and of the same interpretation of the socialist criterion. In dealing with the interest rate, Lange suggests that its determination is arbitrary under socialism, in the sense that the state can influence its level as an instrument of public policy. He suggests that the short run balance of resources and uses would follow Barone's description, but that in the long run the aim would be to make the marginal productivity of capital zero, thus marrying Marx and Barone. And, in the sphere of distribution, Lange points out that allocation of the social dividend is subject to the constraint—noted in passing by Barone—that it must not interfere with the marginal

[20] More recently Michael Polanyi has revived the impossibility thesis in the new context of computer solutions. See below, Chap. Three.

[21] Fred M. Taylor, "The Guidance of Production in a Socialist State," *Proceedings* (American Economic Association, 1928); reprinted in Lange, *op. cit.*

[22] Lange, *op. cit.* This piece originally appeared as two articles in the *Review of Economic Studies* in 1935.

evaluations of work, goods, and leisure by the participants. In discussing price policy, Lange says in effect that wherever the terms differ on which the same alternatives are offered to different participants, there is implicitly a multiple price system—again following up Barone's discussion.[23] Lange briefly discusses one of these multiple price systems, in which consumer goods are produced according to one price system but allocated to consumers by another. Let average direct cost of production, based initially on capitalist prices, govern pricing in the production sector. Then let prices at retail be fixed so as to just clear the markets. This close cousin to the Soviet model is used as an illustration of the possibilities by Lange. One consequence is that consumer goods need not be produced in response to consumer preferences but can follow some quite different preference system laid down by the state.

At two points Lange mentions possible difficulties in achieving convergence to the social optimum by following the rules.[24] The example he uses is that of the cobweb in which supply responds jerkily and with a lag to market price. He suggests that this is not the dominant situation and that the Ministry will counter it by the deliberate use of "anticipations," i.e., by studying the properties of supply and demand reactions when participants follow the rules so as to anticipate responses. This would permit skipping steps, to shorten the adjustment process, or the substitution of new rules for specific products with a view to preventing oscillations. These problems are only mentioned, not analyzed.

In a brief discussion of the existence of a difference between private and social costs, Lange points out the possibility of differences arising under both capitalism and socialism, notes that taxes and subsidies can be used to adjust output to the optimum under capitalism, but claims that socialism can do this

[23] Hayek, *op. cit.*, pp. 282–84.
[24] Lange, *op. cit.*, pp. 71n and 89n.

"with much greater thoroughness."[25] The nature of the advantage claimed is not clear. Part of it seems to stem from the greater scope for intervention possessed by the state. For example, Lange argues that though socialists will make mistakes, these need not be transformed into cumulative upward and downward movements of output, thus avoiding one of the major external diseconomies of private capitalism: large scale and persistent unemployment. Presumably such action would involve at least occasional abrogation of the adjustment rules, since it is a response to failure of the adjustment rules.

Lange is almost as cryptic as Barone on the organizational problems of socialism. He speaks in passing of the "bureaucratic degeneration of the Soviet economy"[26] and at one point states that *"the real danger of socialism is that of a bureaucratization of economic life,* and not the impossibility of coping with the problem of allocation of resources."[27] The position is not elaborated, except to assert that the problem is at least as serious under monopoly capitalism. There is a brief discussion of the effects of bargaining under capitalist conditions but this is not extended to socialism.[28]

In response to the development of economic theory in the intervening period, Lange improved on Barone's arguments at a number of points. The basic lines of the argument remain the same, however, and despite their diametrically opposite conclusions about the feasibility of socialism, the hopes and fears aroused by both discussants are quite similar.

Hayek and Dobb

Hayek in his 1935 essay[29] added to the discussion[30] two important new issues, but made no serious attempt to assess their

[25] Lange, *op. cit.*, pp. 103–108.

[26] *Ibid.*, p. 97n.

[27] *Ibid.*, p. 109. Italics in original.

[28] *Ibid.*, pp. 117–18.

[29] "The Present State of the Debate," Hayek, *op. cit.*, pp. 201–43.

[30] He had some word-of-mouth knowledge of market socialism but does not appear to have been familiar with Taylor's article. See below.

importance. The first is the role of information in resource allocation. In contemporary economics the starting point for the discussion of information is Hayek's work, and its significance appears to have first occurred to him while studying the socialist controversy. He does not seem to understand how the Taylor adjustment rules might be used in practice, so that his estimate of the difficulty of centralized planning is based on the assumption that the plan must be made in some central agency. However, he does point to one obviously important difficulty: a good deal of information must be collected centrally even though the plan is not made there, since it will be needed in order to evaluate the performance of the national economic management.[31]

His second contribution has to do with the role of risk taking. Does the attitude toward risk taking change when there is a shift from private to nationalized property, and if so is it in the right direction? Hayek feels that "nationalized" managers will be overly cautious; whether or not this is true, the question is important as one of the few propositions in the socialist controversy which relate changes in organization to changes in behavior.[32]

Maurice Dobb participated actively in the socialist controversy, but since, being a Marxist, he did not accept the basic framework for discussion as established by, say, Wieser's posing of the problem, it is difficult to evaluate his contribution. He appears essentially to be making two criticisms of the participants: they ignore the dynamic problems associated with market adjustment, and they ignore the widespread existence of external effects. The dynamic problems are the result, he argues, of the way in which ignorance is distributed among firms in a capitalist

---

[31] See especially Hayek, *op. cit.*, pp. 208–14.

[32] *Ibid.*, pp. 233–37. Hayek's discussion centers on the contrast between capitalist and market socialist managers in risky situations. Barone may have a similar principle in mind on the consumer side when he suggests (*ibid.*, p. 286) that the "premium for deferred consumption" will be higher under socialism.

economy, the ignorance being an inevitable consequence of market organization.[33] Expectations are contagious (and may influence marginal cost estimates), and small individual producers are unaware of what is going on elsewhere at the time that they make key production and investment decisions. Dobb feels that this time lag between the making of decisions and the collection of the relevant information, plus bandwagon effects, accounts for much of the fluctuation of price and output in markets, a fluctuation which is wasteful and which would not be avoided under market socialism.[34]

The external effects argument is not strongly put for production. He argues rather that collectivism in consumption is a principle that is being ignored by market socialist analysts.[35] Socialists, in Dobb's view, are collectivists and want to collectivize consumption. They would presumably feel that consumers' tastes will change in the direction of interdependence under socialism, as commodity fetishism disappears and people relate to people rather than to goods.

Rejecting as he does the importance of value theory for a socialist economy, Dobb does not put his ideas in the language of marginalism, so our translation may be faulty. Whether or not Dobb really meant the above, these criticisms appear quite legitimate, revealing areas of danger and possible failure for a market socialist economy which protagonists on both sides seem largely to have ignored. Dobb does not provide any solutions—indeed, his comments on planning under the assumed conditions are naive in the extreme—but, like Wieser, he has posed an interesting problem.

[33] Dobb offered a summary statement of his position in Chap. Eight of *Political Economy and Capitalism* (London: Routledge, 1937); the discussion of dynamics occurs at p. 277 *et seq.*

[34] As was noted above, a deliberate effort to avoid such fluctuations, if they occurred, would require different rules than those of market socialism, and almost certainly a greater stock of centrally processed information.

[35] Dobb, *op. cit.*, pp. 311ff.

Lerner

Abba Lerner in his *Economics of Control*[36] is playing Marshall to Barone's Walras. Lerner stays within the partial equilibrium framework, an approach which perhaps was logically more satisfying at the time. Much of Lerner's book consists of a rather detailed working out of the implications for production of having firms which are applying the Taylor-Lange rules. However, Lerner is more explicit than Lange, in that he has in mind the use of the rules in a market context, rather than thinking of them as a paper-and-pencil approximation technique. Because he plans to keep markets to allocate resources wherever possible, he adds a discussion of optimizing in public finance and foreign trade. Indeed functional finance is one of his most interesting pieces of analysis, though the principle is applicable to capitalist as well as socialist economies.

Lerner discusses external effects in consumption briefly but he feels that they are primarily tied up with income inequalities, which he proposes largely to eliminate. External effects in production are discussed only obliquely; at least a rule applicable to their analysis is propounded under the heading of indivisibilities, which can occur in factors, products, and techniques of production. The idea is simply that one must find a sufficiently comprehensive basis for valuation to insure that all social costs and benefits (including those that will influence relative prices) are being taken into account.[37]

From the point of view of the socialist controversy Lerner has two novel arguments. The first results in the assertion that incomes should be distributed equally in the absence of good interpersonal measures of the marginal utilities of income. The claim is that the rule of equality maximizes the expected value

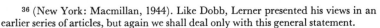

[36] (New York: Macmillan, 1944). Like Dobb, Lerner presented his views in an earlier series of articles, but again we shall deal only with this general statement.
[37] See *ibid.*, Chap. 16.

of the total utility of the participants in society, which serves as a surrogate for the unknown value of total utility. Equality has this property because utility functions are similar among individuals, which Lerner takes as evidence that movements away from equality are more likely to reduce total utility than movements toward equality under conditions of diminishing marginal utility of income. When moving away from equality those who are losing will be losing more utility than those who are gaining are gaining, unless the gainers are more sensitive (i.e., their marginal utility functions are scaled higher). But these latter people are hard to identify, so that the argument for inequality holds only when there is reason to believe that the sensitive types *can* be identified. For the given criterion—and under the Bayesean assumption that redistribution processes, whose selectivity with respect to levels of individuals' marginal utilities of income are unknown, are unbiased in their selection of this property—the argument seems to be logically consistent.[38]

The second novelty is a simple specification of what would be called today the supply system. The market socialist rules provide for the determination of total levels of production and consumption and individual levels of output and factor use by firms and families. But how are the goods transported from one factory to another or from factory to family? Lange does not discuss this question despite the great importance it had already assumed in the Soviet economy at the time he was writing. For Lerner, who preserves the market mechanism and, wherever efficient, private enterprise as well, the answer is simple. There are firms who engage in socially productive "speculation," taking as inputs goods available at one time and place and as outputs the same goods at another time and place. Prices are parametric, either because there is a competitive market or because the state is setting them. Transfers are made by speculating firms up to the point at which price equals marginal

---

[38] *Ibid.*, Chap. 6.

cost.[39] There is, of course, really no more speculation in this
activity than there is in producing goods conventionally for
markets in which prices are subject to variation. The form of
Lerner's argument was doubtless influenced by the negative
attitudes of many socialists, especially Marxists, toward the distribution system. In substance the argument is a good one; that
is, it "solves" the problem of distribution within the context of
the classical static economic analysis by describing equilibrium
properties.[40] It also suggests a place in which explicit consideration could most fruitfully be given to the process of information
collection, certainly a crucial matter for the Lernerian speculator.[41]

The manner in which price adjustment would occur in the
Lernerian system is quite unclear. Of course the remaining
private firms would be free to vary their prices at will, which
would provide an adjustment mechanism both for private and
mixed industries. But what of industries in which all firms are
socialist? Lerner makes no reference to a price board, such as
Lange uses to adjust prices in response to supply and demand.[42]
If there is no price board and firms follow Lerner's rules, there
will never be any price changes in fully socialized industries
(except in those special markets where state speculation occurs),
for the rules provide only for output and input changes. If we
take the rules seriously, however, it does appear that an inefficient equilibrium would result. Suppose that at the initial
prices, firms adjust output so that there is excess supply. Inventories build up, but production and maintenance of steadily
increasing inventories are quickly recognized as an addition to
marginal cost. This schedule shifts up for firms, and continues to
do so until supply and demand are in balance and the marginal

---

[39] To ignore the factor version of the rule, which is the version Lerner prefers.

[40] In his Preface Lerner states that he "intended to provide a theoretical solution
for each economic problem" of his sort of liberal socialist economy. The word
"theoretical" presumably serves to limit his solutions to this special framework.

[41] Lerner, *op. cit.*, pp. 69–71 and Chap. 8.

[42] See, for example, Lerner's discussion of prices in *ibid.*, pp. 63, 64, and 85.

cost—including the marginal cost of maintaining inventories at the given level—just equals price. A similar adjustment in the opposite direction could occur, with inventories drawn down in response to excess demand, but there is a definite limit to cost reduction in this direction. Permanent excess demand could be the result.

Of course buyers might react in either situation by offering lower or higher prices respectively. Socialist firms under instructions to remain price takers would respond in this way, leaving still unsolved the adjustment when socialist industry bought from socialist industry. There is no need to labor the point, and it is certainly not claimed that the problem is unsolvable (within the theoretical framework to which Lerner limited himself). A price board could be created, or prices manipulated by rule by the participants in the market.

The Present State of the Debate

Such were the main developments during the course of the socialist controversy, which might be said to have formally ended with Bergson's summary of the issues in 1949.[43] By that year Wieser's problem could be posed for a more precisely described environment and objectives, and considerable progress had been made at describing imputation schemes. Despite all this, there appear to be no clear-cut answers about the feasibility of the socialist form of economic organization. This is because of many important gaps and failures in the arguments. In listing these briefly below no direct criticism is implied of the participants in the controversy. These are gaps and failures from the point of view of contemporary economics; to apply them as

[43] Discussants are omitted, either because I am not familiar with their work, or because they have contributed nothing to this controversy beyond the points already mentioned. The choice of authors included is not intended to constitute an implicit settling of any claims for priority. Abram Bergson's "Socialist Economics," appeared in Howard Ellis, ed., *Survey of Contemporary Economics* (Philadelphia: Blakiston, 1948), Vol. I, pp. 412–48. Much relevant work has been done in the past fifteen years, but little of it has been explicitly related to the controversy.

criticism to the authors we have been discussing would be to criticize them for not having developed economics better and sooner. The list begins with what might be called analytic issues, and ends with questions about the effects of organizational change.

(1) As a first question to address to a theoretical model we may inquire: Is it logically consistent? Barone offered the weak test of equality between the number of variables and equations, with some consideration as to whether some of the equations were mutually independent. Only in the thirties were serious attempts made to find a range of functions, reasonably shaped with respect to the empirical data they describe, for which a solution could be shown to exist in general. More recent work has shown that the range of such functions is quite large.[44] Perhaps it is reasonable to speculate that this is not likely to prove a serious barrier to constructing economic models of socialism. However, there may well be multiple equilibria and the assumptions necessary to obtain a model with a unique solution are possibly unrealistic.

The consistency problem has a different bearing on the centralized socialist economy than it has on the Lernerian one. In the former case the mathematics plays an explicit role in the economy. It implies that a mathematical model of the economy is actually being used to calculate an optimal plan. If such a model were inconsistent the results would be nonsensical, and the plan, in all likelihood, a blueprint for disaster. In the decentralized economy, however, the model serves only an interpretive role; it purports to describe the results of applying the market socialist rules to firms and price boards in a decentralized economic environment. Inconsistency in the model may mean no more than that the model does not describe well actual behavior in the economy. In both cases consistency is an initial test which any model must pass; passing or failing need have

---

[44] The standard work on equilibrium theory is Gerard Debreu, *Theory of Value* (New York: Wiley, 1959).

nothing to do with the empirical relevance of the model in the latter case, but is empirically crucial in the former.

(2) In every market there is an adjustment process, by which either price or quantity or both are varied in response to changes in the environment. This process is called convergent if it tends to move the values of price and quantity, from whatever starting point, toward an equilibrium point, i.e., a point from which there is no further tendency to move unless the data change.

The problem of convergence is rather difficult to analyze at the general equilibrium level, and was never seriously attacked by participants in the socialist controversy (at least not as participants). During the past decade a number of studies of the stability and convergence properties of general equilibrium models have been made.[45] The results have not been especially reassuring to those who thought their socialist counterexample was established. Convergence has been demonstrated only for special classes of functions which are known to be unrealistic. In particular, general equilibrium models converge if all goods are gross substitutes.[46] Since many goods are thought to be gross complements, and since nonconvergent models have been found when one steps outside the realm of gross substitutes,[47] the question of the convergence of realistic competitive models remains open.

The way in which price and quantity adjustment would occur within the general equilibrium framework is likely to be different for a choice-centralized and a choice-decentralized economy. In the former, Walrasian tâtonnement might well be applied; that is, no goods would be traded until the adjustment process, carried out by paper and pencil, or rather computer, had arrived at the optimal plan for quantities and prices. In

[45] Cf. Takashi Negishi, "The Stability of a Competitive Economy: A Survey Article," *Econometrica*, 30 (1962), 635–69.

[46] Two goods are gross substitutes if *ceteris paribus* the excess demand for one moves in the same direction as the price of the other.

[47] Herbert Scarf, "Some Examples of Global Instability of the Competitive Equilibrium," *International Economic Review*, I (1960), 157–72.

the decentralized, or market socialist version, exchange would presumably occur at nonequilibrium prices during the course of adjustment. Until quite recently studies dealt only with the tâtonnement process. Hahn and Negishi have recently studied these nontâtonnement processes.[48] However, their conclusions are quite similar to those for Walrasian tâtonnement, and for this type of process too the question remains open whether there will be convergence to equilibrium in all reasonably well-behaved markets.

(3) The Lange-Lerner rules, as indeed Walrasian general equilibrium itself, suffer from a temporal indeterminacy. Marginal cost, for example, is defined with respect to flows of goods and services during some time period of unspecified but definite length. What is the appropriate length for this time period? Also, the chosen form of analysis leaves stock-flow relationships virtually ignored. For example, the rules do not provide a basis for establishing an optimal inventory policy. This is a serious problem for a price-fixing agency, since the price board's action is governed by changes in inventory levels (excess demand). Thus in Lange's scheme the regulation of inventory levels would seem to be carried out centrally via price changes, while much of the information needed to determine optimal levels is generated at the firm and industry levels.

(4) Lerner's approach is open to the objection that it effectively ignores the possibility of multiple equilibria. There is no procedure for deciding whether a stable equilibrium, assuming it is reached by Lerner's method, is the best equilibrium available

---

[48] "A Theorem on Nontâtonnement Stability," *Econometrica*, 30 (1962), 463–69. Other adjustment issues may also be raised. For example, what role does price variation by individual participants play in market adjustment? Both tâtonnement and nontâtonnement processes assume a standardized reaction to a common situation on the part of all participants. It may be that the adjustment path is strongly influenced by the behavior of a few key individuals who play the same role in the adjustment processes as Schumpeterean entrepreneurs do on the larger stage of innovational change. There are many other possibilities as well, one of which was discussed by Dobb. See above, pp. 25–26.

by the standards of his society.[49] The problem of identifying alternative equilibria is not easy. In principle, it involves the use of those millions of equations, since one must know their formal structure in order to find out whether other equilibria can exist and what their properties are. And in practice, there is the usual problem of defending the as yet unexperienced alternative against the known *status quo*. The prices of the existing equilibrium may be quite misleading in making this judgment, as is suggested by the example of Figure 2.1, where two equilibria exist because of a concavity in the production transformation line. Position B provides a larger product than A in terms of the prices appropriate to A, though the social welfare function W gives preference to A over B.

(5) Where there are external effects, such as interdependencies in tastes or technologies among decision units, the socialist imputation schemes break down, as indeed do the competitive capitalist ones. Figure 2.1 may again be taken as an illustration of what happens: prices may send you to the wrong place in product space. As yet no general schemes for dealing with external effects in an optimal way have been devised. Again it is a problem which requires the solution of the millions of equations. Though equally true of capitalism, this has special force for a socialist society which envisions group or collectivist activities as playing a much more important role than under capitalism. If interdependencies are to be greatly increased under socialism, then the difficulties in finding the best alternative in the economy are also greatly increased.

The problem of efficient market adjustment is likely to become acute when information becomes a highly valued input in the production process. The Lernerian speculator provides an example. Knowledge is the stock in trade of the man who is buying cheap and selling dear. But before communication he

---

[49] One might argue that Lerner's rule for dealing with indivisibilities and external effects provides a basis for this decision. But this is no solution by his standards; all it really says is: "Watch out!"

has little knowledge of the value of the information to him, while after communication he has lost his incentive to pay for it.[50] Markets have been known to work under this disadvantage, but they need not work well in comparison with alternative kinds of organization.

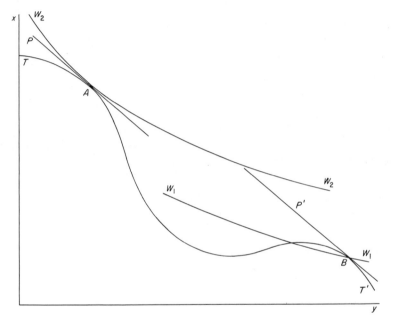

Figure 2.1

(6) External effects pose another problem which is largely avoided in the controversy. Either they must themselves be ignored or some social decision process other than the market must be used to take account of them. There is a variety of these processes, dictatorship and majoritarian democracy representing two examples, and the ways in which they may influence

[50] See the analysis of Kenneth Arrow, "Economic Welfare and the Allocation of Resources for Invention," in National Bureau of Economic Research, *The Rate and Direction of Inventive Activity* (Princeton: Princeton University Press, 1962), pp. 609–25.

outcomes seem to be a rather important aspect of allocative comparisons. These decisions require rule-making behavior. The appropriate twin questions are: (1) What rules will yield an optimal (or merely an acceptable) outcome? and (2) What social decision process will most likely generate these rules or come closest to generating them?

(7) The same thing may be said about objectives, that is, the form of the social welfare function. The practical equivalent of a social welfare function is established in every society by a social process. Presumably it has an important bearing on economic outcomes; if anything a more important effect in a socialist than in a capitalist society. How are the relevant objectives to be formulated, and what outcomes will they generate? Here there has been a little more discussion, but it is generally of the kind that compares some ideal with the worst aspects of reality. The libertarian is appalled at socialist liquidations, the socialist equally appalled at the callousness of the self-seeking marketeer.[51]

(8) The problem of incentives, though frequently raised, remained essentially in the background of the discussion. Bergson's comment on this issue, "Provided the question of controls could be disposed of satisfactorily, our impression is that the question of managerial incentives would not present any serious difficulties,"[52] is a conclusion that a reading of the controversy seems to point toward. Perhaps the problem seemed easy because it was posed as: Can you get people to follow rules to a fair degree of approximation? If the question had been: How will people be likely to react, given some set of rules?, the answer might have been quite different, for this question requires that you look at the effects of some given rules on the actor's environment and objectives.

Attitudes are still not well studied. Though we know more

---

[51] Two striking examples of this are Lange on innovations (see below) and Dobb on investment (see above).

[52] Ellis, *op. cit.*, p. 435.

about the nature of the attitudes of various groups in society, especially American society, we still know relatively little about the determinants of these attitudes or their stability. Nevertheless they are crucial to the question of whether and when people will do as they are told, which in turn is crucial to the understanding of the consequences of adopting a hierarchic organization. At this stage even speculation may be useful.

(9) As Bergson implied, the problem of incentives is closely related to the problem of controls. Participants in an organization are aware that their behavior is being observed and that these observations are likely to be the basis for the issuance of future instructions. As a result, observation of the system by those at the center may lead to simulation by the other participants. This is the heart of the control problem, and yet, though control is a central function of all hierarchies, it plays no role in the socialist controversy.

(10) Last to be mentioned is perhaps the most surprising of the omissions in the controversy: the effect of organizational change on the rate and nature of innovation. The environment of the discussion was a static one, so that innovation was inevitably an exogeneous activity. Aside from Dobb's claim that capitalists invested out of ignorance (if this has any connection with innovational activity) and Lange's claim that capitalists squelched innovations, both of which only implicitly say anything about socialism, there is nothing to go on. Presumably one shifts from capitalism to socialism for long run rather than short run benefits, and in the long run innovations are crucial. In today's technologically fluid environment, one might imagine that *any* modern industrial society would do a good deal of innovating, or at least a good deal of innovation borrowing. But the question as to whether organizational change will lead to changes in the rate and direction of innovational activity is no less interesting for this.

The universe of discourse which was accepted by participants in the socialist controversy seems an especially appropriate one for analyzing the economic consequences of adopting alternative organizational forms. One might note that it is quite different from that often used these days by the organization theorist. The latter typically develops models of organizational decision making within a restricted environment, such as that of a large corporation. In addition, he is much concerned with organization itself, for example, with the specification of the functions of each member of a table of organization and the kinds of interactions that result. Often this is very useful. But a major criticism of this literature to date has been that it is rarely able to relate these organizational variables to economic outcomes, for example to use the interactions within a large organization to explain the values of market variables.[53]

The protagonists in the socialist controversy were also concerned with organization, but always as a means to the end of demonstrating connections with economic outcomes. A criterion was thereby provided for making descriptions of organizations: the aim was to characterize organizational differences in terms of resulting differences in economic behavior. This kept the discussion on the subject of comparative economic effects of alternative organizational forms. The study of organizations per se undoubtedly has a great deal to teach economists about how specifically to make such characterizations. But the interaction between organization and economic behavior is likely to be of more central interest to economists.

However, a problem of diversity immediately arises. There is at present no way of characterizing organizations in terms of continuous variation over a spectrum. Instead there are a large number of discrete descriptions of organizational forms, each apparently leading to a discontinuously differing set of economic outcomes. At the same time, each organizational form seems to be amenable to similar types of economic analysis. The method

---

[53] A striking exception is Oliver Williamson, *The Economics of Discretionary Behavior: Managerial Objectives in a Theory of the Firm* (Englewood Cliffs, N.J.: Prentice-Hall, Inc., 1964).

of dealing with this in the present work is to choose three strikingly different forms of socialist economy, one highly centralized with respect to choice, one in an intermediate position, and one highly decentralized. Two questions may then be asked: (1) How will economic outcomes be affected by modest changes in the organization?, and (2) How do economic outcomes differ among the three key forms?

The choice of basic organizational forms was suggested by those presently or recently existing in Yugoslavia, China, and the Soviet Union. There is a fair amount of information available as to the problems and achievements of these economies over extended periods of time, including a decade or so of relatively normal postwar operation for two of them. In all three societies the question of organizational reform arises recurrently and in ways that are of great interest to the economist. And analytical work on these economies is still relatively rare.[54]

To discuss these economies within the framework of the socialist controversy requires some shift in emphasis. The approach is to make simplifying assumptions which will suggest the operating principles of the three types of economies when they are functioning as well as can be expected. That is to say, there is an element of idealization in the characterizations, just as there is in the characterization economists have provided for competitive capitalism.

Though the discussion centers around socialist economies, the approach may be applied to almost any other kind of economic organization. Beyond the discussion of pricing in Illyria lies the more general problem of the effects of group decision making on the economy. And beyond that there lies hopefully some glimmer of a theory of rule making in human society—a theory which, should it ever develop usefully, would provide the basis for designing optimal social systems for given environments and

---

[54] Two important recent examples of analytical work are Peter Wiles, *Political Economy of Communism* (Cambridge: Harvard University Press, 1962); and Bergson, *The Economics of Soviet Planning, op. cit.*

moral principles. At this stage of such a study, the distinct possibility that many types of socialist societies will prove to be nonoptimal social choices is of small import. Besides, a wise decision as to their optimality can be reached only if they are taken seriously as alternatives.

Part 2

*Centralized
Socialism*

CHAPTER THREE

Making
the Central Plan

The primary argument that central planning is impossible hinges upon the proposition that modern economies comprise a very large number of activities which are mutually interdependent, and therefore an impossible burden of collecting and processing information is imposed on the planners. The large number of activities implies that it would take a large number of equations to describe economic conditions, while the interdependence implies that the equations would have to be solved simultaneously if a consistent plan were to be produced.

Lange's version of market socialism might be taken as a counterexample to this argument; indeed that is how Lange himself characterized his study. However, as was pointed out in the last chapter, market socialism is an incomplete model of central plan making, because for example the adjustment process may not converge to the optimum under reasonable assumptions. Also it may fail, or at least converge slowly and after much oscillation, where constant returns to the production sectors occur widely.

In evaluating various forms of socialism it is desirable to have a clear picture of the plan-making process used in each variant. Without this picture it would be rather difficult to discuss the compatibility of the procedures with the given organization, for example to settle the question of whether the solution to the planning process produces enough information to determine the instruments needed to implement the plan. In this chapter we describe three alternative planning processes, each of which might be used in a socialist economy, but which have sufficiently different properties that they are by no means interchangeable.

The first scheme is the simplest. It produces a plan with a minimum of calculation, so that it could be applied to an economy producing thousands of goods without using any complex computing equipment. The second provides a more realistic description both of production and of goals but requires a good deal of computation. The third is still more realistic and computation-intensive. These techniques bring within the range of practical vision the solving of "millions of equations" in order to produce a plan. After describing the three schemes, this chapter will close with a discussion of their significance for the socialist controversy. In later chapters their compatibility with other aspects of the socialist economy will be treated.

Planning Without Computers

In all three of the planning schemes we will assume that the economy is organized into a number, n, of production sectors and a planning bureau. However in this chapter we will avoid all organizational problems except those which relate to information transmitting and processing for plan making.

An essential element in the description of technology in all three schemes is a table, A, of input-output coefficients. Each column of this table gives the input-output coefficients for a particular process of production. Thus a_{34}, the fourth element in the third row of A, tells how much of good 3 will be needed to produce a unit of good 4.

In the present scheme A is a square array, indicating that each sector is described as if it were a single process of production.

It is also assumed that each sector produces a single output and that each output is produced in a single sector.

The planning bureau starts with a known bill of final demands for each sector. Its task is to find a bill of gross outputs for each sector which is consistent with this bill of final demands and with the production technology. The procedure is as follows:

(a) The bureau reports to each sector its corresponding final demand.

(b) Each sector calculates its input requirements if it is to produce this final demand. To do this it simply multiplies each coefficient in its column of A by the final demand. The results are reported to the bureau.

(c) The bureau adds the requirements for each good in each sector together and reports these to the sectors as additions to the previously assigned output level (the final demands in the first round).

(d) The process continues until further additions to requirements become insignificant. The bureau then takes its total requirements for each sector as the desired plan and assigns these as targets to the individual sectors.

This process is equivalent to the power series expansion solution to a system of linear equations.[1] The process converges for reasonable technologies, that is, it produces an approximation to a solution of the balance equations (with given final demands), the equations which state that the amount of each good produced equals the sum of the amounts used in producing other goods and the amount allocated to final demand. Some features worthy of note:

(a) The calculations are extremely simple. Each sector makes no more than n multiplications at each iteration. The bureau makes no more than n sums of n (or less) numbers each during a single iteration.

[1] This procedure was first interpreted as a planning process by J. M. Montias, "Planning with Material Balances in Soviet-type Economies," *American Economic Review*, 49 (Dec., 1959), 963–85. Montias suggested the procedure was a close analog of planning in the Soviet Union, but has since modified his views. Cf. his *Central Planning in Poland* (New Haven: Yale University Press, 1962), Chap. One. Another version of Soviet planning is presented in Chap. Four below.

(b) A minimal amount of communication is involved, therefore plan making becomes a highly separable activity. At each iteration the bureau sends out one number to each sector, and the sectors reply with n or less numbers each. The bureau does not need to know the technology, A, and each sector needs know only its own column of A.

(c) Prices play no role in plan making. If there is some aggregation at the sectoral level, prices may be used as weights in combining goods and processes, but these prices play no explicit role in the making of the central plan. The final plan may be expressed in terms of physical output levels of individual goods which in principle could be the targets assigned to individual sectors.

(d) The iterative process injects an element of flexibility into planning. For example, eventual decreasing returns to scale in individual sectors can be handled quite easily. Suppose a sector contains some modern and some older, higher cost, equipment. The plan can be begun with the use of the technical coefficients of the modern plants. When their capacity is reached in later rounds the sector can simply shift to the higher coefficients of the older equipment for further rounds. This can be done without any communication between bureau and sector or among sectors during the plan-making process.[2]

(e) In other respects, however, this scheme is inflexible. There are assumed to be no technological options for the sectors. Also the plan can only be adapted to changes in data by running through the whole process again (if consistency is to be preserved). There are no short cuts to plan modification.

(f) No account is taken of limitations on the attainable level of production. For example, if there is a labor shortage in the economy and this was not taken into account when the final demand targets were produced, the resulting plan may be infeasible.

(g) Finally, there is no optimizing. The final demands are given a priori, and any opportunities that may exist for achieving higher performance levels are ignored.

[2] This is true because the center makes no use of the technical coefficients during iteration. Presumably the center would want to know when changes of this kind were being introduced; also, the planners would almost certainly need much technological information in estimating final demands before the iteration starts. The possibility of taking account of decreasing returns to scale in this way was suggested by Hollis Chenery in a public talk at Berkeley some years ago.

Let us now modify the planning scheme to take some account of the last two points. First, there is assumed to be a single scarce resource which exists in fixed amounts over the plan period. Each sector uses some of this factor. An additional row might be added to A which gives the input-output ratios for this factor in each of its uses.

Secondly, we assume that the planners are under instruction to maximize the final demand produced by the economy. However, final demands for each good must be produced in fixed proportions to one another, these proportions being given a priori to the bureau.

Even with these modifications an optimal plan can be generated with a minimum of computation. Figure 3.1 gives a picture of the problem faced by the planners. y_1 and y_2 represent final demands for goods 1 and 2. DE is the familiar transformation line, indicating the limitations to production possibilities in the economy. OA and OB depict the production processes for goods 1 and 2 respectively. Their direction is a consequence of our assumptions about technology. No production ray can lie in the positive quadrant because that would mean, contrary to assumption, that the process turned out not one good but two. OA lies below the y_1 axis because some of good 2 is used in the production of good 1. Point C on OA represents the outcome when activity 1 is operated at unit level and activity 2 is operated at zero level. Some y_1 is generated, but stocks of good 2 must be drawn down to provide needed inputs for activity 1. Since a change in stocks is a part of final demand, this shows up as a negative level for y_2.

Ray OA ends at point A, indicating the limits to operating activity 1 imposed by the limited availability of the primary factor. At point A, all of the factor is being devoted to activity 1. Similarly OB describes activity 2 and at point B all the primary factor is being consumed in activity 2, with activity 1 being operated at zero level. Other points on AB represent mixed allocations of the primary factor, part going to activity 1 and the

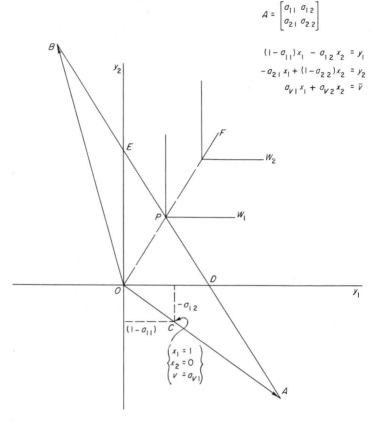

$$A = \begin{bmatrix} a_{11} & a_{12} \\ a_{21} & a_{22} \end{bmatrix}$$

$$(1 - a_{11})x_1 - a_{12}x_2 = y_1$$
$$-a_{21}x_1 + (1 - a_{22})x_2 = y_2$$
$$a_{v1}x_1 + a_{v2}x_2 = \bar{v}$$

Figure 3.1

rest to activity 2. Clearly the optimal plan lies somewhere on the transformation line, *DE*.

OF represents the acceptable proportions between final demands, in the criterion assigned the planners by the leadership. The indifference lines W_1 and W_2 have a shape which expresses the leadership's desire for fixed proportions. From the diagram it can be seen that the optimal plan is at point *P*.

The diagram does not describe the planning process, but this differs very little from the process already described. Now, as an initial bill of final demands, the bureau chooses at random a point on the ray *OF* (a point other than *O* of course). The iterations are carried out as before. When a solution has been produced, the bureau calculates the primary factor requirements for this bill. Since a proportional variation in all final demands implies a proportional variation in gross outputs,[3] the bureau then scales up or down its initial bill of final demands, until the primary factor is exactly used up. This will be point *P*, the optimal plan.

The optimizing feature plus the addition of a primary factor make this a somewhat more realistic planning scheme than the previously described variant. The added realism is bought at very little price in additional calculation—an optimal plan for some thousands of sectors could certainly be produced without computers. About the only significant loss is in flexibility. Because of the scaling up or down of targets at the end of the process, it is no longer possible to vary technical coefficients from one iteration to the next. As before, prices play no role in the process, and changes in the plan are not easy to make. To summarize, the output of the planning process is a bill of gross outputs which is consistent with the production technology and which maximizes the provision of a fixed assortment of final demands, subject to the fixed availability of some generally used input such as labor.

Malinvaud's Scheme[4]

This scheme improves in two directions over the last one. The criterion is more general in form, so that final demands

[3] The equations of the two-sector model are written out on Figure 3.1, where it can be seen that the two final demand equations are homogeneous in the gross outputs.

[4] What follows is a diagrammatic description of the process developed by E. Malinvaud in "On Decentralization in National Planning," *Working Paper* No. 36 (Berkeley: University of California), Management and Science Research Center, sns. 3 and 4 (Aug., 1961); and "Decentralized Procedures for Planning," *Technical Report* No. 15, same center (Nov., 1963), sn. 3. Some properties of less restrictive models are also presented there.

need not be produced in fixed proportions. For example, welfare indifference curves derived from the criterion might be quadratic or linear logarithmic. In addition, some technological choice is allowed in production. Table A is now expanded so that each sector in principle has a number of production processes, and may choose any one of them to operate at a positive level. Constant returns are still assumed, each production process provides only a single output and there is but one primary factor which is not produced by the system. The problem is to find a bill of final demands and gross outputs which is consistent with the technology and the factor limitation and which maximizes the value of the criterion.

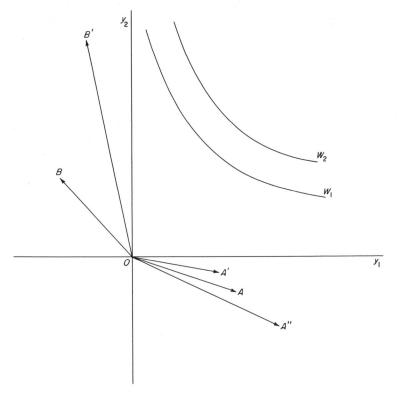

Figure 3.2

A picture of the situation is presented in Figure 3.2. In sector 1 there are now three possible activities represented by the rays OA, OA', and OA'', while in sector 2 there are two processes, OB and OB'. Also the kinks are removed from W_1 and W_2, which represent the criterion or objective faced by the planners. The adjustment process is as follows:

(a) The planning bureau starts with a feasible plan; that is, it knows of a production process for each sector which will produce positive amounts of all final demands. Using this technology, the bureau finds the corresponding set of prices (assuming the price of the factor to be unity). This is equivalent to solving an input-output problem. In Figure 3.3, if OA and OB are the given technology, then

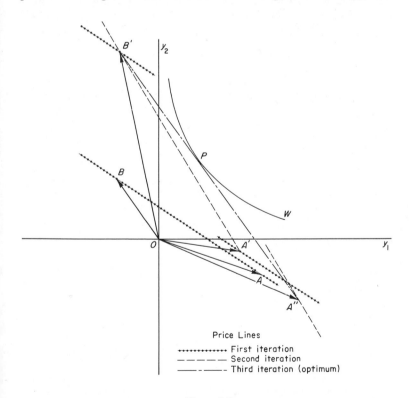

Price Lines

••••••••••••• First iteration
————— Second iteration
———-——- Third iteration (optimum)

Figure 3.3

by a familiar argument the slope of the transformation line AB represents the relative prices of goods 1 and 2 which such a solution would produce. The planning bureau reports these prices to each sector.

(b) Each sector then chooses that process of production which maximizes the value added per unit of the factor for the assigned prices.[5] In Figure 3.3 sector 1 would choose that process which permits the farthest outward parallel shift of AB, given that AB continues to touch at least one of sector 1's production rays. Sector 1's choice is now OA'. Similarly sector 2 selects OB'. These choices are reported to the bureau.

(c) The bureau now finds the set of prices that correspond to this new technology and reports them back to the sectors. In Figure 3.3 activities OB' and OA'' are chosen in the second iteration. The iterations continue until each sector reports the same activity to the bureau as it had on the previous round, which happens on the third round in Figure 3.3. The bureau now assumes that this is the optimal technology.

(d) The final step is taken by the bureau. It maximizes the value of the criterion, subject to the constraint that the solution not lie outside the last transformation line derived in the iterative process. In Figure 3.3 this is $A''B'$, with the maximum occurring at P. Given these final demands it solves the input-output problem based on the final technology for the appropriate gross outputs and reports these to the sectors as their production targets.

Notable features of this scheme are the following:

(a) It converges monotonically to an optimal plan.

(b) Each stage in the process improves on previous stages with respect to the value of the criterion until the optimal plan is reached. Consequently if the process is stopped short of full optimality, because of time or other costs of optimal plan generation, the stopping point will be an improvement over the plans generated by previous iterations.[6]

---

[5] In the diagram each sector maximizes value added, on the assumption that all the scarce factor is utilized in that sector. But the lengths of these rays are proportional to rays whose lengths are determined by per unit factor use. Therefore the choice of technology will be the same in either case.

[6] More precisely, utility will not be decreased by adding an additional iteration to the plan. Cf. Malinvaud, "Decentralized Procedures for Planning," *op. cit.*, pp. 40–46.

(c) Only one process is selected for each sector (though there may be ties) because the transformation line need be supported in each sector by only one process. This suggests that each alternative activity will generally be an aggregative description of several processes, some of which will be contained in more than one of the formal processes used in plan making.

(d) The transformation line or production possibilities surface will be linear or planar. This is a consequence of the restriction of each process to production of a single output. It brings about a major simplification in the calculation routine: the separation of the process of generating an optimal technology from that of generating an optimal bill of final demands. Thus the sectors report to the bureau, not a bill of goods they will produce, but merely the technology they will use to produce goods. Only at the end of the process are production assignments "discussed" in this scheme.

(e) Since the Malinvaud scheme produces a set of shadow prices it offers greater flexibility than the previous scheme. Because of the planar shape of the production possibilities surface, these relative prices (and the optimal technology) are unchanged in response to shifts in the criterion. The shadow prices can be used to measure the effect on the criterion of relatively small shifts in production schedules. They can also be used with some justification to measure the effect of shifting technologies, when the shifts have relatively small effects. This situation may arise, for example, if a plant included in the optimal scheme must suddenly be taken out of operation.

(f) A modest extension of the calculations would produce the inverse of the optimal technology matrix. This will make calculation of the gross output effects throughout the economy, of changes in the bill of final demands, a quite simple calculation—adding greatly to the planners' flexibility of response to changing data.

The Decomposition Principle

A major drawback to the use of the Malinvaud scheme, especially as a device for making short-term plans, is its inability to deal effectively with capacity constraints on individual sectors. In Figure 3.4 the rays *OA* and *OB* represent as before the maximal levels of operation of their respective sectors, under the constraint of a limited supply of some primary resource such as labor. But suppose that the capital stock in each sector also imposes an upper limit to short-run operations. This might be represented by points C and H on the rays and by lines CP and HP. These latter are parallel to the ray in the opposite sector because some of one sector's output must be used in the operation

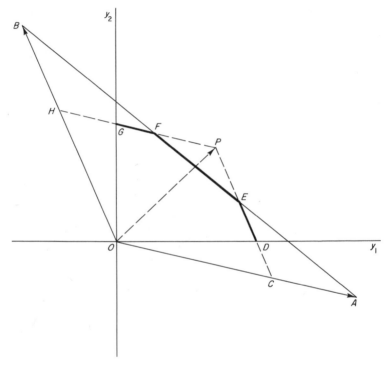

Figure 3.4

of the other sector at a positive level. It will be remembered that at point D, for example, sector 2 is producing a positive level of output, all of which is being used up in sector 1. Thus a consequence of the capacity constraint is that the production possibilities surface, $DEFG$, is now a bent line instead of a straight one. A shift in the criterion will on occasion change the marginal rates of transformation, and hence the optimal technology. It is because the introduction of capacity constraints destroys the possibility of separating the choice of technology from the choice of output level that the Malinvaud scheme cannot formally handle these constraints.

The decomposition principle can be used to take account of these capacity constraints.[7] In addition, a more general characterization of production is possible: Individual production processes may be capable of producing positive amounts of more than one good. This generally has the same effect on the production possibilities line as do capacity constraints. Suppose that a new activity ray is introduced, such as OP in Figure 3.4. Since P is in the positive quadrant of the diagram, this means that positive amounts of final demands of both goods can be produced by this single activity. It can be combined with either of the other activities, OA and OB, in any desired proportions, which would be represented on Figure 3.4 by the new production possibilities line BPA. (Not drawn in. Note that we are ignoring capacity constraints now.) BPA clearly is not a straight line, except in the very special case in which P lies on AB.

Choice of processes remains an option for each sector.

Plan making now follows a somewhat different pattern:

(a) Sectors are assigned the task of choosing a production plan for outputs and inputs to their sector which maximizes profits.

(b) The plan bureau sends a set of price weights to the sectors to use in their criteria. Each sector then searches its production set for the process that is optimal. Formally this entails solving a linear program in each sector. The resulting plans are reported to the bureau.

(c) The bureau begins with a knowledge of at least two complete plans which are feasible. These may be previous plans (in a static

---

[7] Developed by George Dantzig and Philip Wolfe. For an account which includes a planning-model interpretation by Clopper Almon, see George Dantzig, *Linear Programming and Extensions* (Princeton: Princeton University Press, 1963), Chap. 23.

society) or the result of computations which we may ignore. The procedure followed by the bureau is based on a fundamental property of linear programs: The optimal solution may be characterized as a convex combination (a weighted average with all weights lying between zero and one inclusive) of the finite set of extreme points (vertices) generated by the constraints.

(d) When the bureau receives a new set of plans from the sectors it solves a special linear programming problem. It finds values for a set of weights to be used for combining the already known solutions to the problem with the new set of plans from the sectors. This weighted average of solutions satisfies the general economic constraints of balance for production and use of each good over the entire economy, and also maximizes the overall criterion with respect to feasible combinations of this limited set of solutions. The criterion is linear, a weighted average of the final demands. The solution weights determine a new feasible solution to the overall problem. The solution of the dual provides a set of prices from which new weights for the sectoral criteria may be found. These price weights are reported to the sectors.

(e) The process continues until an optimal plan is reached. This occurs when a further iteration fails to improve any of the subprograms.

Some properties of this procedure are:

(a) The increase in realism of the economic description, as compared to the previous schemes, is clear. The only cost in comparison with the Malinvaud scheme is in the criterion, which for linear decomposition problems is linear. However, some nonlinearities can be introduced into the model without eliminating the "decomposed" nature of the sectoral constraints.

(b) The bureau may have to solve a fairly large linear programming problem if there is a large number of sectors. A problem of comparable size is solved at each round of the process. A priori, one would expect that for a comparable number of sectors the bureau faces a larger computational task using the decomposition principle than using the Malinvaud scheme.

(c) Again, prices are produced that may be used to evaluate alternative adjustments to relatively minor changes in data.

(d) The bureau need not be provided with complete technological information about the economy. However it does need the input-output coefficients for each process that enters into a solution which is used in the bureau's calculations. Thus it has been suggested that the sectors need not develop a complete description of their respective technologies before the start of plan making. Instead they may guide their search for alternatives by means of the successive price weights they receive from the center, exploring only those alternatives which appear to have some chance of being chosen, given the assigned criterion. However, when a new process is selected, its formal description in input-output terms (that is, the coefficients that relate to goods acquired from, or delivered to, the rest of the economy) must be reported to the bureau.[8]

(e) Information transmission is on a relatively modest scale. The sectors report plans and included technologies, the bureau reports price weights, and sectors need not communicate with one another. Communication between sector and bureau can hardly be a bottleneck in this scheme.

(f) The bureau's problem does not grow indefinitely as new solutions are reported by the sectors on successive rounds. The structure of the problem sets an upper limit to the number of solutions that must be considered at each round. Once this limit is reached it is always possible to drop some solution whenever a new one is added.

(g) How quickly the process converges to an optimum is not clear. It seems likely that the more sophisticated the assumptions about technology and the more interdependent the sectors, the slower the process will be.

Planning Routines: An Evaluation

The schemes described above all have a number of things in common. They are static, in the sense that they produce a plan of production for a single time period based on data pertaining to that period. They essentially use linear activities as the basic elements of the description of production. They do not deal with

[8] See Clopper Almon's description in *ibid.*, pp. 462–66. Note that in this account no aggregation and disaggregation of variables occur. The bureau's plans deal explicitly with all goods that are used or produced in more than one sector.

final consumption (or other elements of final demand) in any detail; in particular no account is taken of alternative possibilities for allocating final demands among decision units. They can all be used to solve large-scale problems involving thousands of variables.[9]

As a conclusion to this survey it may be useful to discuss briefly some of the implications of the oversimplifications introduced in these schemes and some of the problems of central plan making that may have been partly or wholly solved. Organizational problems will be deferred to later chapters.

Why not make planning schemes dynamic and nonlinear? In principle it is perfectly possible to do so. For example, dynamic input-output models have already been applied to national planning,[10] while the linear logarithmic model offers considerable computational convenience in dealing with certain nonlinearities.[11] However there are two reasons why these types of planning models are not suitable. First, there are no general solutions to nonlinear problems. Consequently one must specify the production sector in considerable detail before anything can be said about optimizing techniques. A parallel consideration applies to dynamic problems: the dynamic interactions must be specified in detail before deciding if there is a solution routine.

---

[9] A Soviet writer takes a highly optimistic view of the computational possibilities. He appears to favor a two-stage version of the Malinvaud scheme, optimized with respect to a quadratic objective (social welfare) function, and asserts that such a system could be used to calculate a solution for a model containing five million constraints and fifty million variables by using a computer system no more capacious than that presently available in the United States. V. N. Pugačev, "Voprosy optimal'nogo planirovaniia narodnogo hoziaistva s pomošč'iu edinoi gosudarstvennoi seti vyčislitel'nyh centrov," *Voprosy Ekonomiki*, No. 7 (1964), 93–103. For a discussion of the proposal see B. N. Ward, "Linear Programming and Soviet Planning" (Berkeley: University of California, 1965 [mimeo]).

[10] For example a sixteen-sector model covering 1960–70 was estimated recently in the Soviet Union for use in constructing the 1966–70 plan, though apparently the results were not in fact acceptable because of flaws in the model. See Alfred Zauberman, "The Optimality Test in the Mathematical Model for the Soviet 1966–70 Plan" (London, n.d. [mimeo]).

[11] See Roy Radner, *Notes on the Theory of Economic Planning* (Athens: Center of Economic Research, 1963).

For this reason it is not possible to specify the properties shared by modern economies in a way that will permit general conclusions as to the feasibility of central planning. Second, the nonlinear and dynamic systems require a good deal more information and, usually, a good deal more calculation than do linear problems. Consequently there is a relatively large cost, in terms of scope and detail of results, that must be paid in order to get the potentially greater descriptive accuracy. As will be discussed later, the most probable implication of the above is that economies making use of central planning for short-run allocative purposes will choose to make a hierarchy of plans embracing time periods of different duration. One might hope that the series of decisions which produces, over the years, a number of these plans will be self-correcting, but the properties of this plan-making hierarchy do not yet seem to have been discussed.

Aggregation raises a special set of difficulties. On the one hand, the plans of different duration tend also to be at different levels of aggregation. This is perfectly proper. When variables are introduced which represent events far in the future there is bound to be greater uncertainty as to their values. A higher level of aggregation is a natural response to this increased uncertainty. Also the higher level of aggregation in the longer-run plans reflects the lesser interest of the planners in the details of plans other than the current operational one, the one from which instruments will ultimately be derived which will guide current production decisions.

But within the static framework, plans must be disaggregated too. There is an upper limit to the number of variables that can be manipulated in these schemes which is far below the millions of distinguishable goods produced in a modern economy.[12]

---

[12] Michael Polanyi in his *Logic of Liberty* (Chicago: University of Chicago Press, 1951), Chap. 10, and in later works has emphasized the problem of rounding error in computation. His own estimates greatly exaggerate the size of the computational limit imposed by this problem because he does not take account of the very large fraction of the cells in a technology matrix which are zeroes. Also there are routines for improving the accuracy of solutions which are subject to rounding error;

Within each sector there will be organizational subunits such as firms and plants, whose decision variables will not be explicitly described in the central planning scheme.

These aspects of aggregation and disaggregation cannot easily be accounted for formally in a planning model. The discussion of aggregation by economists has centered around the determination of the conditions for consistency of aggregation, that is, the conditions under which aggregative solutions will be the same as aggregates derived from the direct solution of the disaggregated data. Since it turns out that aggregation is consistent only in relatively uninteresting cases, it is not possible to say anything about the overall effects of aggregation in these models, except that its use will generally result in nonoptimal plans.

These remarks about aggregation apply to the criterion or objective function also. By using as a criterion a function of a set of variables aggregated over the decision units which consume final demands, a special assumption is implied. Clearly goods in themselves are not ultimately valued; somehow the criterion must be tied to the values of decision units (consumers, the political leadership, or whatever). The assumption is that whenever the criterion function increases from one possible plan to another, it will be possible to allocate the resulting final demands among decision units in such a way that the implicit "ultimate" criterion also increases. This is a plausible assumption only in a very rough sense.

Aggregation also causes problems for a centralized distribution system. One easily derivable output of the planning schemes is a bill of intersectoral deliveries. But given that most sectors

---

see for example V. N. Fadeeva, *Computational Methods of Linear Algebra*, trans. by C. Benster (New York: Dover, 1959), pp. 99–102. Nevertheless it is quite possible that, for the kinds of large-scale calculations required in central plan making, rounding error will pose a serious problem and perhaps even an upper limit to the size of a computable problem. But only experience with specific problem structures will tell. Some other reasons for believing in an upper limit to the practicable number of variables are discussed below.

contain plants located in a variety of places around the country, these numbers are of limited help in scheduling interplant deliveries. One might be able to produce an optimal feasible schedule of interplant deliveries, given the intersectoral deliveries derived from the optimal plan, but clearly these would not be elements of an overall optimum unless there were some inter-action between the supply system and central plan making.

The errors introduced by the linear static activity analysis of production have already been mentioned. Dynamic interaction among production activities, seasonality of some production, optimal inventory policy, etc.: in these and many other ways dynamics suggest alterations in the given models. In addition uncertainty has been ignored. One might assume that the model is based on expected values, but this gives no assurance of opti-mality; it merely offers the opportunity of being more precise about the ways in which such plans will be in error.

These charges all fall under the rubric "lack of realism," and they are certainly serious. Nevertheless they are not a basis for rejecting the schemes out of hand. One must remember that the models do accomplish some desirable objectives in a central planning process. Some of their properties, such as flexibility, model size, and formal optimality have already been mentioned. A further comment on the informational properties of these models, is however, in order.

First, it should be noted that communication between sectors and plan bureau or among sectors cannot be a bottleneck to extension of the schemes. There is none of the latter kind of com-munication, and the former involves at each round sets of num-bers that should not exceed n^2 for any one unit, where n is the number of sectors, and is generally much less.

Secondly, if time prevents completion of the iterations needed to generate an optimum, the process can be stopped at an inter-mediate round and will produce a plan which is consistent and an improvement over the starting feasible plan. (This is true for the Malinvaud and decomposition schemes at least.) This can be important if data are changing rapidly, so that the plan should be produced as closely as possible to the planning period to avoid data obsolescence.

Thirdly, learning can take place to some extent during the planning process. Relevant here is the possibility mentioned already that under the decomposition scheme individual sectors will not begin with complete information on their production possibilities but will develop their information about particular areas of the production set in response to the price signals from the bureau. One implication of this is that a great deal of the imperfect, intuitive knowledge possessed by people in the sectors can remain in that form and need not be communicated to the center.[13]

Finally, it should be noted that nothing has been said here about the implementation of plans or about starting-up costs, the problem of reorganizing an economy and training the participants to operate a planning routine effectively. The major points here are that: (1) there are currently available planning schemes which can produce fairly detailed optimal plans with respect to moderately sophisticated descriptions of the economy; and (2) there are still enough questions about various aspects of these schemes that the issue remains open whether national plans produced by such formal processes will have an acceptable level of reliability. As yet there is no direct experience with short-run application of large-scale models to help inform the judgment.

[13] This partly meets another objection to central planning made by Michael Polanyi in his *Personal Knowledge* (Chicago: University of Chicago Press, 1958). However, there may be serious communication problems within the sectors resulting from the phenomenon of intuitive knowledge or inexpressible (without considerable cost) information.

CHAPTER FOUR

Classical Soviet Economic Organization

The last three and a half decades of Soviet economic history have possessed some basic elements of organizational stability despite the great changes that have occurred in the size and nature of the economy, of the economic organization, and of the political environment. Most obvious is the preservation of hierarchic decision making as a substitute for the market throughout the industrial sector. However, another persistent feature has been the use of market allocation, especially for consumer goods and labor. Though the border between market and hierarchy has shifted—consumer-goods rationing, and direct allocation of labor or at least restrictions on its free movement, have been much more important during some times than others (and indeed the border area itself is somewhat fuzzy)—both systems have continued to have a central place in the economy. Still another element of stability has been the centralized control of investment. Both formal decision making and initiative with respect to investment have tended to be placed at a very high level in the Soviet hierarchy, while a large diversion of resources for rapid expansion of industry has been a persistent feature of economic policy. These aspects of the Soviet system were transferred to the East European socialist economies, where they have also shown resistance to change.

The present chapter presents a highly simplified and stylized description of the soviet type of economic organization, and discusses some of its implications for economic efficiency and responsiveness to control. Emphasis will be on these stable elements and their impact on the industrial sector of the economy. Hopefully the approach affords some insight into central features of the system, and in particular into the different range of problems that emerge as a result of the use of hierarchic rather than market forms of organization. This description is also a basis for comparison with alternative types of hierarchic organization and with some of the more decentralized organizations which have received wide discussion in recent years. However, the latter comparisons will be reserved for later chapters.

Hierarchic Organization

A hierarchic organization is a group of specialized decision makers and their assistants. Each decision maker has responsibility for choosing among a restricted range of alternatives according to some criteria. There is a partial ordering of participants in a hierarchy such that each is either subordinate to or a subordinate of some other participant, or both, and such that no participant, directly or indirectly, is both subordinate to and a subordinate of another.[1] All are linked by a communications system and the decisions are usually interdependent in the sense that a change in the decisions made by one participant will tend to alter the decisions made by others.

Where decisions are complex and interrelated a hierarchy

---

[1] Many organizations are much less cleanly hierarchic than this. In a very indirect way superiors may be subordinate to their formal subordinates, as in a corporation when the subordinate owns voting stock in the company, or among voters in the civil service hierarchy of a democracy. At times the connection may be much closer, as in the relation between members of a Yugoslav workers' council and the factory manager. However, in most cases, and in particular in the soviet type of organization, this reciprocal control can be ignored. It should be distinguished from organizational interaction as a result of multiple membership in organizations, which is an important feature of soviet organization.

may be a very useful device. However, the way in which economists have traditionally looked at decision making tends to develop an antibureaucratic bias. For a hierarchy is clearly inefficient as compared with a dictatorship, given that each has the same goal and that information is costless to collect and process. The decision units of most economic theory are dictatorships, perhaps because economists usually ignore information costs; hence a comparison with the market alternative must be made under different assumptions than those used by the authors discussed in Chapter Two. The comparison in this and subsequent chapters will therefore concentrate on the reasons for deviations from efficiency under each alternative rather than attempting to derive efficiency conditions. But before making a brief initial market-hierarchy comparison several points need to be made about general problems of interpreting hierarchic decision making.

The first has to do with the nature of the human beings who inhabit hierarchies, and in particular with the relevance for bureaucratic behavior of that dependable human motivation: self-interest.[2] The various versions of economic man employed by economists all have one property in common: His behavior is assumed to be governed by personality, that is, by motivations that are in some sense fundamental, part of the nature of the individual. Occasionally, as in some of the writers of the classical school, it has been argued that the criterion of acting independently of others in seeking personal material reward should be chosen as a matter of principle in making economic decisions, in which case the criterion might be assumed as a role by principled individuals. However, this is polemics rather than economic analysis, and it remains true that the assumption of materialistic self-seeking is not treated as a role in modern economics.

---

[2] James March and Herbert Simon, *Organizations* (New York: Wiley, 1958), p. 201, conclude that, on the basis of current evidence, one cannot say simply that "self-interest is the only dependable human motive." Self-interest does nevertheless play a central role in much of the rationalizing of behavior observed by the authors surveyed by March and Simon.

Indeed, economists have found very little use for the concept of role.[3] The reason probably is that so long as individuals act with reasonable consistency there is no need for the economist to explore the inner process of their criterion formation. The individual, even the family, is a "black box." In particular, in a market economy the participants in any one market play a large variety of roles and in irregularly changing proportions, so that role analysis is not likely to improve the quality of the results of market analysis. In a few areas, however, and especially in those situations in which stable hierarchic relations occur, there may be some real benefit to using the role concept.

In a hierarchic situation a dualistic version of human motivation becomes useful, because there is often a conflict between the criterion of choice which the participant personally prefers and that which his role as a member of a hierarchy enjoins. Indeed, students of bureaucracy such as Max Weber and Chester Barnard have emphasized compliance as a key problem for any bureaucracy. Where the hierarchy makes economic decisions, the internal conflict of participants may become a matter of importance to economists. In the soviet type of economic organization, where hierarchy is important in most economic decisions, the problem of compliance has been recognized as being of vital importance by nearly all observers.[4] Clearly any analysis of hierarchies must give close attention to the extent to which criteria assigned the participants lie within the zone of compliance. In this book it will be assumed that self-interest—describable roughly in terms of the utility attached to real income—is

[3] Two notable exceptions are R. A. Gordon, *Business Leadership in the Large Corporation* (Washington, D.C.: Brookings, 1945), esp. Chap. 11; and Harvey Leibenstein, *Economic Theory and Organizational Analysis* (New York: Harper, 1960), Pt. III.

[4] The problem of compliance includes not only the conflict within the participant and its resolution, but also the problem of designing bureaucracies in such a way as to obtain acceptable levels and ranges of compliance. Perhaps the most percipient analyses of the latter problem for Soviet society have been Joseph S. Berliner, *Factory and Manager in the USSR* (Cambridge: Harvard University Press, 1957); and Alec Nove, *The Soviet Economy* (London: Allen and Unwin, 1961), esp. Pt. II. On the former see Raymond Bauer, *Nine Soviet Portraits* (New York: Wiley, 1955).

a fundamental attribute of the personalities of the participants.

A second aspect of the analysis of hierarchies is the relevance of the concept of equilibrium. James March and Herbert Simon, whose framework for analyzing bureaucracies has been adopted here,[5] speak of organizational equilibrium as occurring when the membership in the organization tends to remain stable. However, organizations may also be said to have reached an equilibrium with respect to their decisions when, given that the environment does not change its properties, the organization continues to make the same sorts of decisions in the same sorts of ways. Of course not all organizational forms may possess decision equilibria with respect to all environments, while in many situations equilibrium is not approached because of frequent change in the environment. Nevertheless the concept seems useful and will be employed to elicit certain properties of hierarchic decision making.

As a final introductory remark reference is made to a property of complex organizations which has been noted by a number of recent studies: the tendency for unanticipated consequences of actions of participants to affect the equilibrium decision pattern. This point can be illustrated by a very rough model of bureaucratic behavior which incorporates features studied in some detail by Merton, Gouldner, and Selznick.[6] First, in an environment of imperfect knowledge the leadership is uncertain as to whether its orders are being carried out. To increase the reliability of subordinates' response to given orders, standardized routines of communication and response are developed. This in turn leads to some rigidity in the responses of subordinates, some lessening in the effectiveness with which unanticipated, "unroutinized," information is incorporated into their decision processes. The leadership recognizes the limitations imposed on its range of choice by this situation, but may be willing to accept

[5] March and Simon, *op. cit.*, esp. pp. 84–89.

[6] What follows is a modified version of the discussion in *ibid.*, pp. 36–46. In particular, the notion of a decision-pattern equilibrium is incorporated into the model.

a certain amount of response rigidity because of the relatively high cost of routinizing additional patterns of response. The equilibrium in this case does not require a perfect repetition of the past pattern of stimuli into the organization. Rather it requires that the stimuli not result in a disturbance of the expectations which have become established throughout the organization. Each decision maker within the organization continues to make decisions that are intelligible and acceptable to the other participants and that do not induce substantial changes in those participants' behavior.

Another kind of equilibrium can result from the specialization of decision making. Subordinates have the authority to make decisions; this authority inevitably gives them at least some limited autonomy with respect to the leadership. In addition, even the most loyal subordinate has some incentive to exploit and perhaps expand that autonomy, since he should possess the best information in the system with respect to the alternatives among which he is empowered to choose. This gives him, among other things, an incentive to preserve his control over the decision. At the same time the subordinate must report his decisions to, and usually evaluate the consequences for, the leadership. This creates incentives to distort the information transmitted. The leadership is of course aware of all this, and must make its own decision as to the proper mix of autonomy and information control that it will permit subordinates. Frequently an equilibrium may be reached such that the leadership will tolerate more limited information about decisions taken than it would like, because it is reasonably satisfied with the reports of their consequences and fears that attempts to get more information will jeopardize the current level of accuracy of these reports.

An organization is not a simple mechanism, nor does information always flow through the organization along established channels. Since the attitudes and expectations of key participants may on occasion be strongly influenced by, for example, a short and informal communication, it would be dangerous to think of equilibrium as a standard property of bureaucracies regardless of their environments and their forms of organization. Another aspect of bureaucracy may serve to illustrate the possibility of persistent disequilibrium.

Not only can new information often be obtained by the leadership through informal and accidental contacts, but even formal communications may have consequences which are unanticipated by the sender. For example, if the leadership has received conflicting reports about a situation it may feel compelled to respond by intervention in the particular case to resolve its doubts. If subordinates recognize that this is not a typical response, they may feel with the leadership that the incident lies outside the general field of expectations, so that direct intervention does not lead to any revision of expectations with respect to other aspects of their work. This kind of limited increase in centralized control in response to a specific difficulty will tend to occur frequently in certain environments, particularly if the organization is so complex that the leadership must live with highly uncertain information as to what is going on at most lower levels of the hierarchy. Once assumed, such centralized control tends to persist, often because delegating and routinizing is more costly than exercising control, at least in the short run.

Over time the consequence of this piecemeal intervention is more and more effort by the leadership. When the burden becomes too great, a general reorganization and redelegation of authority become necessary. Should the situation suggest that the broad lines of organization are effective relative to acceptable alternatives, the reorganization may well take the form of a return to something like the initial situation, which in turn begins again to generate piecemeal intervention and a new reorganization. Thus a cycling rather than an equilibrium occurs.

The above processes appear to occur frequently in actual bureaucratic organizations. They were presented here mainly to suggest the way in which organization will be viewed in what follows. Clearly any propositions which emerge from this analysis will require closer specification, both of the structure of the organization and the environment in which it functions. Before undertaking this in a very rough way for the classical soviet economic organization, however, it will be useful to illustrate the function of organizational propositions about hierarchies by displaying a few of their opposite numbers from market analysis.

Hierarchy vs. Market

Much of the following discussion of economic hierarchies consists of eliciting ways in which the hierarchic decision process produces different results from the traditional norm of static efficiency which has played a central role in the socialist controversy. The aim of the present section is to indicate that these divergences do not in themselves constitute proof that a hierarchy is inefficient relative to a market system. For markets, too, produce many divergences from static efficiency. A few examples of comparable divergences will make this point explicit.

Positions of special influence, not unlike monopoly, can occur within a hierarchy. An enterprise which is the only producer of a product in great demand may have such an influence in a hierarchic system, and may be able to bargain for side benefits in exchange for delivery of the good. Such a firm may also exert its influence to keep "competitors" out, by obtaining control of new enterprises which produce the commodity or by arguing against their construction.

Perhaps the most striking difference between a hierarchic and a market economy lies in the structuring of arbitrage. The price system in a market economy tends to generate a single price for each good through an arbitrage process which destroys the advantages which might otherwise be gained by trading in the good. That this single price be established is a condition for efficiency in the environment hypothesized by the socialist controversy. The plan-making schemes described in Chapter Three produced single prices under hierarchic conditions, too, but by a process of vertical adjustment rather than of price bargaining among consumers and producers of the good. What are the implications of this difference?

Only two will be mentioned at this point. First, the information costs of finding the equilibrium price are very different, and it is not at all clear a priori which will be the more costly. In the market, price signals are broadcast very widely, reaching many for whom they have no interest. Also the equilibrium price is not distinguished in these broadcasts from disequilibrium prices which are in process of adjustment, so that the cost of identifying the equilibrium price may be significant for each potential buyer or seller. In the hierarchic version, these costs are somewhat more easily identifiable—being associated with the costs of plan making, of communicating, and information processing—in the process of producing, among other things, a set of shadow prices.

Secondly, the market very often does not produce a single price. The cost of making all potential buyers and sellers informed as to the states through which a market is passing is apparently far greater than the improvement in formal efficiency which the greater information would produce. Many buyers are willing to pay a higher price rather than spend more time and effort in looking for a lower-priced offer; and vice versa for sellers. Perhaps the opposite number to this effect in hierarchic plan making is the stopping rule. A large-scale iterative planning scheme generally cannot be run until the full optimum is reached. Instead, the process is stopped after a few rounds, and adjustments are then made to bring about balance on the basis of information available up to that time. The presumption is that the efficiency to be gained from an additional round is outweighed by its cost.[7]

The adjustment processes in the two systems are also very

[7] Cf. Thomas Marschak, "Centralization and Decentralization in Economic Organizations," *Technical Report* No. 42, (Stanford: Stanford University Economics Department, 1957).

different. Markets are usually categorized as using contracting adjustment, that is, of seeking the equilibrium by movement of the prices of actual deals toward the equilibrium price. A planning device is usually categorized as involving adjustment by recontracting. The decentralized units report their behavior for a given price, but are not expected to perform in accordance with the report unless the process stops at that report.

These represent extreme characterizations of the actual course of such processes. Through bargaining, a substantial element of recontracting enters into the market process. And in the hierarchic system, the initial instructions will generally be recognized as nonoptimal, and be adjusted during the plan period as new information comes in—thus inserting an element of contracting-adjustment into this system. However, as a rough approximation, the distinction is useful.

One final comparison deals with externalities. It has already been suggested in Chapter One that externalities appear in choice-centralized as well as in decentralized organizations. In hierarchies, it is the division or specialization of decision making, with its accompanying informational separation, that is the primary cause of externalities. One illustration may serve. In a competitive market system the participants have very little incentive to develop innovations which benefit all participants. Roughly speaking, if there are n producers a single producer will try to develop the innovation only if the expected gain is at least n times the expected cost, assuming he captures a share of the gain proportionate to his share of the market. Even if he expects to expand his share of the market this principle continues to hold, though the critical benefit-cost ratio would be lower. Corresponding to this in a hierarchy is an incentive system which rewards individual performance. In responding to the incentive system, the rule for participants would be very similar: an innovation that will benefit many equally under the incentive system will be made by an individual participant only if its total benefit is many times its cost to the participants.[8]

[8] We are ignoring the possibility of cooperation in both cases.

As the above comments imply, this discussion of economic organization will occasionally step outside the bounds of the socialist controversy and consider problems of dynamics, externalities, uncertainty, and technological change, which played little role in that controversy. Unfortunately, limited knowledge of the processes to be studied and their obvious complexity will force us into a rather rough and ready speculative treatment of the problems. Conclusions can be extracted from this mélange, but they will have neither the precision of formalized theory nor the scope of institution-free scarcity economics. Hopefully they will increase our somewhat dim understanding of some currently very important kinds of economic organization.

Plan Making

An essential, and often the primary, function of plan making is to increase the knowledge that the various parts.of an organization possess about their environment. In addition, of course, there is the final product of the process, the plan, which serves as an instrument of organizational policy. In the discussion of planning in the previous chapter the first of these two functions was given rather slight attention. It comes to the fore at this point when plan making and the plan are treated as integral parts of the complex of activities that comprise the economy.

All levels of plans interact with one another. What can be done this year affects what should be done five years hence, just as what can be done five years hence affects what should be done this year. Nevertheless, there is a sense in which a certain priority of place attaches to the longer-term plans. The leadership, which provides the society's goals, is presumably interested in producing ultimately a skilled and powerful and affluent society. But these goals are rather vague; it is not at all clear how many sixpenny nails will be needed for the task. Hence the goals are transmuted into policy in a series of stages, by which the increased information resulting from each stage is converted into a more disaggregated and shorter-term plan.

In this section we will be concerned primarily with the basic operational plan, since it is this plan that is most directly connected with the operating units in the economy. Thus its role is most informative as to the way soviet type economies operate. The procedures used in constructing longer term plans are less unique to the soviet type of economic system and are also less determining of the organizational properties of that system. Not so the annual plan, whose organization has at times been separated into a distinct planning body to emphasize its unique functions, and whose procedures are quite unique.

From the point of view of the annual planner then, the function of longer term plans is purely informational. The information is mainly about priorities; the areas of the economy that are given closest attention and are to grow most rapidly according to the perspective plans are very likely to be principal preoccupations of the annual planners as well. However, the perspective plans do not provide this information in the form of a criterion function, nor is it easily converted into a formal criterion by the short-run planners. The difficulty lies in the fact that two different levels of aggregation are being used, so that the annual planner is not informed as to relative priorities in terms of arguments of the functions with which he must work.

The fact that perspective plans also give aggregative targets in rough balance between sources and uses may provide some limited information about feasibility to the annual planners. However, most of this sort of information comes from past and current performance data. These too are inputs to the annual plan bureau, making their appearance in the form of reports from ministries, the statistical service, and the like. In addition, information on prices and finance is also received from the appropriate agencies.

Formally the annual planners' task is to derive from all this information an optimal feasible plan, in the form of several thousand targeted levels of economic activity for the coming year. However, for at least two reasons the planners cannot simply plug in one of the planning routines described in the preceding chapter. The first has already been mentioned: no formal criterion exists. The second reason is that even the information on past performance is not "hard," especially if it is taken as a basis for estimating current capabilities. This is because of the well-known distortion of communications resulting from organizational pressures, in particular from the fact that subordinates know very well that information they transmit on their own performance is used both to reward that performance and to construct standards of performance for the future. Consequently much of the effort of the planning bureau must be devoted to improving the quality of the information it possesses, and to converting it into a form that is more suitable for the planners' purposes.

The soviet type of planning procedure in effect produces simultaneously an initial bill of gross *and* net outputs (final demands) based on the above data. The initially assigned gross outputs represent estimates of capacity production by the planners.[9] The choice of capacity operation is based on the assumption that the long-run plan is a good one, and that it has hitherto been fulfilled—so that existing capacities are roughly those needed to continue on the optimal long-run path. Of course there is some flexibility in the definition of "capacity" to allow for differences in gestation periods among investment projects and to take account of any special information about the quality of the poorer plants, customary practices as to the number and intensity of shifts, and even changes in productivity. In low priority sectors the initial target may be based on little more than "last year plus 10 percent." In other sectors a very careful estimate of potentialities may be made.

[9] The following is based largely on Western studies of soviet type planning, particularly J. M. Montias, "Planning with Material Balances in Soviet-type Economies," *American Economic Review*, Vol. XLIX, (Dec., 1959), and *Central Planning in Poland* (New Haven: Yale University Press, 1962); and H. Levine, "The Centralized Planning of Supply in Soviet Industry," *Comparisons of the U.S. and Soviet Economies*, (Washington, D.C.: GPO, 1959), pp. 151–75. However, the interpretation differs in important respects.

Net output estimates have a similar *ad hoc* basis. Some components, like material reserves, are estimated by rules based on past experience with shortfalls and their costs, the properties of the goods, etc. Consumption and other components may again be little more than "last year plus 10 percent" for low priority sectors. In other cases changes in retail prices, or other a priori information, may be used to generate a more careful figure. These rather crude estimates are then turned over to product sections within the planning bureau for use in the next stage.

Meanwhile the initial gross output figures have been moving down the appropriate sections of the hierarchy to the firms, going through some disaggregation on the way, and at each stage are used as a basis for generating bills of requirements for the assigned production levels. One may construe this administrative procedure as being roughly equivalent to the development of a more accurate assessment of the technical coefficients of production—the amounts of inputs required per unit of output—which are needed for plan balancing and improvement. A major problem with the planning procedure is that there is a good deal of uncertainty at the planning bureau as to the true values of many of these coefficients. It may be useful to think of this information as being converted in the planning bureau, not into a single number but into a distribution. Suppose it is reported as two numbers ("mean" and "standard deviation") or in some more complicated form depending on the shape of the distribution, i.e., on the relative likelihood that various upward and downward biases dominate. Thus the nature of the distribution depends on the values of the coefficients actually reported, information relating to the bargaining process (recent revisions, changes during the course of the reporting, possibly even reports on the personalities concerned), and information collected in other ways. From this information the coefficient distributions are constructed by the planning board, say by the appropriate product sections.

Armed with these distributions the plan is then made. The interaction (administrative iteration) now is between the planning board and its own product sections. The board first reports a bill of gross outputs and final demands to each product section. If these balance for the set of "mean" input coefficients showing uses of the relevant product, this fact is reported back to the board. If not, the product section must choose from among other possible input coefficients within some prescribed range of the coefficient distributions. Product sections will generally have some discretion in reassigning coefficients. This discretion is defined and limited by a criterion. The criterion is assigned to the product section by the center, which takes account of the relative priorities of the various industries and the effectiveness of changes (i.e., the amount of saving of product available per standard unit of reduction in coefficients). Of course revision may be forbidden for some uses, so that in effect the coefficient distribution is a point. Success in balancing product supply and allocation would be reported to the board at the completion of this step, possibly with some summary statement as to the adjustment which was made.[10]

Should this step fail to yield a balance, the product section reports that the plan is infeasible and by how much. The board then may choose one of three courses of action: (1) it may simply reduce the required final demand for the product by an amount that will bring gross requirements down to gross output; (2) it may lower some aspects of the coefficient-adjustment criterion; or (3) it may raise the target level of production of gross output for that product.

The implications of this procedure may now be illustrated. The material balances for a two-sector economy, in which the x_i are gross supplies (requirements) of the commodities, $\bar{x}_i$ are targeted gross outputs (capacities), y_i are final demands, and a_{ij}

---

[10] A notable omission in this idealization is the effect of regional bodies on plan making. Some brief discussion occurs later (cf. Chap. Seven).

the mean coefficients of input of i per unit of output of j desired, are:

(1)
$$\bar{x}_1 = a_{1\,1}\bar{x}_1 + a_{1\,2}\bar{x}_2 + y_1$$

(2)
$$\bar{x}_2 = a_{2\,1}\bar{x}_1 + a_{2\,2}\bar{x}_2 + y_2$$

Equations (1) and (2) show a consistent set of gross outputs for the given estimates of technical coefficients and final demands. Suppose now that sector 1 is not in balance, the gross output targeted being too low to cover all needs, as described on the right side of the equation. This situation is shown in Figure 4.1. The line α is equation (1) with gross supply, x_1, substituted for gross targeted output, $\bar{x}_1$. Line β shows equation (2), with sector 2's material balance in order (that is, it passes through Q, the plan target). If both equations were in balance, P would define the consistent bill of gross outputs; but they are not. The first product sector, if it follows the first of the above possibilities, will shift equation α to the left so as to bring about a new intersection at Q, consistent with the targets but at a lower final demand, y_1. If this is not permitted or does not suffice, norm adjustment may be tried. α' shows the result of reducing a_{12} (the amount of product 1 needed by sector 2 in producing a unit of product 2). If permissible rotations of this kind will not bring the sector into balance at targeted output levels, the product sector reports failure.

Note that the advantage of operations of these kinds is that they have no effect on material balances elsewhere in the system. Even though a change in $a_{1\,2}$ has some impact on sector 2, it does not affect directly the balancing work of this product sector, which is concerned with targeted gross output and allocations of product 2 only. But if the board is forced to change gross output levels, the impact on other product sections may be widespread. A standard iteration, or perhaps even two, involving the reporting and summation of additional requirements, will then be necessary in most cases. However, the damping of this process, by adjustments in all sectors of the first two kinds described above, sharply limits the overall impact on the plan.

The result of this process is a bill—of some hundreds or even thousands of gross outputs which are mutually consistent in terms of a specified set of final demands—and a technology matrix, both of which are somewhat altered as a result of the

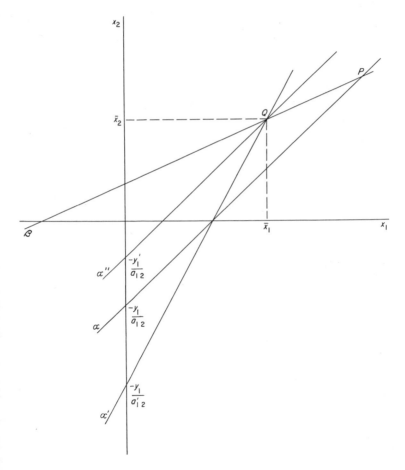

Figure 4.1

planning process. The final step is to convert this highly aggregated bill of goods into production targets and input quotas for each enterprise in the country; however, this phase of the operation is more closely related to implementation than to plan making and will be discussed later.

The above highly simplified description of the soviet-type plan-making process admittedly idealizes reality. In particular it takes no account of the at times quite serious organizational inefficiencies which have stemmed from divided and conflicting authority and poorly designed reporting and information processing procedures. Hopefully it does capture essential features of the process, and omits primarily those aspects which are corrigible without fundamental institutional reform. Assuming this to be the case, a few comments are in order as to the relation between plans produced under these conditions and an ideal plan, from the point of view of the leadership, in which institutional problems are ignored.

Perhaps the most striking feature of this procedure is that it produces a complex result with a bare minimum of calculation; indeed the planning bureau has no need for calculating machines more powerful than slide rule and abacus. No large-scale calculations are made internally by the planning bureau; major operations are separable so that, for example, many adjustments may be assigned routinely to product sections and other specialized subgroups of the planning bureau. The most complex task is the making of criteria for norm adjustment, but intuition and experience play a large role in practice here, and interdependence a small one.

When gross outputs must be adjusted, as a consequence of a failure of the adjustment procedures, it is true that a problem arises which formally entails interdependence throughout the system of balances. However, further coefficient changes provide a strong damping of the adjustment process, unless the maximal permitted adjustments fail to balance product sources and uses quite widely throughout the system. It is clearly this damping feature which is primarily responsible for the absence of any need for large-scale computations, and which virtually ensures convergence to a balanced plan.

If the plan is too tight, and norm adjustment will not work, the planners still have two alternatives available—neither of which requires much computation. They may reduce gross outputs across the board, thus inserting more slack into the norm adjustment, or they may expand the scope of adjustment by altering the criteria. A great danger in the system is the temptation to adopt the latter approach, which can entail a very sharp divergence of the plan from feasibility. One recalls cases from several soviet-type economies in which political pressures not to reduce plan targets apparently have led to adoption of this procedure, thereby creating great difficulties for producers and controllers alike. Of course even if this problem does not arise, the fact that the plan is balanced is no guarantee of feasibility, much less of optimality—a state of affairs of which participants are well aware.

Another notable feature is that, unlike most of the mechanistic planning schemes, this one possesses no dual. Prices are not generated by the planning process, and there does not appear to be any parallel process, potential or actual, by which they could be generated. It is true that one might derive input-output prices from the matrix of coefficients implicit in the final plan; however, if the calculation were performed, given the interpretation placed on these coefficients above, the prices would not possess even the limited rationality attributed to such prices by input–output theory. In the soviet type of economy, price formation is an activity wholly separate from plan making.

Many commentators have observed that soviet-type economies collect at the center a tremendous amount of information which is not used in plan making, and which is not directly relevant to plan making. Our description of the process indicates that much of this information is indeed useful, its aim being to provide better knowledge of coefficient distributions. Bargaining is closely bound up with the procedure because of the expectations of subordinate levels about future tasks. The additional information serves to control distortions in reporting, even when no use whatever is made of it in plan making.

The most surprising aspect of this scheme is the implicit transposition of the way in which technological choice is built into the system. To see how this works we may contrast the choices open to product sectors in making norm adjustments with the technological choices available under the Malinvaud scheme. In the latter case, choice for each sector was among production activities, each of which was characterized by a vector of input–output coefficients. However, in the soviet-type planning bureau, each product sector controls not only the sectoral production activity descriptions but also the allocation coefficients for the sector's output.[11] Indeed most adjustments by a product sector, especially a priority one, will be in values of the latter coefficients rather than the former. But this is equivalent to choosing allocation vectors as activities instead of production vectors. It appears to assume that production is a more flexible process than allocation.

How can such an approach be justified? Actually there are several factors which may mitigate the unfavorable consequences of the procedure. In the first place, it must be remembered that the rigid linearity assumption for productive activities is often a serious oversimplification, especially in industries having a broad age distribution of plants; consequently there is some chance that individual coefficient adjustment improves the accuracy of the description of requirements for the targeted level of activity. Secondly, there is the considerable uncertainty about the accuracy of the coefficients, even if the production process is in fact linear. Over a modest range, coefficient adjustment in

[11] In Gosplan SSSR during the 1950's these two tasks were handled by different bureaus, the former by the industrial departments, the latter by the summary departments. However, each pair perforce worked closely together. See Levine, *op. cit.*, p. 163.

response to the needs revealed by imbalance has some chance of improving the description of production itself. Thirdly, it is possible for a production sector to respond to imbalance by adjusting the coefficients of the production processes it controls; however, this has the effect of causing adjustments in the balances of all input sectors.[12] Finally, there are limits imposed by the planning system on allocation-norm adjustment. These must be reported to the product sections controlling the productive activity. If they are outrageous they will be challenged, and some other form of adjustment may be adopted. Essentially, the planning process uses available information to seek an acceptable compromise, among a group of specialized experts who possess divergent interests which are reflected in disagreements over the plan data.

Crude as this plan-making process is, there are nevertheless at least three ways in which normative, optimizing features are built into it. The first is simply the fact that the result is a formally consistent plan. This means, in the normative sense, that some account is taken of the interdependence that abounds in any modern industrial economy. The second feature is the gearing of short term operational plans to the longer run aims of the leadership. The construction of perspective plans based on social goals as spelled out by the leadership, and the use of information from these plans in setting priorities in the operational plan, serve to point the latter in the desired direction. Finally, the processes of making coefficient distributions and norm adjustments bring current performance data into the plan, and thereby permit some interaction between short run possibilities and long run desires. For all its inadequacies, the results of this scheme might conceivably be preferred to, say, a plan constructed from a perfectly accurate input–output table which guaranteed no more than consistency among gross and net outputs.

---

[12] For downward revisions in a tight plan, the effect is similar to relaxing norm-priority rules: It can be expected to involve a substitution between slack and probable feasibility in the plan.

Enterprise Decisions

We turn now to the operating end of the hierarchy, the enterprise. A model of enterprise decision making will be presented in this section, and its implications for implementation and control of the plan evaluated in the next. The enterprise manager in a soviet-type economy, though he is a subordinate official in a complex hierarchy, is also a man to whom authority has been delegated and consequently who has some scope for choosing among alternatives. In addition, the leadership has provided him not only with instructions as to how to make these choices, but also with strong material incentives which often leave him with clear indications as to how to make his decisions. At times incentives and instructions are contradictory, but we will ignore aspects of this contradiction which cannot be captured by the notion of substitution among goals of varying relative value.[13]

In soviet-type economies a rather complicated system of bonuses has been developed. In the first place, there are bonuses which vary with the extent to which the target for the gross value of output is fulfilled.[14] Another bonus applies to the extent to which average cost is reduced. Still others depend on the level of production of specific commodities, defined in physical terms, and the amount of saving in the consumption of certain inputs. The labor productivity goal is an example of the latter, as is the bonus for saving on fuel consumption. Of course not every firm is subject to all these targets and bonuses at the

[13] Cf. A. G. Frank, "Goal Ambiguity and Conflicting Standards: An Approach to the Study of Organization," *Human Organization*, 17 (1958), 8–13, and footnote 27 below.

[14] There has been a good deal of discussion whether gross or net value of output is the more appropriate maximand. We do not consider this problem, though it can be treated within the framework of this chapter. See below, footnote 16, and Alesky Wakar and J. G. Zielinski, "Socialist Price Stystems," *American Economic Review*, 53 (March and Dec., 1963), 109–27 and 1093–94; and J. M. Montias, "Socialist Price Systems," in *ibid.*, pp. 1085–93.

same time. However, it is a feature of the operation of soviet-type economies that bonuses tend to proliferate, with instances not uncommon in which a single firm may have twenty or thirty or even more such goals at one time.[15]

A calculating manager then will find himself faced with an objective function such as the following:

$$(1) \qquad G = G(Q, \pi, Q_i) \qquad (i = 1, \ldots, n)$$

where G is the income index, Q the amount by which the gross value of output target is overfulfilled, π profits (or cost), and Q_i the amount of overfulfillment of the plan target for the ith good. Suppose that the n outputs and inputs of the firm are listed so that the first k of them are outputs, and that we write

$$G_Q \quad \text{for} \quad \frac{\partial G}{\partial Q}, \qquad G_i \quad \text{for} \quad \frac{\partial G}{\partial Q_i}, \qquad \text{etc.}$$

Then G_Q is positive and G_i is positive for

$$i \leq k,$$

and otherwise negative.

As for G_π, it will be positive where π is interpreted as profits, negative when interpreted as cost.

Gross output overfulfillment[16]

$$(2) \qquad Q = \sum_{i=1}^{k} p_i(x_i - \overline{x}_i)$$

where p_i is the state-determined price of the ith good, x_i is the actual output of the ith good which the manager intends to produce, and $\overline{x}_i$ is the output target fixed by the plan. Prices are

---

[15] Berliner, *op. cit.*, is the standard work on this subject. A pathological case is described by Janos Kornai, *Overcentralization in Economic Administration* (London: Oxford University Press, 1959).

[16] If Q is interpreted as net output, the summation is merely extended to embrace the inputs of intermediate goods.

thus used as a weighting system for aggregating different kinds of products into a gross output measure. Profits

$$(3) \qquad\qquad \pi = \sum_{i=1}^{n} p_i x_i$$

are the usual sum of revenues and costs with the x_i appearing with negative signs when they are used as inputs. As a cost index, the first k terms of the sum would be dropped. In Soviet practice, both profits and cost reduction targets are assigned and have bonuses attached to fulfillment and overfulfillment. On this interpretation, equation (1) describes roughly the bonus system faced by a factory manager in a soviet-type firm.

In equation (3) prices are used as a measure of costs and benefits. This is clearly a different use from that of equation (2) and so a different set of price weights may be used. The Soviets have in fact often used different price systems in these two calculations.[17] At times they have even used different prices in calculating costs and profits. For convenience we will assume that a uniform price system is used within the industrial sector.

The manager must operate within the constraint of his technology

$$(4) \qquad\qquad F(x_1, x_2, \ldots, x_n) = 0$$

for which marginal products have the signs:

$$\frac{\partial x_i}{\partial x_j} \geqq 0 \quad \text{for} \quad i \leqq k, j > k$$

$$\frac{\partial x_i}{\partial x_j} \leqq 0 \quad \text{for} \quad i \neq j$$

and either $\qquad i, j \leqq k \quad$ or $\quad i, j > k$

that is, marginal products are nonnegative and every pair of inputs and outputs is technically a substitute. In addition, second order conditions for determining a maximum are

[17] For a description of Soviet price systems see Morris Bornstein, "The Soviet Price System," *American Economic Review*, 52 (Mar. 1962), 64–103.

assumed to be satisfied. The function F describes, not the production set of the manager, but the efficiency surface. We are assuming that the manager will always choose efficient points, an idealization that permits easy comparison with alternative models and which perhaps does not distort reality more in this case than in those.

The manager's course is now clear: he finds the levels of output which maximize (1) subject to the limitations of his facilities, (4).[18] This is equivalent to maximizing the Lagrangean

$$(5) \qquad\qquad Z = G - \lambda F$$

for which equilibrium conditions have the form

$$(6) \qquad\qquad \frac{1}{\lambda} = \frac{F_i}{p_i(G\pi + G_Q) + G_i}$$

or

$$(6a) \qquad [p_i(G\pi + G_Q) + G_i] = -[p_j(G_\pi + G_Q) + G_j]\frac{\partial x_j}{\partial x_i}$$

where the marginal products are evaluated at the equilibrium point.[19] Before proceeding, this result may be compared with that for a competitive capitalist firm faced with the same prices and production function. For the capitalist, $G = \pi$ and the result of maximizing this subject to (4) is to generate equilibrium conditions of the form:

$$(6b) \qquad\qquad \frac{1}{\lambda} = \frac{F_i}{p_i} \qquad \text{or} \qquad p_i = -p_j\frac{\partial x_j}{\partial x_i}$$

[18] Note that where strict upper limits to scarce inputs are set by the state, the production function can be changed by inserting the fixed level of supply, thereby reducing the number of arguments. However, the opportunities available to a Soviet manager are such that he would probably not be compelled to accept such a rigid constraint. Cf. below, pp. 88–89.

[19] A similar version of this model was presented in my "Planners' Choice Variables," in Gregory Grossman, ed., *Value and Plan* (Berkeley: University of California Press, 1960), pp. 132–51 and 158–61. See p. 160 of that work for references to earlier theorizing about the Soviet firm. See also Bela Balassa, "La théorie de la firme socialiste," *Economie appliquée*, 12 (Oct.–Dec., 1959), 535–70.

which describes the familiar condition that the price of a factor be equal to the value of its marginal product.

It is clear that the Soviet manager will often have an incentive to produce a different output from that provided by the plan. The output bonuses tend to encourage him to produce more, while the cost and input bonuses (and often the profit bonus) tend to encourage him to save on consumption of inputs. During most of its life the Soviet system has emphasized the former at the expense of the latter. The physical rationing of many inputs might suggest that the managers have little or no flexibility on the input side of their decisions. It is well known that this is not the case, that in fact by bargaining, by *sub rosa* trading, and even buying and selling, the managers of a great many firms have some ability to alter the available supplies of various inputs. However, the range of choice should not be exaggerated. Successful firms in heavy industry typically have had more flexibility than textile firms, whether successful or not. And flexibility varies with the kind of input. Finally, even the most successful firm will hesitate to expand its achievements beyond a certain limit, for fear of norm raising by the planners in response. Unfortunately there is no basis for making an estimate of the magnitude of these limits.[20]

In Figure 4.2 a simplified version of the firm model is presented in order to illustrate some of the possible solutions. In this case Q and π are the only arguments of the criterion function, which is shaped so as to give primary but not sole emphasis to rewarding gross output performance. The extreme case occurs when the enterprise is near plan fulfillment, where no substitution of profits for output, on however favorable terms, is rewarded. But given gross output plan fulfillment, such a substitution becomes relatively more favorable the lower the degree of profits plan fulfillment. The wavy line enclosing the diagram indicates that there are rather strict limits set by higher organs

---

[20] See the discussion in Berliner, *op. cit.*, Chap. 6.

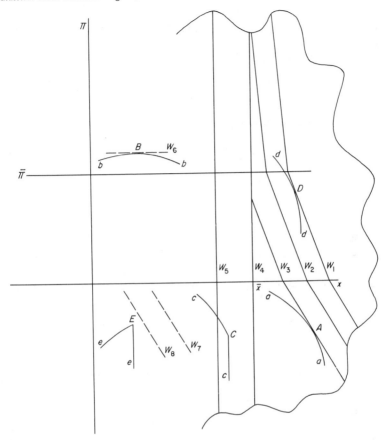

Figure 4.2

to the range of choice open to factory managers. The curved
lines represent alternative profits–output possibilities curves,
A and D showing optimal adjustments when output fulfillment
is feasible, B, C, and E suggesting possible adjustments when it
is not.[21] Point B also represents the competitive capitalist choice
for short run adjustment given profits–output possibilities bb and

---

[21] The latter are the more conjectural, since little is known about behavior
when fulfillment of output targets is not possible.

the same price system. In recent years the reward curves have tended to be shifted in favor of better profits or cost reduction performance, as compared to the "moderate Stalinist" case depicted in the diagram.

Extreme Stalinism

We now take a brief look at a special case of soviet-type enterprise decision making. This may be called the "extreme Stalinist" case since it uses only fulfillment and overfulfillment of the gross output target as an argument of the criterion. Thus

$$G = G(Q)$$

Maximizing this subject to the production function yields two types of equilibrium conditions. The first deals with a pair of goods one of which is an output (and so appears in Q), the other of which is not:

$$\frac{\partial x_i}{\partial x_j} p_i G_Q = 0$$

so that, as expected, each input is used until it can no longer yield any positive marginal product. The second and more interesting case is that of two outputs:

$$p_i = p_j \frac{\partial x_j}{\partial x_i}$$

Since G_Q has dropped out of this equation, output targets and the gross output bonus have no effect on the assortment decision. Prices are now the only relevant parameters for that decision. This happens because the gross output bonus system is symmetric with respect to outputs; that is, the same contribution to gross output is made by the same value of given output increments. Given technology, these values—and consequently the incentive to change assortment—are wholly dependent on relative prices.

This helps explain the great difficulty the Soviet system has had in controlling assortment effectively. Even with a less extreme criterion the problem remains serious, so long as gross output is a major measure of enterprise performance.

Implementation and Control

A scheme of the kind described in the section on Plan Making above clearly produces a plan which contains a good many mistakes in the form of nonoptimal or even infeasible targets. A natural response to awareness of this has been to provide for some flexibility in the implementation of the plan at lower levels. The G-function of the last section defines the terms of the choices open to firm managers. Changes in G serve both as signals that certain changes are deemed desirable by the authorities and as a promise of reward for adopting them. Whether the manager is motivated by commitment to the aims of his society or merely to his personal advancement, changes in G provide a stimulus to changes in enterprise activity.

In addition, the comparative statics of the model presented in the section on Enterprise Decisions show that responses tend to be in the right direction. An increase in the price of a product does tend to encourage increased production, a decrease in the price of a factor to encourage its substitution against other factors, an increase in a physical output target to encourage increased production, an increase in the relative rewards associated with profits vis-à-vis gross output to encourage cost reduction, and so forth.[22]

One obvious difficulty with the enterprise control scheme as described is the absence of a single instrument that can move the system from one equilibrium consistent with a given set of efficient prices to another. Suppose that the competitive equilibrium is the appropriate solution for a given firm. Then if each of the terms in brackets in equation (6a) can be made equivalent to the shadow prices of competitive equilibrium, the enterprise

[22] Formal comparative static analysis has not been included, since the qualitative results are straightforward and conventional.

will be guided by the incentive system to choose the right bill of outputs.[23] But such a change, in general, cannot be brought about by varying prices, since prices play roles of differing significance within the bracketed terms for differing firms. In principle the adjustment could be made by appropriate change in the Q_i, but this requires a separate calculation by the controllers for each firm. A direct instruction to produce the appropriate amounts would be much simpler.

A related problem occurs with respect to the assortment of output in the case of multiproduct firms. A price adjustment will not work.[24] Suppose sources and uses of the product whose production should be altered are at present balanced. A change in the price of that product will generally have a weaker effect on production and consumption than under comparable conditions in a market economy, so the change will typically have to be much larger. Also a given price change will usually change production by a different amount than consumption. This is handled in markets by flexible price response, a groping toward equilibrium. But in this administrative system such frequent price changes are too costly. So the price change will typically lead to some persisting imbalance, unless the Q_i are adjusted as well. Indeed, direct adjustment of the Q_i seems preferable, if only because these instruments are relatively more powerful. But the effects of a change in one of these instruments on outputs of *other* goods produced by the same firm cannot be easily calculated by the controllers. One of the most serious problems the controllers face in the soviet-type economy is precisely in these secondary effects on relative outputs of adjustments in targets.

To bring out clearly the major control problems let us assume that there is only one level of organization between the enterprise and the planning bureau, the ministry. Each ministry

[23] Assuming there are not multiple optima to the solution of the set of equations consisting of the equilibrium conditions and the production function.

[24] In the extreme Stalinist case, price adjustment can be used in principle as indicated in the last section. The present argument deals in part with a different aspect of the problem, and applies also to this case.

controls the enterprises producing a particular class of goods.[25] The ministerial incentive is to perform as well as possible with respect to the aggregate targets assigned it by the plan. It must disaggregate plan targets and allocate targets among enterprises under its control. It is also the major procurement and supply agency for the inputs and outputs of its enterprises which are exchanged with other ministries. The ministry thus bears major responsibility for constructing and adjusting the G-functions for enterprises under its control, given that aggregate targets measure its own performance and that it can only adjust prices of goods which are produced and consumed largely within the sector.

The restriction on price adjustment by ministries is an essential one, for otherwise the planning bureau's version of the plan would impose no constraint whatsoever on production by a given sector, if disaggregation of the targets was necessary. Figure 4.3 illustrates this point. $\bar{x}$ is the target assigned the min-

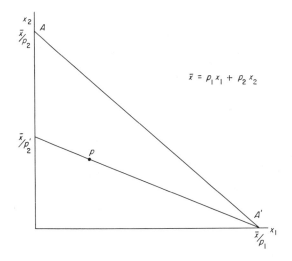

Figure 4.3

[25] The problem would be rather similar if we were to substitute regional economic councils for ministries. The differences are discussed in Chap. Seven.

istry, which is an aggregate of goods x_1 and x_2. At prices p_1 and p_2 any bill of the two goods represented by points on the line AA' will fulfill the ministry's target. But if the ministry controls prices it can fulfill its target by producing at *any* point on the diagram, such as P, simply by varying one or more of the prices.[26] Thus even though prices are not produced by the planning process, and output targets are basic determinants of choice throughout the system, some price stability is essential in stabilizing expectations, at the plan bureau level, as to the effects of choosing different values for the variables which are manipulated by the planning process. And the particular choice of prices has a considerable influence on the relation between the plan bureau's plan on the one hand, and the enterprises' targets on the other.

Given these limitations and restrictions on the use of prices as instruments, the ministry will tend to rely primarily on output targets. In disaggregating the plan the ministry would probably first make a rough allocation among firms in terms of the generalized (gross) output instrument, Q, and would then carry out finer allocations using the appropriate Q_i. Past experience in most cases will provide guidelines for these allocations, with some modifications to take account of learning and of the presence of new capacity.

Nevertheless the process of making allocations is almost inevitably costly and time consuming. There are bound to be some conflicts of interest between ministry and enterprise. Though both ministry and enterprise have an interest in keeping targets within ranges that can be easily achieved, once the ministry's task is fixed (and its expectations of minimum acceptable performance are established during the course of bargaining with higher levels in the hierarchy) it must find enterprises to whom it can assign targets which will generate at least

---

[26] We are considering here the price weights used in constructing the aggregate variables which measure ministry performance. In a multiple price system, variations in other prices would not be excluded.

that performance. Bargaining, whose aim explicitly or implicitly is to alter relative target ratios among enterprises, is the
result.

The ministry will find it in its own interest to reward firms
which have done well in the past; usually these will be the newer
enterprises whose plants are more efficient. Having established
good relations with ministerial personnel it is easier for such
enterprises to maintain them. There may even be some incentive
for the ministry to make inefficiently large allocations to such
firms, since it has generally proved useful for a unit in the hierarchy to be able to report outstanding levels of performance by
individual subunits. On the firm's side, its special influence is
rather like a form of monopoly. Its position in the ministerial
organization enables it to obtain a relatively more favorable
position with regard to the arguments of its criterion. However,
monopoly does not in this case imply a reduction of individual
enterprise output; quite the contrary, since output figures prom-
inently in that criterion. Only to the extent that at the *industry*
level there are inefficient allocations among enterprises is there
likely to be a comparative reduction in output as a by-product
of monopoly position.

The enterprise criterion is manipulated at two different
levels, since most prices are under high-level control, as are
allocation quotas for some inputs, but output targets are under
ministerial control. No doubt this causes difficulties in controlling
firms; probably it is not a fundamental difficulty, since price
manipulation is an infrequent instrument of policy and its
impact is rather weak, except on assortment decisions. But
clearly, even ignoring this problem, the ministry has a very
difficult task in providing appropriate forms and parameters for
its enterprises' G-functions. Partly it is a matter of the technical
difficulty of the problem. As we have seen, the ministry would
have a hard enough time stimulating enterprises to produce at a
competitive optimum; but at least in this problem one knows in
principle what values to assign the "true" prices, namely the

shadow prices. The task is to adjust the Q and Q_i so that for each product "true" and shadow prices coincide. But in terms of the model, "true" prices should not equal shadow prices. Rather they should equal values which will stimulate the firm to produce the right amount of each good with the right technology. This set of prices is not easily derived from the ministries' own targets, but depends in important ways on the specific technology of each firm under its control. Even with accurate information on hand this would be a tremendous problem. And it would be wasteful to solve it since direct controls would be much cheaper to administer.

But of course information is not accurate, being subject to the distortions of the bureaucratic bargaining process. The firms withhold as much information on maximum attainable performance as they can and the ministry, no more than the planning bureau, can be sure how good past performance was relative to potential. The information available to the ministry is that its own targets are probably not optimal, and the capabilities of its own units are known only with a large margin of error. Consequently it can treat manipulation of the G-functions only as a crude device suitable for making gross adjustments in the performance of enterprises. The ministry can get a firm to adjust output of a good by changing a Q_i, but only if it accompanies the instruction with clear indications that it is to be taken seriously. And even then it cannot be at all sure as to how much actual adjustment will occur in relation to the amount demanded.

Uncertainty on the enterprise side compounds the difficulties involved in effective incentive manipulation. Armed with a large number of instruments, and functioning as an important cog in short run adjustment to changes in the environment, the ministry is bound to make fairly frequent changes in its demands on the firm. Almost inevitably there will be conflicts and contradictions among the instructions. This creates ambiguity in the minds of the enterprise managers, and tends to weaken the average impact of instructions on their behavior.[27] In such an uncertain environment there are no instruments which can be effectively used to make the fine adjustments that are required to adjust assortment appropriately.

A notable feature of the soviet type of economic system is the large number of what might be called "Irish pennants" that the system generates. These are loose ends of connections among elements of the system which ideally should be connected to the rest of the system in feedback loops but which instead are left dangling—being influenced by, but not influencing, the rest of the system.[28]

Some examples will indicate the significance of this phenomenon. We have already noticed the high level of uncertainty in ministerial control over enterprises. The consequence of this is that large amounts of information are absorbed at each level, thus limiting responses of each unit to a relatively small number of strong signals from other units.

Another case occurs with the transportation plan, which must provide schedules for intersector and interfirm deliveries of the more important commodities. Ideally the final plan would be the result of close interaction between the production and distribution aspects of economic activity. However, this does not generally occur. Instead the planners produce their production plan, taking at least implicit account of relevant distributional information from past operations. The transportation plan makers then take the new plan, for the most part in disaggregated form, and apply rules for allocation which in effect are the counterpart of the second stage in plan making as described above.

---

[27] A. G. Frank (cf. footnote 13 above) has suggested that goal ambiguity serves a useful role in fixing the attention of managers on instructions. The combination of rather heavy sanctions against nonperformance and uncertainty as to the nature of intended performance leads to intense search of each instruction for clues as to its real meaning. Even if this is true it may not improve ministerial control, since the risk of unanticipated consequences from such close perusal of instructions would probably be rather high.

[28] A variable of this kind is endogenous to the system but appears in only one equation (or subset of equations) of that system.

Rules governing the direction of flow of various kinds of goods from producer to consumer, rules governing the typical pattern of seasonal operation, etc., are incorporated into this decision process either directly or by norm-adjustment. Much is left open, to be settled by direct negotiations among various supply and procurement agencies. However, to a much greater extent than the annual plan makers, the transportation plan makers take the production plan as given and adjust their schedules appropriately. There are much sharper limits to norm (*zaiavka*) adjustment in this case.[29]

A final example comes from the consumer sector. A notable feature of the soviet type of economy is the short-run rigidity of response of production to changes in consumer demand. The typical responses to an increase in demand for a consumer good are either to raise the retail price or simply to allow empty-shelves rationing. The distribution system for consumer goods has virtually no leverage on the production sector over the time period of the operational plan.

This is sometimes interpreted as absence of consumer sovereignty, but that is a misleading conclusion. What it really says is only that the immediate or short run response to consumer desires is very weak. From one operational plan to the next, consumer desires are unquestionably taken into account, as the quite rapid rise of consumer goods production in most soviet-type economies and the notable variations in the rates of increase among consumer goods testify. The most significant criticism of this form of organization is not absence of consumer sovereignty so much as the production inefficiency it entails, especially when undesired goods are produced and excessive inventories result.

Is There an Equilibrium?

In the first section three kinds of organizational interaction were cited, illustrating the notion of organizational equilibrium.

[29] A description of the procedure can be found in I. Birman, *Transportnaia zadača lineinogo programmirovaniia* (Moscow: Ekonlitizdat, 1962), pp. 96ff.

Examples of each of the three instances have been found in the preceding sections to occur in soviet-type economies. For example, the leadership in a soviet-type economy is aware of the large amount of institutionalized response built into the process of plan disaggregation. In order to preserve some minimum level of confidence in its expectations as to responses to alternative aggregate plans it must encourage this rigidity in response by subordinates, because changes will have uncertain consequences until they too have become institutionalized. Therefore the rigidity in response tends to persist. That is to say, there is a point beyond which the addition of resources devoted to the preparation of a better plan no longer pays in terms of alternative uses of those resources.

Examples of the second effect—conflicts stemming from divergence of interest between different levels of the hierarchy such as ministry and enterprise when there has been some delegation of authority—have also been described.

The third example, consisting of a cycle of creeping centralization followed by redelegation of the accumulated authority, also seems to have a counterpart in the soviet type of economic organization. The necessary conditions are present, in particular the relatively high cost of collecting information about performance at the center, which requires not only some delegation of authority but also some trust, a recognition that not all actions of subordinates can be controlled. Particular bits of information about unwanted outcomes are likely to generate piecemeal recentralization, for example by expanding the number of commodities planned at the center or by increasing the number of ministries; this increases work pressures at the center and finally leads to reorganization. If overall performance has been satisfactory it is quite possible that this cycling will remain always within the same general organizational framework.[30]

[30] The pressures pushing both toward and against choice-decentralization in the Soviet Union are analyzed by Gregory Grossman in "The Structure and Organization of the Soviet Economy," in D. Treadgold, ed., *The Development of the USSR* (Seattle: University of Washington Press, 1964), pp. 41–60.

Other responses are possible however. An improvement in the quality of information available at the center can be achieved by setting up a secondary hierarchy whose primary function is to collect information more or less autonomously of the existing hierarchy and report up. Both the party and the financial organs, not to mention the statistical service, have performed this function in all soviet-type economies. The problems associated with the use of secondary hierarchies will be discussed later. Here we only note that when these organizations are given some authority to control results as well as report them, serious conflicts can occur with the primary hierarchy. To some extent the effect of this conflict is to negate the usefulness of the secondary hierarchies, since it introduces a further element of uncertainty into the process of response to signals from above.

Enough has been said so far to make it clear that within the operational planning period the soviet type of system has surprisingly little flexibility of response, except to the strongest signals. An indication of this, as well as a significant cost, is the high level of inventory accumulation which characterizes economies of this kind.[31] One might speculate that there is an equilibrium inventory level for given levels of output in the system, which depends on the average level of uncertainty as to deliveries and the effectiveness of the inventory reporting system. As with the other equilibrium properties, this too is a rather rough-and-ready one, which would probably vary depending on the economy's place in the centralization-delegation cycle.

It seems that there is a strong systemic element in the pressure under which subordinates typically operate in soviet-type economies. A natural consequence of the leadership's uncertainty as to what is possible is to overstate their demands. The difficulty lies in their very restricted ability to observe the "reserves" that are not being utilized. As long as the pressure does not create a divergence between actual and reported behavior so great as to

---

[31] Robert Campbell, "Soviet and American Inventory-Output Ratios," *American Economic Review*, 48 (1958), 549–65.

seriously reduce the accuracy of the plan as a measure of economic potential, the pressure would seem to be a net benefit to the leadership in reducing capturable reserves.

However, this conclusion is not independent of the specific properties of the soviet type of economic system. For example, persistent pressure is likely to be relatively more effective at the enterprise level when the G-functions are weighted toward output targets, than when they are weighted toward profits or cost-reduction targets. A major problem is that the achievement of enterprise cost reduction may not contribute to economy-wide cost reduction, given the dubious nature of the prices used, and the balancing problems which can lead to inventory accumulation even if each firm is highly successful in reducing cost. Cost reduction is too indirectly related to the goal which inspired it (presumably an increased ability to produce certain goods) to be transmitted through such an "absorptive," multilevel hierarchy as exists in soviet-type economies.

In contrasting the planning system of this chapter with those of Chapter Three it might appear that there are heavy costs to be borne in terms of plan accuracy if the plan is to be fitted into an organization which is concerned not only with finding out where the optimum is but also in achieving it. But in this chapter we have been discussing only a single type of plan making, and not all conceivable organization schemes would produce the levels of uncertainty under which officials in a soviet type of economy operate. In the next two chapters we shall consider a somewhat different, though not unrelated, form of organization, one that is calculated to require a minimum of communication within the hierarchy, and then contrast it with the soviet organization.

CHAPTER FIVE

The
Command Society

The term "command economy" refers to a form of economic organization in which the allocation of resources is carried out by the extensive use of orders to produce and deliver goods. Of course commands or orders or instructions play an important role in all industrial economies. At the plant level, organization is nearly everywhere that of the command economy. But the soviet-type economies are distinctive in that they use the command economy extensively in interenterprise allocation processes. In the last chapter we explored some of the implications of that system.

The general concept of hierarchy provides a basis for comparing command and market economies. But it does not capture the differences that may exist between command economies. From the point of view of individual behavior, one might differentiate hierarchies according to the degree of their participants' dedication to the goals of the system. The most dedicated will behave differently from the "undedicated"; for example the former may accept orders without question while the latter complain, cajole, or threaten in their effort to get the orders modified or accepted.

A distinction of this kind has played a very important role in the history of communist societies and economies. This distinction appears to be sufficiently important that the two kinds of hierarchies will perform very differently when used to control the economy, or a large portion of it. Also, a hierarchy consisting primarily of highly dedicated participants represents probably the greatest degree of authority centralization that is feasible for a society. Consequently this kind of hierarchy is worth studying for two reasons: it is an interesting extreme form of social organization and is at least a potential organizational choice for communist leaderships, an alternative they tend to recognize rather explicitly.

Unfortunately no description of the properties of such an organization exists in a useful form—for discussion of its effectiveness in controlling an economy. In this chapter we present a sociological model of this command society, and in the following chapter consider its applicability to an economy, and contrast it with the classical soviet organization.

Properties of the Command Society

Gregory Grossman and others have done much to develop the idea of a command economy, and to explore the economic problems associated with the use of directives from a center as a means of organizing economic interaction.[1] By emphasizing the sociological aspects of command we hope here to be able to add something to the understanding of this distinctive type of social organization. Command societies operating outside the economy have a long history and provide the best available material. It is for this reason that the present chapter leaves the economy temporarily aside.

A command society is an integrated hierarchic organization. By "hierarchic" is meant that there is at least a partial ordering of levels such that a member of a higher level has some responsibility

[1] Among others, see Gregory Grossman, "The Structure and Organization of the Soviet Economy," in D. Treadgold, ed., *The Development of the USSR* (Seattle: University of Washington Press, 1964), pp. 41–60; and "Notes for a Theory of the Command Economy," *Soviet Studies*, 15 (Oct., 1963), 103–23.

for and influence over some members of a lower level, and that the hierarchy pyramids in the familiar way. Although authority and responsibility are pyramided, it should be noted that the position of each member with respect to every other member is not necessarily fixed by a hierarchy. There will usually be individuals who neither give nor take orders from some other member. A hierarchy may be said to define a partial ordering of the members of a group with respect to the property of being empowered to give orders to members.

By "integrated" is meant that the entire society or hierarchy is controlled by a single person or group, and that these leaders are (typically) members who worked up through the hierarchy to their present position. It also is meant to imply that the society does not contain parallel hierarchies; that is, there must be some significant probability that some member of the hierarchy employed in one part of the system will be transferred (possibly with promotion) to one of the other parts.

Specific rewards and penalties are, generally speaking, not tied to short-run performance in the command society. Instead, short-run performance is influenced by instructions. There are rules which may prescribe activities or conduct. Among the activities with which rules may be concerned, decision making is of prime importance. Instructions may simply enjoin the performance of certain acts ("Produce 500 flanges on your lathe this morning") or may enjoin the use of certain criteria in decision making ("In production planning, choose the least-cost technology"). Instructions may be personal communications from superior to subordinate, in which case they are often called "commands," or impersonal communications from the upper hierarchy to the lower, often called "regulations." The form of the instruction is not relevant, except that formal acceptance of authority relationships within the social system is probably necessary; instructions may be minatory in mood, flowery in language, or simple declarative sentences ("Members maintain their own equipment"). The essential feature of an instruction is that it be recognized as such by the parties concerned.

The separation of rewards and penalties from the specific properties of short-run performance is the heart of the command society. It has fundamental effects on the communication process as well as leading to an entirely different incentive system. However, it is not meant to imply that there are no sanctions or rewards associated with individual acts. Another important element of the command society is that there are strong sanctions against disobedience of instructions. Disobedience, however, is treated as a generalized act, the sanctions being fixed, within broad limits, without reference to the specific nature of the instruction violated.

The command society's incentives are not entirely negative. Promotion to a higher position of command within the hierarchy is the major positive incentive. Promotion being periodic, it is based primarily on average performance levels over an extended period of time. In special cases promotion may be awarded for specific acts, but this is done infrequently enough so that it does not arouse expectations. Promotions generally are accompanied by an improvement in the standard of living, either in terms of ordinary material benefits or of status goods whose primary purpose is to identify and ornament the level attained, or of both. Many command societies offer additional rewards which appeal to some emotion other than self-gratification. But the societies which are mentioned below all make at least supplementary use of material rewards of the above two kinds.

Four fundamental properties of the command society have been distinguished: (1) integrated hierarchic organization; (2) separation of rewards and short-run performance by the use of instructions; (3) strong and generalized sanctions against disobedience of instructions; and (4) promotion within the hierarchy as the major interest-oriented incentive. These are taken to define the necessary characteristics of a command society; they are also sufficient; that is, all social systems which possess these characteristics will be called command societies.

The command society is a kind of rational bureaucracy, in the sense of Max Weber, and also a kind of formal organization, in the sense of Chester Barnard. In fact, the Weber and Barnard conceptions are closely related, with the former emphasizing problems of authority and the latter emphasizing communication problems.[2] However, in three respects the command society represents something of a special case: (1) the emphasis on integration within the hierarchy,[3] (2) the emphasis on long-run rather than short-run rewards, and (3) the emphasis on a generalized disobedience sanction. The latter is probably the most important, and accounts for many of the special features of the command society.

As briefly set out above, the intent behind this definition of command society properties may not be wholly clear; this vagueness can be somewhat remedied by looking at a couple of social systems which do not qualify. First consider a local public education system in the United States. It is certainly a bureaucratic system, with a hierarchy ranging from the teacher through the principal up to the superintendent of schools. The school board would not be considered a part of the bureaucracy since its members have not typically worked their way up through the hierarchy. Promotion is a major incentive for at least some of the participants, and no one is on piecework. However, both integration and the generalized disobedience sanction are weak or absent. There is much movement from one school system to another, and no hierarchic control over groups of school systems. All hierarchies are interested in compliance, but training and exhortation toward obedience of orders as a cardinal virtue is hardly a common feature of public school hierarchies in the United States. Also, probably the majority of the teachers have no serious ambitions toward administrative work, which tends to weaken the promotion incentive.

[2] As has been pointed out by Terence Hopkins, "Bureaucratic Authority: The Convergence of Weber and Barnard," in Amitai Etzioni, ed., *Complex Organizations: A Sociological Reader* (New York: Holt, 1961), pp. 82–96.

[3] Though in Weber's case the emphasis on career orientation of the bureaucrat seems quite similar. Cf. Peter Blau and W. R. Scott, *Formal Organizations* (San Francisco: Chandler, 1962), p. 33. We return to this question below.

The public school itself has some features of a bureaucracy, with its periodic promotions of students from one class to another, the emphasis on obedience to the teacher, and the student–teacher–principal range of hierarchic levels. In a stable community the typical student and teacher would expect to complete their service in the same school. However, promotion in the sense intended above really does not exist in a public school. Movement from one grade to another does not give the newly advanced student any significant power to command students in lower grades. The promotions for teachers too are primarily in terms of salary, not power. In sum, promotion from class to class does not involve advancement to a new level of command in the hierarchy, while promotion from student to teacher status is generally not integrated.

A somewhat different case is presented by a prison. Here all the trappings of a total institution, as Goffman has called it,[4] are present: participants are separated from the larger society around them, and are subject to rigid controls from above in almost every aspect of their lives. Strict obedience is demanded of inmates, and compulsion is freely used to obtain compliance. Furthermore, a kind of hierarchy seems to develop among the inmates, with the leading positions often going to those who can obtain favors from the guards, the latter tending to manipulate this situation in order to maintain and enhance their own authority. The formal administrative hierarchy of a prison may in some instances constitute a command society. However, the total institution, including the inmates, does not. There is, after all, a mobility barrier between inmate and guard which is rarely bridged—such a "promotion" does not constitute part of the hopes or expectations of inmates. One is promoted to the outside. Prisons and asylums—considered as institutions consisting of both staff and inmates—do not qualify as command societies because

---

[4] E. Goffman, "The Characteristics of Total Institution," reprinted in Etzioni, *op. cit.*, pp. 312–40.

of the absence, or great weakness, of integration and of promotion incentives.

The prison as described can serve to illustrate a frequent misunderstanding with respect to the operation of command societies. In many social systems, including asylums, and some military organizations as well as prisons, the disobedience sanction is associated with the institutionalized use of force to obtain compliance. This resort to force is not, however, an inherent part of every command society. Usually it is a substitute for the positive incentive of promotion within the hierarchy. Many command societies have seemed to function effectively while making even less use of force in obtaining compliance by their members than is typical of the greater society in which they are embedded.

There is bound to be an element of speculation in any attempt to decide what is useful and what is not in any given type of social system. However, differences on this score may be reduced somewhat by checking the ways in which actual command societies have operated. This will be our procedure here. For this check two societies have been chosen. The particular choice was partly governed by availability of information to the writer, but partly also because these two exemplify the strong case: the command society at its best, or very nearly so.

The first of these is the Society of Jesus.[5] Established formally in 1540, the Society has had a more or less continuous existence since then, serving as a leading instrument of the Church Militant. Organized from the beginning as a hierarchy, the Order has a General in Rome, who is elected for life by a group of professed

---

[5] Among the more useful works on the Jesuits are: Louis Baudin, *L'état jésuite du Paraguay* (Paris: Génin, 1962); Joseph Brucker, S.J., *La Compagnie de Jesus (1521–1773)* (Paris: Gabriel Beauchesne, 1919); T. J. Campbell, S.J., *The Jesuits 1534–1921* (New York: Encyclopedia Press, 1921), 2 vols.; Rene Fülöp-Miller, *The Power and Secret of the Jesuits*, trans. from the German (New York: Viking, 1930); John La Farge, S.J., and Margaret Bourke-White, *A Report on the American Jesuits* (New York: Farrar, Straus and Cudahy, 1956); Denis Meadows, *Obedient Men* (New York: Appleton-Century Crofts, 1954).

members of the Order. Next in line to the General in the chain of command are the provinces, which are territorial divisions, each headed by a provincial. Within each province are the primary institutions, nowadays primarily educational, with their rectors and members of various kinds, including various administrative assistants. Promotion is unquestionably a reward for effective service as a member of the organization, and material reward in the short run can play no significant role in a Jesuit's motivation. The hierarchy is integrated, in the sense that transfer to and from other orders is not a regular practice (though transfers between provinces do occur). Finally, obedience has a special status in the Society of Jesus, one which the quasi-military form of organization was designed to support.

The second organization which will be used to illustrate the functions of the command society will be the officer corps of the interwar United States Navy.[6] The interwar period was a time during which the dreadnought type of battleship had become the primary official measure of naval power. The line of battleships with its support of aircraft carriers, cruisers, destroyers, supply train, submarines, and land installations, required the fine coordination of tens of thousands of men operating some of the most complex modern equipment. Both environment and goals are thus entirely different from those of the Society of Jesus. The naval officer hierarchy was integrated in a sense that some navies and armies are not, because of the great flexibility required of line officers and because the overwhelming majority of officers were graduates of the same institution, the Naval Academy at Annapolis. It was expected that every line officer should be able to assume any job appropriate to his rank on the major types

---

[6] The picture of the interwar Navy presented here is partly based on conversations (not interviews) with members of that society. The most useful general source of information is the *Proceedings* of the United States Naval Institute, a semi-official periodical. F. R. Bichowsky, *Is the Navy Ready?* (New York: Vanguard, 1935), is a useful locator of material in the *Proceedings*. Also very useful: H. F. Cope, *Navy Shipboard Administration* (New York: Norton, 1944); and *Naval Leadership*, rev. ed. (Annapolis, Md.: United States Naval Institute, 1939).

of ships,[7] and the career patterns of officers typically reflected a wide variety of duty. There was no bonus system, and promotions at roughly seven-year intervals were the primary material incentive. Obedience was emphasized, as is typical of military organizations.

Institutional Support

The great advantage of an effectively functioning command society is that members do as they are told. As a result, the leadership is able to bring about substantial changes in the behavior of vast numbers of people swiftly. This permits a great concentration of power in the hands of the leadership, which can thus manipulate the social system with considerable flexibility. Of course some price must be paid to create and maintain such a social system. Competent members of this sort of hierarchy are made, not born; not all such hierarchies do function successfully; when they are bad they tend to be very bad; and their prospects for success vary considerably depending on their environment. Let us consider some of the elements which seem to be necessary to the successful performance of assigned tasks by such a social system.

Separation from Society-at-Large

Chester Barnard used the term "zone of indifference" to describe the range over which a hierarchy member is willing to comply with authority, that is, the range of instructions he is willing to obey without question. The indoctrination of the command system is oriented toward the development within participants of an adequately large zone of indifference. This is accomplished partly by inculcating pro attitudes toward the

---

[7] Except the operation of aircraft and submarines. However, those who qualified for these specialties were expected to maintain their other skills, and an officer who spent too much of his time on either specialty was jeopardizing his career.

broad goals of the system, partly by emphasizing the differences between members and outsiders, partly by instilling abhorrence of disobedience.

The attempt to influence attitudes in these three directions began from the moment of entry into the society. In fact it began before, since adaptability—one might almost say malleability—is an important criterion in selecting new members.[8] The Navy and the Jesuits both have a strong preference for the young. This is formalized in the case of the Navy so that entry into the officer corps beyond the age of twenty-four was virtually excluded, exceptions occurring only for a relatively small number of temporary commissions granted during World War I which were subsequently made permanent. The Jesuits do not have such an age limit, but the training system is designed to take younger men, and reports on the novitiate show an overwhelming majority of men in their teens and early twenties. It seems reasonable to infer that primary attitudes are more easily changed at this age than later, and indeed some of the most virulent attacks on the Jesuits have come from ex-members who entered at a later age and apparently could not fully adapt.[9] Though the Navy did not have complete control over admission to the Naval Academy, its control of some of the entrance rules constituted a limited right to veto the nominations of Congressmen. The result of this selection process seems to have been a relatively homogeneous product, with backgrounds concentrated in the middle reaches of the middle class.[10]

After some initial selection of human material, the process of

[8] Anthony Downs has recently prepared a RAND Corporation report on bureaucratic theory, which is concerned among other things with the selection of personality types by bureaucracies operating in various environments, suggesting that selection occurs on both sides. In his terms an effective command society would probably be led by Advocates but staffed by compliant Zealots. The peculiar nature of the society stems from its attempt to manufacture and then to control Zealots. See his "A Theory of Bureaucracy," *American Economic Review*, 55 (May, 1965), 439–46.

[9] For example, Count von Hoensbroech, *Fourteen Years a Jesuit* (London: Cassel, 1911), 2 vols.

[10] C. Wright Mills, *The Power Elite* (New York: Oxford, 1956), Chap. 8.

indoctrination began. In both societies it appears to have been effective, at least in the sense that observers frequently note differences in the behavior of its products as compared with members of society-at-large. During the years of training, members are separated from society in institutions designed to provide environmental support for the indoctrination. In both the seminary and the Academy the candidate is kept fully occupied with appropriate activities, and only very limited access to the outside world is granted. That the Jesuits carry out a special set of "spiritual exercises"[11] over a thirty-day period has been frequently commented on as a vital factor in establishing commitment to the aims of the Society; however, Church dogma in general provides a continual source of exhortation, tacit and overt, toward these goals. In the case of the Navy, no such body of ideology is at hand—in fact it seems that not much was made of patriotism, perhaps because this could be taken for granted in the group selected. However the traditions of naval service and the quasi-aristocratic trappings of military life seem to have provided at least a partial substitute.[12]

The successful product of this training has had his previous loyalties weakened by lack of contact with their objects over a period of years. At the same time, he is being intensively exposed to a new set of loyalties which are constantly being tested in action, for example by demanding cheerful obedience to the frequent assignment of unwelcome chores and, more important, to the regular accomplishment of a strict and imposed daily regimen. His zone of indifference has been greatly expanded, perhaps even transformed, in terms of attitude, into a zone of "active compliance."

[11] For an English edition see W. H. Longridge, *The Spiritual Exercises of S. Ignatius of Loyola*, 3rd ed. (London: Mowbray, 1930).

[12] In the case of the Jesuits, the attempt to recreate to some extent the parent-child relationship is quite explicit, with relations between superior and inferior described as like that of father and son. The special devotion to Mary might also be noted, but we will eschew Freudian interpretations. In the Navy these things were less explicit but by no means absent.

One of the most striking features of the indoctrination is the imprecision of the dogma in terms of many aspects of behavior. The goals of the system—promotion of the aims of the Church or service to the Navy—are defined in terms which are quite general and nonoperational. As stated, the goals do not provide a basis for action by the individual, at least during the early stages of his career. Rather they serve to increase the candidate's receptivity to orders from his superiors, who are to be accepted as the practical interpreters of the goals in action. It seems almost true that the distinctive features of the command society are aimed wholly in the direction of establishing an effective zone of compliance as a permanent part of the attitudes of participants.

Incentives

Training for a Jesuit usually lasts from twelve to fourteen years. The permanent vows of poverty, chastity, and obedience, which are taken at or near the end of this period, were a novel feature of Catholic orders in Loyola's time, though they are now a commonplace. However, the professed Jesuit generally takes a fourth vow of special obedience to the Pope, and his training continually emphasizes the special attitude of obedience appropriate to a Jesuit. Support for similar attitudes in the Navy comes from the idea of a code of honor appropriate to a gentleman, as well as from simple appeals to the practical necessity of quick responses by the fleet in battle. Much of the routine of daily life, such as the salute and customs of precedence in talking and walking in groups, seem designed to provide continual assertion and acceptance of hierarchic relationships among participants.

However, in both cases it is recognized that participants from the beginning of their regular careers will have to exercise judgment in obeying superiors. The environments in which the participants find themselves are too complex to permit each act to be commanded. The functions of intermediaries in a hierarchy inevitably involve judgment in essential ways, since they are constantly dealing with human beings. In Jesuit literature, passages abound which exhort the subjection not only of the will but also of the mind of the novice to the wishes of his superior. In handbooks for naval officers, there is usually a distinction made between obedience and blind obedience, though the distinction is not really operational; and it is recognized that many commands leave considerable discretion as to the means to be employed so that knowledge and judgment must play an important role in generating successful execution of the command.[13]

Obedience has its limits for every participant. The Jesuit is not required formally to obey an order if performance would entail an act of manifest sin, and similar qualifications apply to the naval officer's obligation to obey. In both cases some formally acceptable procedures by which juniors may relieve seniors of their authority exist. These rules are seldom invoked, however, and informal sanctions against their use appear to be very strong.[14] The support which daily observation of the obedience of others provides is of a different order of magnitude than the qualifications which apply only to extreme and unusual situations.

An aspect of obedience is the acceptance of assignment to any post. I have no evidence on the frequency of transfer of Jesuits, but in the interwar Navy regular transfer at not more than three-year intervals was the rule. Mobility of this kind should weaken any tendencies to develop secondary loyalties and especially loyalties to particular individuals, though this danger seems to be a very real one in the best of circumstances.[15] The Jesuits had an additional weapon against such tendencies in the statement of

---

[13] Cf. *Naval Leadership, op. cit.*, pp. 59ff. and 106 for some naval homilies on the subject.

[14] Herman Wouk's *The Caine Mutiny* (Garden City: Doubleday, 1951), deals with this issue, but may well understate the strength of these informal sanctions, especially in the peacetime Navy.

[15] In the interwar Navy there appears to have been at least one secret association of officers, the Green Bowlers, centered in the Bureau of Ordnance, which lasted a number of years and had some influence on promotions, and possibly on such fundamental policy issues as the role of the carrier as a fleet weapon.

conscience (*ratio conscientiae*), which was made to the superior periodically and was not made under the secrecy of the confessional.[16] Reporting questionable acts of other participants to superiors was strongly encouraged. Even superiors were not free of the criticism of inferiors, as the rule of censorship of all mail did not apply to letters sent over one's immediate superior's head. At least during the long training period, a series of public admonitions (*lapidationes*) were arranged in which a participant was singled out and publicly (i.e., before his peers and superiors) admonished for his failings by each member of the group in turn, in a sort of asymmetric *kritika i samokritika*. The Navy does not seem to have had anything comparable, possibly in part because the environment provided a more public demonstration of failings in many situations.[17]

There is no reason to question the assumption that promotion provided the primary incentive for a naval officer. Not only were material and status rewards largely tied to promotion, but the alternative to successful promotion was separation from the service. In the case of a Jesuit earthly rewards are rather more difficult to evaluate. Secondary vows were taken not to seek "dignities" either within the Church or outside, nor even to report those who do. Nevertheless status differentiae exist, such as the role-vocatives of various ranks in the hierarchy; and the lure of power in order to further the aims of the Society may be hard to distinguish from seeking after dignities. It seems reasonable to infer that the strongly hierarchical structure of the Society is not without influence on the aims of participants. If such a system is to function effectively, the criteria for selecting members for advancement must have some influence on the behavior of the members.

---

[16] Meadows, *op. cit.*, p. 298f.; Hoensbroech, *op. cit.*, Vol. I, pp. 342–46. The Navy, with its less formalized world view and less self-conscious participants, made little or no use of this institution.

[17] Also, no doubt, because humility was not a proper attitude for a gentleman. It is quite possible that the weak use of ideology was a defect of the system. Comparisons with the interwar Japanese Navy might be revealing.

Training and Communications

The successful operation of a command society is an impressive achievement, involving as it does the manipulation of large numbers of people performing a variety of tasks. The simulation of a naval battle by upwards of a hundred ships acting in concert provides an obvious and striking example. The Jesuits, especially since their reconstitution, have been engaged primarily in the less spectacular work of education—but education which aims to instill certain standardized attitudes and attributes in its products. The preservation of a reasonably uniform world view among teachers who are themselves the products of many cultures and who are expected to assimilate the development of secular knowledge in the fields of their specialty is in its own way a most impressive accomplishment.

The role that training plays in careers in these two organizations is very great. Perhaps a quarter of a Jesuit's active life is spent in the status of a trainee. For the interwar naval officer there was, in addition to the four years at the Academy, a year or two of postgraduate specialization, a junior and a senior course at the War College, plus several shorter training courses such as that provided at torpedo school.[18] Each major promotion through captain was accompanied by a battery of written examinations, and keeping up with changes in regulations and equipment was a matter of almost daily concern.

Of course in a sense a navy between wars is engaged exclusively in training. However, the participants themselves probably did not view their situation this way. The training provided skills which were tested and used and made the basis for promotion within the service; that is, they were means to ends which were of importance to the Navy even if it never again went to war.

---

[18] No officer would receive all of this training. But formal training programs which a successful officer would almost certainly have completed total seven years: four years at Annapolis, two in postgraduate school (of which one might be at the Postgraduate School in Annapolis, the other at a university), and a year at the War College.

An important and specifically bureaucratic aspect of the command society is its emphasis on routinizing actions. High levels of skill were sought, but a high standard of performance by all participants was of more value than spectacular performance by a few stars; for routinizing and standardizing tend to enhance predictability. When the leader knows roughly what the effects of issuing a given command will be regardless of the person of the inferior, his own ability to design an efficient course of action is increased. The idea of the hierarch as an impersonal building block was emphasized by Weber. Much of the operation of a command society is aimed at achieving this state.

In particular environments the means for standardizing differ. For the Jesuits the rules of theological dialectic are apparently an important part of the process,[19] while for the Navy simulation of wartime performance by component parts of the system was of great importance. Communications of course are at the center of the effort to standardize and impersonalize. The development of a laconic style of speech, the emphasis on truthfulness, and the discouragement of close personal relations between superior and inferior—all were considered important to both societies and all serve this purpose. Set phrases serve to signal set responses. Orders are questioned only if not understood. Repeated simulation is one of the most important devices for developing such a communications system.

In personal behavior, perhaps the most striking difference between successfully functioning members of a market society and a command society lies in the attitude toward bargaining. Bargaining is an accepted part of normal behavior for the former; it is anathema to the latter. To bargain successfully requires the simulation of preferences, something which runs counter to the codes of behavior of the command society, which emphasizes truthfulness and simplicity.[20] This attitude has its functional base

---

[19] Meadows, *op. cit.*, provides an account of seminary instruction procedures and dialectic; the principles are set forth in the *Ratio studiorum*, available in English in E. A. Fitzpatrick, *St. Ignatius and the Ratio Studiorum* (New York: McGraw-Hill, 1933).

[20] Though this may not apply in dealings with "outsiders."

in the special communications problems of a command system. The major source of information is those lower down the hierarchy, so that keeping the leadership informed inevitably requires a good deal of communication. Since in addition much action requires the issuing of orders, there is generally a real communications bottleneck in command systems. For this reason the successful inculcation of ideals relating to communications is vitally important in preventing the clogging of lines of information flow, in keeping accurate and up-to-date information available to the leadership.

Related to this is the danger that bargaining will lead to the evaluation of orders. It obviously threatens the authority of a superior to have an order questioned; for an inferior to counter an order with a proposed alternative order is little less than mutiny. However, a more insidious form of altering orders is to accept the order but to put one's own interpretation on it. To do this requires that the inferior have some criterion of his own by which to evaluate his situation. This is a kind of bargaining, especially in terms of the aftermath in which it must be decided whether or not the given order actually has been obeyed. The consequence of such alteration if it becomes widespread is to increase the leadership's uncertainty as to the effect of giving an order, and also to reduce the amount of accurate information available to it. If making judgments as to whether orders have been obeyed or not is frequent, the quasi-judicial discussions needed to come to a decision are a further drain on scarce communications channels. For all these reasons it is essential to attempt to eliminate bargaining from interpersonal relations within a command society.

One of the consequences of the separation of members of a command society from outsiders and the concentration of emotions and incentives on the internal hierarchy seems to be the development of attitudes of contempt and distrust for outsiders. At times this is interpreted as license for suspending standards of conduct in dealing with outsiders—the rule of truthfulness is apparently a rather frequent casualty. Especially if outsiders have some power to influence the scope of action of the society, a natural incentive is created to conceal information about its internal workings. The separateness of the society's members and the absence of vital need for information from outsiders in the process of internal control of the society can make a considerable degree of secrecy relatively easy to achieve. Information is not available in quantity to the outsider, and the insider's attitudes have been tampered with. The resulting mutual ignorance is likely to contribute to the tension between members and non-members. It also reduces the confidence one can have in assertions as to how command societies work in practice, since observers are all either outsiders or products of a strong indoctrination.

The Leadership and Environmental Change

Most of the active career of even the most successful members of a command society is spent in intermediate positions in the hierarchy; that is, in a situation in which the member commands some participants and is commanded by others. Almost all his training is devoted to helping him operate efficiently in these intermediate levels. However, sooner or later some small fraction of the membership nears the top. These members must begin to adapt to a situation in which there is no one above them within the command society, so that they will be expected to provide both the broad definition of goals for the society as well as basic operating instructions for attaining them. To some extent they are now expected to learn to act and react in ways which their social system has gone to some lengths to eliminate from their personalities.

One might get around this difficulty by selecting members who have not been successfully indoctrinated in the behavior code to begin with. However, if the promotion incentive is at all effective this choice would in the long run destroy the distinctive features of the command society, for the effective selection criterion could not be concealed for long from the participants. On the other hand if the indoctrination has been successful, leaders would seem to be ill equipped to deal with the problems they would be likely to face.[21]

One problem the budding leaders face comes from their separation from society-at-large. Most of a member's experience is with men who react somewhat differently than do those on the outside. This can lead to errors of judgment as to the behavior to be expected from outsiders. In particular, lack of experience with bargaining situations may be especially troublesome.

Another difficulty stems from the very different kind of decision process expected of a leader and an intermediate in a hierarchy. The latter is often given open-ended orders in which he must in effect choose among a number of possible courses of action. However, he has a rather clearly defined set of alternatives among which to choose, and a fairly explicit imposed criterion of choice, especially with respect to situations whose occurrence has been anticipated by the leadership. The process of search for the best alternative is a highly structured activity which is generally sharply restricted in scope. The leader, on the other hand, is in a position in which search for novel approaches to a problem and even for more expedient—for ultimate goals— criteria is one of his primary functions. Though of course much of this activity would in fact be delegated to a staff, it is still the leader's job to make the decision, and this is in an entirely different context from that of an intermediate.[22] This problem of adaptation at the top appears to be more serious for command

[21] It may be that aging itself assists this process of transforming the followers into leaders. To the extent that the early emotion of commitment wanes with age and experience (perhaps because of the father-figure symbolism; perhaps because familiarity breeds a certain complaisance) the senior participants may be better equipped to deal realistically with the outside world and with the goals of the organization.

[22] Staff positions thus become an important training ground for future leaders, serving in Down's language (cf. *supra*) as a means of debriefing Zealots. Typically, full admirals had some staff experience while still in the intermediate ranks.

societies than that of providing effective training for intermediates.[23]

Related to this problem is the occasional need to react to a radically changing environment. If the responses trained into members become inappropriate as a result of fundamental change in the environment, it will be very difficult to bring about the appropriate alterations in behavior. It is no longer a matter of issuing commands, but of changing attitudes. Whether retraining of those well past the more malleable age of entry is at all possible is a moot question. The techniques to employ are not known with any confidence. In addition there is the reinforcing conservatism of the old guard, of those who tend to resist any fundamental changes within the system because of the vested interest which their own training in the old ways gives them.

The need to respond to radical change may impose a constraint on the basic ideology and goals of a command society. These goals have as their primary functions to differentiate members and nonmembers of the society and to support compliance by members. If they are sufficiently vague as not to prejudge the changes to be introduced by the leadership, the command society is less likely to suffer from this particular form of hardening of the arteries. The ideal ideology is emotionally inspiring and practically tautologous. In this form it need never interfere with attitudes to compliance toward commands.

However, when a command society is caught in a vicious circle of stagnation, there does appear to be one other possible way out: the hurrah period, as it has been called.[24] When the environment favors it, as when a war occurs or a wave of evan-

---

[23] An interesting instance of this problem can be found in Husband E. Kimmel, *Admiral Kimmel's Story* (Chicago: Regnery, 1955). Kimmel's defense of his conduct as commander-in-chief of the Pacific fleet at the time of Pearl Harbor is essentially that he obeyed the orders he had, and that that is sufficient vindication of his performance. Though a *post factum* defense, the facts suggest strongly that this is actually the way he viewed his job at the time.

[24] By Naum Jasney. However, our implication is somewhat different, namely that hurrah has its functional aspects in providing social support for adaptation to fundamentally changing environments.

gelical zeal comes to sections of a population, the opportunity arises to rededicate the command society to new goals, to place emphasis on new blood, to pull the sting of the old guard. Whether this type of resuscitation can be *deliberately* imposed on a command society by the leadership is problematical. Again the techniques for the confident generation of desired outcomes are unknown.

A final point with respect to leaders versus intermediates concerns the financing of the command society. Military and religious societies have generally been dependent financially on other agencies. This means that a budget grant is made to the central leadership of the society from agencies which control the organization. The effect of this form of financing is to remove the intermediate members still further from contact with society-at-large. The individual Jesuit does not have to depend on the whims of donors to carry on his work effectively, though of course donors are important to him in many situations. Similarly the typical naval officer was aware that congressmen had some indirect influence over his future, but usually he was not directly concerned with humoring congressmen in the ordinary performance of his duty.

Not so the leaders. Here again, they must learn or relearn social techniques that they have had little opportunity to exercise during much of their career. The effects on the leadership of this large-scale immersion in society-at-large must be very great, and a constant threat leading toward secularization of the entire society.

Appropriate Environments for the Command Society

The adoption of a particular organizational form is never a sufficient condition for the effective operation of a social system— and is not usually a necessary condition. But the choice of organization always makes some difference, and in certain circumstances may be crucial. A relatively rigid form of organization, such as the command society, is especially likely to be limited in the environments in which it can function effectively—where by environments we mean the set of problems with which the social system is expected to deal. In what follows the issue will be discussed in an *ad hoc* and speculatively. Thus it provides a counterpart, though only partially developed, of the more formal discussions of the environment in which the competitive capitalist model yields pareto optimal outcomes. The resemblance is unfortunately rather distant because of the less precise nature both of our description of the command society and of our conception of social effectiveness.

The interwar fleet at maneuvers provides a good example of a routinized but very complex environment. The primary actions of a ship which concerned the fleet admiral were its movements and its gunnery. Both types of activity could be controlled by issuing relatively simple orders, chosen from among a rather small list of possibilities, the execution of most of which had been the subject of frequent drill. Of course some maneuvers of a line of battleships were quite difficult to execute, and there was always some chance of failure—(which would require novel commands and responses) but this does not alter the basic fact of habituation to the execution of the most important commands that were likely to be given. On the other hand, a good deal of the work of standardizing actions required long and complex communication, which could be completed only during an extensive training period.[25] The situation was somewhat more complex within a large ship, where over a thousand men of varied specialties were being coordinated. Even here, training to routinize even such actions as damage control was feasible, and in general seems to have been controllable from above. The dangers in the situation often stemmed from misapplied success indicators. For example, gunnery officers became too involved in

[25] And even then, not always. The problem of optimal choice of targets by individual ships, in actions between fleets, called for coordination and communication which could not be handled within the available time, while the possibly optimal patterns were too numerous to be anticipated. As a result, a combination of rules of thumb and discretion was installed.

winning the fleet competitions to devote adequate attention to training under unfavorable sea conditions.

Many commands enjoin performance, that is, they order a participant to execute a particular act. Such commands often call for judgment, as, for example, the order to a captain to maintain station while executing a maneuver—which is to say that success is problematic. As a consequence it is important that these commands be feasible for the average executor; otherwise pressures will be established to evaluate and reinterpret orders. It is one of the chief advantages of a command system that it has the facilities to manufacture a successful response to a wide range of performance-enjoining commands. The environment then should continue to reward the society for the successful execution of these commands and responses. Again, the Navy provided a good example of this sort of environment. The ability to handle the ship and to maintain reasonable standards in gunnery provided a basis for successful performance of commands and were the instruments by which the admiral controlled the course of battle. In addition, success or failure in performance was easily observed, making reinterpretation of orders difficult to justify. Thus the environment tended to support this particular division of labor and of authority.

The Society of Jesus faced a rather different situation. The results of their education processes were attitudes, which were of prime importance to the leadership but very difficult to observe. This led the Society to resort to close control of the educational process of the teachers themselves, and especially of the teachers' attitudes, through such contacts with superiors as the confessional and the *ratio conscientiae*. Formalized activities such as the administration of the sacraments were also controlled, and a special and distinctive style seems to have been developed by the organization. Since interactions among Jesuit units were not so great as with the Navy, the chief function of routinizing was to ensure the maintenance of standards while on distant missions. Also this meant that performance-enjoining commands were relatively less important. Propagation of the faith could be enjoined with confidence; "convert ten thousand heathen" could not—though at times the Society seems to have faced success indicator problems in this area.

The environment must remain sufficiently stable that the routinized commands do not lose their usefulness before some gain has been reaped from the costly training process. The inter-war Navy faced a number of technical innovations of which the most important, indeed revolutionary, was the introduction of the aircraft as an offensive fleet weapon. There is no doubt that the interwar Navy's reaction to this was far from ideal. However, it is easy to exaggerate the extent of this failure, and to misjudge its location and impact on the officer corps. That there were not more carriers or a better appreciation of their function in future wars was not the fault of the middle and lower rank officers but of the leadership (and Congress). Aerial tactics were highly developed; the officer corps did not show any serious inertia or conservatism in this respect. And the modifications called for in the action of the overwhelming majority of officers during war-time appear to have been made relatively promptly. Gunnery, engineering, navigation: developments in these areas were quickly transmitted to officers and absorbed by them. The re-sponsiveness of the hierarchy below the level of the top leader-ship to rather rapid change in their already complex technical environment seems to have been quite good.

The argument then is that rapid technical change may be absorbed efficiently by such a hierarchy, provided it does not threaten the basic operation of command as a function. It remained true for the interwar Navy that unit commanders could not generally feel that orders from superiors were inappro-priate in that the unit commanders themselves had more of the relevant information than their superiors. Coordinated action, based on information communicated up through several lines to superiors, remained vital to effective operation of a fleet—indeed of the Navy as a whole. Failures seem largely attributable to

inertia in the leadership itself. The Navy's relative isolation from
the world at large and from the strategic implications of new
weaponry suggests that the conversion of middle rank officers
into effective leaders of the organization was the primary
systemic failure. This is especially striking in view of the fact that
opponents, notably Japan, had appreciated some of these
changes. The leadership had become too absorbed in the maintenance of its old guard status to respond even to quite overt
challenge.

Another important environmental condition can be stated
about the boundaries of the society's operation. These must be
such as to preserve incentives to high level performance and to
prevent serious erosion of attitudes through excessive contact with
secular society. In order to do this, the hierarchic pyramid must
not have too low a peak. If a very large fraction of hierarchs at a
particular level cannot be promoted to the next higher level, the
less competent will come to recognize their own limitations and
may lose a primary motivation. Within the Society of Jesus this
may be a serious problem, though there is no evidence to this
effect. In the interwar Navy it appears that relatively few officers
were washed out of the lower grades. In the middle grades
perhaps half were weeded out at each promotion, while only a
small fraction of captains achieved flag rank. Through the rank of
captain, the majority of officers could legitimately maintain
their expectations of promotion to the next rank upon successful
performance of current duties. The Navy was distinguished from
the Army during this period by the stringency of its selection procedure, for by and large at each grade it was "up or out." A
certain lottery element was also introduced into the system. Since
standardized performance was emphasized, there was often
relatively little to distinguish the relative performance of officers
eligible for promotion; most would have performed their duties
with acceptable competence. The effect was to increase anxieties,
but also to spread more widely than would otherwise have been
the case a reasonable hope for promotion. However, a large

number of captains (and perhaps an even larger fraction of rear admirals) recognized that they had reached their peak in the system and may well have been converted into time servers. To a considerable extent the environment itself determines the shape of the pyramid. *Ceteris paribus* a sharp narrowing at the top can be expected to weaken the average quality of the leadership.[26]

A more serious boundary problem may occur at the bottom of the pyramid. A command society is almost inevitably an elite corps, and is likely to need to make use of men who generally are not qualified to become members of the society. This sets an upper limit to the reasonable aspirations of those below the mobility barrier. In addition, the maintenance of effective control over this group by members of the society limits the nonstatus rewards that may be given them. One possibility is the resort to material and status differentiae among members of this lower group, which has been the reaction of military services. Another response, also practiced by the military, is greater resort to coercion as an instrument for securing compliance. This approach, and in particular the joint resort to material reward, promotion, and coercion, seems to have been reasonably effective in the case of the interwar Navy. However, its great advantage stemmed from the shortage of alternative employment for discharged seamen. Where alternative employment exists, coercion becomes less feasible.

Horizontal boundaries between the command society and other parts of the society-at-large for whom status, relatively to the membership of the command society, is undetermined or ambiguous must be established for reasons already discussed. This is not just because of attitude erosion, but also because of the lesser effectiveness of members of a command society in dealing with outsiders they distrust. Joint decision making with outsiders

---

[26] Whether this is compensated for by the quality of the very few selected for the highest positions depends on the selection process, which may not be under the control of the society. It appears a priori that sharp narrowing at the top creates a large fraction of time servers in all but the topmost rank, and that this in turn increases the difficulty in converting hierarchs into top leaders.

under these circumstances would seem likely to be inefficient and fraught with conflict.

These comments can only suggest a few aspects of the environmental requirements of a command society. They are all oriented toward one overriding goal: that of creating and maintaining the effectiveness of a hierarchy as a joint decision-making body. Only where the making of all basic decisions is consistent with hierarchic coordination can a command society hope to function efficiently.

CHAPTER SIX

Two Command Economies:
A Comparison

Surely the overwhelming majority of western students of soviet-type economies believe that these economies could be made more efficient by choice-decentralizing economic control. Their views seem to be shared by a large and growing number of eastbloc economists. As a consequence, when revision of economic organization in these economies has come under discussion, the more decentralized alternatives have occupied the participants almost exclusively.

There are some indications that this is a mistake. Clearly there is considerable opposition to decentralization within the hierarchies of these countries. Partly this reflects the views of those with a vested interest in current procedures. Partly it reflects uncertainty as to the effects of any particular decentralization scheme, both on the grounds of efficiency and of the danger that a choice-decentralization scheme will entail some authority-decentralization. And partly it may reflect a basic ideological commitment to a more integrated and solidary society than seems to be consistent with substantial delegation of authority. If a feasible highly centralized alternative exists it should have considerable appeal.

Consequently it may be worthwhile to explore some of the properties of such an alternative: this is the subject of the present chapter. After a few remarks in justification of our particular choice of centralized scheme we will turn to the applicability of the command society to the economy. This will be followed by a comparison of this scheme with the classical soviet system as described in Chapter Four. The final section contains comments on organizational equilibrium and stability under the two schemes.

Communist Parties as Command Societies [1]

Established Communist parties everywhere seem to satisfy the basic prerequisites for a command society. They are hierarchic in form. In the Soviet case there is a system of co-opting election to higher positions in the party bureaucracy. However, descriptions of the process clearly indicate that the wishes of the leadership are not ignored when they are expressed and that they generally *are* expressed. The typical process may well be the presentation of a slate approved by higher authority which is then approved by acclamation. Integration of the hierarchy is achieved since party members must be willing to accept any assignment and are subject to fairly regular reassignment. Promotion brings both power and substantial material rewards, and is generally a strong incentive, though there are cases where it is not an overriding consideration—as perhaps it is not with the typical factory manager.[2] The disobedience sanction appears in the notion of party discipline, the violation of which is a dismissal offense. Discipline need not be invoked on all questions, but this is a device which in one form or another appears in other command societies as well.

---

[1] Especially helpful in writing this section were: Carl J. Friedrich and Z. K. Brzezinski, *Totalitarian Dictatorship and Democracy* (Cambridge: Harvard University Press, 1956); Wolfgang Leonhard, *Child of the Revolution*, trans. from German (Chicago: Regnery, 1958); Leonard Schapiro, *The Communist Party of the Soviet Union* (New York: Random House, 1959); Merle Fainsod, *Smolensk under Soviet Rule* (Cambridge: Harvard University Press, 1958); Alfred Meyer, *The Soviet Political System* (New York: Random House, 1965); Raymond Bauer, *et al.*, *How the Soviet System Works* (Cambridge: Harvard University Press, 1959).

[2] That is, typically his probable motivation is not to advance within the *party* hierarchy, but within the industrial hierarchy.

As in all bureaucracies, the delegation of authority for certain decisions is often essential. The distinction between suggestions and orders provides needed flexibility in such situations.

There seems to be less separation of a member of the Communist party from society-at-large than in the other two cases of command societies. The process of becoming a party member in the Soviet Union takes a long time and a lot of work, from the Pioneers and Komsomols to the indoctrination meetings and candidacy. However, new members often have had no experience of special party schools and quite a large number are above age twenty-five upon admission to candidacy.

Partly this reflects the extent to which society-at-large is controlled in the Soviet Union. By subjecting all youth to a large measure of indoctrination in the ethos of the command society the need to separate out candidate members is reduced. On the other hand, Soviet society is widely thought to have become highly secularized—that is, its members are less influenced by and accepting of the ideology—especially in the years since the purges of the late thirties. The result of such a process may even be to make new party members more adept at manipulating the formal command environment in their own personal interests than would be the case if recruitment were from a society where political socialization is more effective, since the former have more opportunity to observe and practice manipulation. Since early indoctrination appears to be a crucial feature of the command society, this is a serious lapse.[3]

Ideology seems to be in a somewhat similar position. Marxism

---

[3] One might speculate that the reason for this lapse is a failure to adapt from the status of a revolutionary underground group to political leadership. When society-at-large was hostile, and party membership constituted a commitment to revolutionary overthrow of existing institutions, there was a natural selection process which ensured some dedication in party members. No one—aside from police spies—joined the party unless he had already become alienated from society-at-large and was willing to risk at least his freedom in serving party goals. In noncommunist countries this has often provided a highly effective surrogate for the novitiate. After the revolution it gradually ceased to operate, and a really effective substitute was never created.

has proved to be a tremendous ideological force, offering both a world view and a general program of change which many find inspiring, but without a program specific enough to have prevented effective policy making after the revolution. Its impact on pre-revolutionary intellectuals in Russia was exceptionally strong. However, in the years since the revolution the leadership for a variety of reasons has interpreted Marxism in ways which appear at times to have hindered effective policy making. And there is some doubt whether a body of thought whose social content is a critique of capitalism can in the long run be an effective inspiration to citizens of a socialist society. At any rate, it has neither been replaced nor efficiently modified for the functional requirements of the command society.

The incentive system within the party seems to be reasonably effective in rewarding effort. Reports about party officials tend to emphasize their energy in the face of very great demands on their time. However, a major problem has stemmed from the tremendous size of the party—close to ten million in the Soviet Union in recent years, with perhaps a quarter million full-time party workers. Controlling an entire political and economic administrative apparatus is an undertaking which has promoted the development of secondary loyalties, to branch or region or person, which have interfered with the basic lines of authority. The central party apparatus controls assignment of members, but in an organization of this size the personal contact that is an important element in the superior-inferior relationship in a command society is necessarily weakened.

The purges of the thirties may have begun at least partly as an attempt to preserve command relationships in an unfavorable environment.[4] For whatever reason, there is wide agreement that

---

[4] As the second five-year plan was nearing its end some substantial gains had been achieved in production and (compared with 1932) in consumption standards. The earlier, revolution-inspired, hurrah attitudes were fading, and many of the shock workers began to think of reaping the rewards of their effort. To some extent this would find reflection in the attitudes of some leaders. But this is not to minimize the irrational aspects of the purges.

the actual effect of the purges was to further secularize the party hierarchy and to create the attitudes of mutual distrust which must be a continual hindrance to effective joint action. Nevertheless a large measure of commitment remains within the hierarchy, and there seems to be no way to get a good measure of the extent to which these factors have reduced the relative efficiency of the CPSU with respect to other command societies.

One condition which has been most unfavorable to preservation of command relationships has been the fluctuating demand for members to man administrative posts. Especially in the Soviet Union, party admissions have come in bursts, generally followed by a slow process of weeding out undesirables. This is an extremely inefficient process, by the standards of other command societies. Rapidly changing demand seems to have been somewhat less of a problem in the postwar period, and perhaps the days of mass admissions are past.

One of the important functions of a party member is indoctrination and exhortation of nonmembers. The training in ideology and in defending party stands appears to be quite effective in the Soviet Union. However, the press of administrative duties seems often to push agitatorial work into the background, and leaves the member spending most of his time acting like an official in an ordinary bureaucracy.

There are a large number of party schools designed to provide the ideological training and appropriate background for administration. I have seen no estimates as to the amount of party schooling a typical member gets, but perhaps he is likely to get some in almost every five-year period of his membership in the lower and middle ranks. The manifold duties of, for example, a regional party secretary make it rather difficult to routinize this work after the manner of other command societies.[5] It appears that non-command relations often exist, and that the evaluation of commands is very common. However, it is difficult for an outsider to get a clear idea as to the role bargaining plays in political

[5] His responsibilities are most clearly described in Fainsod, *op. cit.*

administration. The powers of higher party officials are and always have been very great; the defenses of inferiors are largely limited to the control of information essential to decisions higher up.

The nature of top leadership structure in the Soviet Union since Stalin's death is a matter of much controversy. However, whatever its nature, there is evidence of the existence of dilemmas typical to command society leaderships. The problems of getting accurate information, and the difficulties of revising dogma, combined with a certain narrowness of perspective may all be associated with the expected pattern of malfunctioning of a command system. Unfortunately they may also be associated with other things, such as the proletarian overtones of the movement, the relative crudity of many aspects of Russian culture, and the isolation of the Soviet Union itself from other countries during much of the lifetime of current leaders. Besides, the problems at the top of any highly centralized structure are likely to be influenced by particular personalities in ways which may dominate the systemic influences.

Though there is much less information available on the Chinese Communist Party, its differences from the CPSU appear to tend in the direction of strengthening the command features of the organization. Indoctrination is taken rather more seriously, both when a potential member is still outside the party and throughout his period of membership. Explicit expression of enthusiastic agreement, both with the general party line and with particular aspects of policy, is demanded of everyone—and its elicitation is a major function of party agitators. Indeed this is carried over into society-at-large, so that the distinction between party member and mere citizen is less significant in China than in the Soviet Union.

The ideology appears to retain a more inspirational force in China also. Partly this stems from the relative ease with which the external threat to China can be tied to Marxist ideology. Partly no doubt it stems from the general recognition of the tremendous difficulties China faces in carrying out a program of modernization, which makes arguments for the subjection of personal inclinations more compelling. The puritanical dedication of Chinese communists has been noted frequently, even by other communists.

Of course the Chinese party has a much shorter history of power than the Soviet; also it has not yet faced the potential disruptions of a change in leadership. Scattered evidence suggests that the period of the Great Leap had the effect of diluting the commitment of many communists. Nonetheless the Chinese appear to have established a more strongly integrated and committed party organization than the Soviets possessed at any time in their history, possibly excepting the period of World War II.

On the one hand then, communist parties are, roughly speaking, command societies—though many of them have been under strong secularizing pressures in recent years. On the other hand, a survey of their ideological literature, of Marxism-Leninism, such as that admirably performed by Peter Wiles,[6] suggests that something very like the command society constitutes an ultimate ideal or utopia within this literature. The key elements are indoctrination to produce an internalized commitment to similar goals by all the citizenry, and a firm belief that industrial administration would be carried out within a hierarchy without any resort to money or markets.

These remarks are hardly to be considered a serious evaluation of the operation of communist parties. Rather it is suggested that there is some connection between the model of the command society of the last chapter and the attitudes of communists and some aspects of communist organization. For communists to give up intensive, centrally controlled attitude manipulation would be to abandon a key instrument—both for achieving their ultimate goals and for current social control. Hence it is not quixotic to explore the possibilities for its further extension.

[6] *Political Economy of Communism* (Cambridge: Harvard University Press, 1962), Chaps. 17–18.

The Command Economy as
a Command Society

As an economic organization the command society may be considered a means to the end of a solidary society, such as, for example, Maurice Dobb has depicted. (See Chapter Two.) Such a society would be greatly concerned about distributive equity because of the strong externalities of consumption. As a consequence, control of consumption patterns would be desirable. This might be achieved by an arrangement like that in soviet-type societies, whereby the quantities of consumer goods to be produced are fixed by plan, and allocations to households are made by some combination of income and physical rationing. With consumer goods thus channeled through the planning system, a hierarchy would be used to organize production and the remaining aspects of distribution.

Our concern is with the production system and in particular the modern, factory-based sector. We again ignore transition problems and assume that a command society has been installed in this sector. Given our conclusions about the properties of such a society, what can be said about organization in this sector?

To take the planning system first, it is clear that the soviet type of planning is inconsistent with the preservation of a command society. Bargaining—with its erosive effect on command attitudes—is an integral part of the soviet procedure. This erosion is furthered by the poor instruction making and the frequently infeasible instructions. A comparable disobedience to instructions would be tantamount to insurrection under the command society. In addition, there is the informal trading which serves to patch up some of the inflexibility and error in the soviet system: this also has a powerful erosive effect on command attitudes.

For a somewhat different reason market socialism cannot be sustained by a command society. Even in the Lange version there is little support for command as a function in the system. Essentially, enterprises are instructed to set price equal to marginal cost and that is the end of it. Price adjustments by the center are not so much commands as bits of information. The continual support that command relations seem to require would be absent in such an organization. Also the instruction: "Set output at the point at which price equals marginal cost!" is a quite complex order which makes checking on obedience very difficult. Finally there are the technical uncertainties with respect to this scheme which were mentioned in Chapters Two and Three.

Much more effective under the conditions of a command society would be one of the schemes described in Chapter Three. The assignment of physical output and input targets and control through a branch hierarchy seems more appropriate to the command function than market socialism, while the standard routines of interaction in plan making are preferable to soviet-style bargaining. The big question, of course, is feasibility. Even with a very large commitment of resources to plan making and information collecting the result is doomed to nonoptimality because of the highly simplified assumptions of these schemes. In order to avoid infeasible instructions, the planners would have to adopt a more cautious attitude toward estimating maximal performance. Also some aggregation of targets at the planning bureau would be inevitable, with its probable consequences for nonoptimality and planners' uncertainty.

One of the main causes of uncertainty at the planning bureau, under soviet conditions, is the distortion of reports by enterprise management which, in turn, is in large measure a consequence of the incentive system. Somehow the linkage between planning and control must be altered if a suitable environment for the command society is to be created. One possibility lies along the following lines:

The enterprise manager is given a plan and is instructed to fulfill it if possible. In addition he is informed of a price system, which is derived from the plan. In making secondary decisions, the search for profits under this price system is his assigned objective. Thus if he could fulfill and have some resources left over, profit calculations would determine whether, for example, he should increase output or reduce cost.

This is a rough approximation to a scheme proposed some years ago by Boris Kidrić for the Yugoslav economy.[7] A variant of the scheme was actually given legal sanction but because of technical errors was never actually installed. From our point of view the trouble with such a scheme is that it is hard to apply a rule to cases in which the plan cannot be fulfilled. One possibility is to instruct the manager to choose a production pattern that minimizes the difference between profit at the planned level and achieved profit. But in cases where profit increases with underfulfillment this would lead to wastage. Another might be to maximize profits, but in that case the plan targets lose all significance and command functionality is lost.

For such a system to operate effectively within the command society context, the use of profit as a criterion would have to be relegated to a genuinely secondary position in the manager's criterion. But there is some reason to suppose that such an aim might be accomplished by the command society. Because of the absence of short run rewards, the manager's motivations must be dominated by longer run considerations. A criterion which judged managers on the basis of average performance in fulfilling the plan over a period of several years, and also on the basis of improvements in performance observable over the period of tenure in a given enterprise, might fit this bill quite well. Though such a manager would not be unduly disturbed by temporary deviations from the plan, his overall level of performance would be a matter of concern. The incentive to distort reports of short run performance, though by no means absent, would be considerably weakened.[8]

[7] "O nekim teoretskim pitanjima novog privrednog sistema," *Komunist*, No. 1–2 (1952), 42–69.

[8] This will be discussed further in the next chapter under the rubric "target socialism."

Naturally, emphasis on fulfillment rather than overfulfillment implies that a fairly effective planning system has been designed. Also the plan must be flexible, capable of adjusting to the changes in data which affect feasibility. Any hierarchy which requires aggregation and disaggregation of data before a decision can be made is likely to be somewhat unwieldy; but the price calculations that can be made should be at least rough and ready indicators of the directions in which reaction is most desirable. A planning system which produces shadow prices has at least this great advantage over the soviet system of planning.

If members of a command society are forced to work closely and regularly with outsiders, it has been suggested that their attitudes toward the society are likely to be affected unfavorably, from the point of view of efficient operation of the society. To what extent can this be avoided when the economy is the society's assignment? First, if the entire society is under a uniform centralized control, the problem of hostility toward outsiders would presumably be considerably lessened. However, it would not be eliminated, because in general incentives toward effective horizontal cooperation are weakened both by the command society itself and by the barrier between suborganizations. Second, the natural way to deal with outsiders is through the top of the hierarchy. As was suggested earlier, this might be accomplished for the process of allocation of consumer goods to households, given a highly solidary attitude toward consumption. A similar approach might be feasible in the case of scattered, small-scale industries (agriculture, crafts) which would be difficult to integrate into a command hierarchy. The result might be very inefficient, but we are concerned here with the operation of the command society rather than other portions of society-at-large. Thus the planning of inputs and outputs to these dispersed sectors would have to be funneled through the planning bureau, and instructions would reach individual firms with respect to inputs to and outputs from these sectors via the normal hierarchic lines.

Labor however will not fit into this scheme, since it is used on the spot by the enterprises. Here a mobility barrier problem would arise, since the command society itself could not efficiently run its members through the various grades of manual and supervisory worker on their way to top executive positions. Given comparable circumstances, the command society might deal effectively with this problem in much the same way the interwar Navy did. The situation to be avoided is erosion of reward differentials through relative excess demand for below-the-barrier labor. Given the barrier, discipline—perhaps including some physical coercion—would have to substitute to some extent for the promotion incentive. A scarce worker is a valued one, who has alternatives available to him which reduce his willingness to take orders. This could not only weaken effective control in the factory but erode attitudes among the hierarchs as well. This reason alone suggests that it would be very difficult to preserve a command society for industrial control in a more or less open, full employment economy.

In this description of probable properties of a command society undertaking the operation of the industrial sector of an economy, an attempt has been made to present difficulties as well as advantages. Clearly there is no basis for any absolute judgments about the feasibility of the system under all circumstances. However, perhaps enough has been said to lend plausibility to a few comparative remarks about the two types of command economies that have now been described.

The Two Command Economies

As an alternative to the soviet type of planning and control scheme, the command society can hardly be said to "solve" the problems of central planning. Nevertheless, given the appropriate supporting environment, the latter has certain advantages over the former, such as the greater accuracy of the plan and the longer perspective of the enterprise managers. Perhaps the most striking ingredient of the soviet system that is missing in the command society is the element of pressure, of constant urging of all participants to improve performance.

Holland Hunter has argued that this tautness is an essential element in good planning, regardless of the organizational environment in which it functions.[9] This is because of the ignorance and inexperience of many of the participants in an underdeveloped economy, and also because, within limits, people tend to do more as more is expected of them. To the extent that this is true, tautness is not specific to the soviet organizational form, but should be found in every good development plan.

In the early stages of the use of an organizational form to promote economic development, there is undoubtedly some measure of truth in this argument. But we are concerned with the economic system as a going concern. After cadres have been trained and given some experience, uncertainty stems primarily from the physical and economic environment rather than from the defects of background of the participants. In other words, as time goes on tautness declines in usefulness as a reaction to other than organizational conditions. This applies a fortiori to the command society, where homogeneity of the human material is achieved to an unusual degree.

However, in the soviet type of organization there is a systemic reason for preserving tautness, in the deliberate simulation of performance and the distortion of claims which the system encourages in participants. As knowledge of the technology grows it does not necessarily follow that knowledge of the capabilities of the economy grows among members of the planning board. This information is generated at the firm level, and must pass through the hierarchic filter before they receive it. And the managers at both firm and branch level have a fairly clear picture of the effects on the planning board of various kinds of information. At

[9] Holland Hunter, "Optimal Tautness in Developmental Planning," *Economic Development and Cultural Change*, 9 (1961), 561–72.

the same time there are limits to the extent to which performance and capabilities may be simulated, since the hierarchy is not without power to collect some information from the lower levels. Under these circumstances there is a very strong need to preserve tautness as a device to compel higher performance from the participants. And this tautness is itself an argument against the introduction of sophisticated, but costly and organizationally rigid, planning schemes which rely heavily on accurate data for their success.

In a command society these problems would seem much less severe. Once established, a command society could hardly make much use of tautness to stimulate participants to greater efforts. The essence of the command principle is the enjoining of feasible acts, the rationalizing of choice, and the transmission of accurate if stylized descriptions of the environment. Indeed to the extent that tautness is desirable, the command society is undesirable as an economic control organization. Its inaccuracies and impossible demands would inevitably force the participants to evaluate commands, thereby destroying any positive effects on attitudes which the indoctrination procedures might have achieved.

However, it would seem that tautness could be avoided in the command society without much cost. Assuming the problems of inexperience largely solved, there is no reason to impute any substantial bias to the planners' estimates of the economy's capabilities. Managers would have less incentive to understate capabilities since they would not be judged primarily in terms of finely graded estimates of short-run achievements. And once the expectation that excessive performance standards were going to be assigned was eliminated, a manager could speak reasonably frankly as to the capabilities and requirements of his organization in the short run. Indeed to the extent that his incentives became associated with longer-run performance, he might find biases in the opposite direction developing, for example, a strong inclination to make a new investment in his firm in order to increase long-run productivity.

Naturally these are merely tendencies in the command society relative to those in the soviet type of organization. Simulation and disingenuousness are to be found in all human situations; but in the command society the pressures encouraging simulation are more strongly countered than in its soviet counterpart.

The two systems differ strikingly in the nature of their financial and supply systems. The problem with both the soviet-type finance and supply systems is that they are integrated neither into the plan itself nor into the institutions that exercise primary control over production units. As a consequence they are in constant danger of being overruled by more powerful control bodies. They are also in a poor position to institute action against a firm because they work with ambiguous control criteria.

The corresponding problem in a command society is posed differently: Secondary control organizations cannot be allowed to function in such a society, or at least must be subject to effective control by the primary hierarchy. Command as a function cannot survive if legitimate bodies outside of and parallel to the hierarchy are permitted to countermand orders. Since the supply system certainly, and a financial system most likely, will be indispensable to the operation of the economy, some way of integrating these decisions into the primary hierarchy must be found.

The problem of financial control might be settled for the command society by placing banking functions under control of the production sectors. Each sector in effect would be extended a line of credit as a part of the plan, and would be free to allocate the funds as it wished within the sector. Presumably the money would be of use partly as a seasonal control instrument over the firms and partly as a floating reserve for emergency procurement. Any excessive credit grants over the planned line of credit would require approval from above. In this way monetary stability, effective use of credit for usual control functions, and the preservation of the command function could be achieved. We will not consider this question further, since in the command society it seems inevitable that the control functions of money would be relatively marginal. To the extent that they are used, they would seem to be at least as effective as they have proved in the soviet type of organization. Indeed, to the extent that a more rational planning scheme would permit the improvement of the price system as a means for measuring social opportunity cost, the command society should get more expedient control out of its financial system.

The supply system seems doomed to pose one of the most intractable problems for a centralized form of economic organization. There would be no difficulty if the plan were perfect. Every participant would try to do exactly as the plan required, and everyone would find that he could just succeed. But there are errors and ambiguities in every plan, the ability and diligence of officials vary unpredictably, and the data of the economy change in unexpected ways during the course of the plan period. All of this requires a continuous series of adjustments and revisions by all participants.

But even this is not the whole story. Within the producer goods sector, there are a number of intermediate products whose specifications will vary somewhat from one use to another. Often there are some variable properties of a product which are very useful to the consumer but rather difficult for the producer to incorporate into the product. There is no great incentive on the part of the producer to satisfy such demands, even though they may be in the interest of the economy as a whole as well as in the interest of the consumer. Conflicts arise and someone must solve them. If the consumer is from the same sector of the economy as the producer, the hierarchy is well organized to resolve such conflicts in the social interest. However, if the consumer is from another sector the decision, following the command principle, must be made by the hierarchic level which commands both producer and consumer. This is near the highest level in the command society as we have depicted it. If such conflicts of interest are common, and in a modern economy they surely will be, a literally impossible burden is placed on a level of the hierarchy that is already loaded down with problems of information processing. And plainly the level is too high; most such problems are not important enough to be decided efficiently at the top.

What can be done? In a market economy it seems that there are three social processes for dealing with such conflicts. The first and most common is negotiation between firms, with the profit incentive and the threat of taking one's business elsewhere the limiting factors to acceptance of a solution on either side. Thus by negotiation a determination of the controversial properties to be incorporated in the product is, so to speak, built into the plan via the contract. Frequent resort to the same process is had in both types of centralized organization, but the circumstances of the negotiation are quite different. The consumer has no direct claim on the producer's loyalty in the soviet system, and so neither the producer's current profit (incentive) levels nor his fear of losing future business plays much of a role in negotiation. Instead there is simply a requirement that contracts for delivery must be made by firms or branch supply agents. The consumer has far the stronger incentive to make a contract because of tautness in planning. But even here, irreconcilable differences are frequent. When the relative strength of the consumer's incentive is lessened, as would be the case under a command society, one might expect this means of reconciling differences to be even less frequently effective.

Note that even if one were willing to ascribe to participants' feelings of loyalty to the system which transcended all personal or localized sentiments, the problem would be far from solved. Under the soviet organizational form, lower levels in the hierarchy are in no position to judge the social benefits of alternative courses of action. In general this would be true of the command society also. Under the best of circumstances the plan can hardly provide enough information to determine all product specifications. The choice-decentralized output-quality decisions of enterprise managers are a major source of interest divergence among managers, and the incentives to carefully compromise these divergences by negotiation are weak. Furthermore, even without tautness some asymmetry between producer and consumer is likely to exist.

A second market process for resolving performance conflicts is resort to the courts. This technique is used in soviet-type economies and could be used even in a command society, though hierarchic review of decisions and perhaps even integration of the courts into the formal command hierarchy—as with military courts—would be desirable. However this is a very expensive decision process. The judges must become informed as to many aspects of the economic operation of both conflicting parties, and be sufficiently aware both of precedent and of the plan's requirements to render an expedient verdict. That is, for such centralized societies the criterion would probably not be justice, defined in terms of the behavior of the participants, but consequences, defined and evaluated in terms of the goals of the leadership. The costs, both in time and skilled manpower in reaching judicial decisions on conflicts, make this a rather inefficient social device, and one which could hardly be expected to take up the slack resulting from less frequent agreement by negotiation.

The third process is reorganization. In a market society persistently unsatisfactory results from using market suppliers create pressures on the firm to integrate lines of activity under a single managerial roof. Or, more positively, the advantage of having a guaranteed buyer and of knowing the market is an incentive toward vertical expansion. However, what is "vertical" expansion in a market economy is "horizontal" expansion in a command economy. A consumer located in a different hierarchy is a firm at a comparable level to the producer—horizontal in this sense. Entry by the consuming firm complicates economic planning and control. In fact, with respect to the planning and control system, the existence of a firm producing products for two different branches constitutes an external effect. The reason for this is that alterations in the plan or the control instrument of one branch will have consequences for the production by that firm of products of the other branch. One might well imagine that this is the greatest source of external effects specific to the choice-centralized economy.

These external effects are probably more serious in a command society, in which we assume that there is greater reason to strive for more accurate planning than in the soviet type of organization. But there is yet another reason why organizational internalization is a poor approach to interfirm conflict in the command society: by producing for more than one branch, the firm acquires a dual set of superiors. Perhaps nothing can destroy command effectiveness sooner than such a dualism, which could be expected frequently to present the manager with conflicting orders.

The problem of determining product specifications stands as a crucial instance of the fundamental problem of centralized economic operation: the difficulty in finding generalized routine processes for settling details efficiently. The specific problem here is that, because of the particular organizational partitioning, the details must be resolved very high up in the hierarchy or they will not be resolved efficiently; but it is not efficient to resolve them at this high level either. However, given that the range of choice is limited to our two types of centralized organization, it is not clear that one has any significant advantage over the other. The command society cannot make much use of reorganization. Though the soviet form can and frequently does, the results are not satisfactory and can lead to organizational chaos. Nor is it reassuring that the reason for the greater organizational flexibility of the soviet form is that it cannot hope to plan or control with very great accuracy.

Thus neither the command society nor the soviet type of organization shows up very well in dealing with this class of decisions. On the other hand there is no clear reason to prefer the way in which either one of these two systems handles the problem. It is always possible to set up a routine for making decisions which will in fact generate decisions; the difficulty only comes when they are also required to be good decisions. The command society could, for example, assign authority arbitrarily to specific sectors in making this type of decision with respect to other sectors. It can integrate sectors in which such problems are very frequent at some level below the highest. And it can call for relatively more standardization of products than is generated under other organizational forms. But present information is not sufficient to make any comparative judgment.

In Soviet society the role of informal decision making is known to be quite substantial. The combination of an inaccurate plan, great pressure, and ubiquitous bargaining opens the door to informal processes for mitigating their consequences. Among the most interesting of these processes is the informal but tacitly accepted market for producer goods which is operated by *tolkachi* functioning rather like salesmen in a market or influence peddlers in other bureaucracies. As has been noted already, this informal market system can be a help to firms in fulfilling their obligations, being particularly useful in compensating for mistakes in the distribution system.

Informal contacts among participants in a command society cannot be avoided. Indeed the development of patterns of horizontal loyalties is a by-product of the indoctrination system in which classmates share the rigors of the early training routine.[10] The question is whether these loyalties will be disruptive of efficient operation of a command society in an economic environment.

First it should be noted that a command society could not survive the development of an informal market. If it did exist it would indicate strongly that the system of attitudes appropriate to the society had been seriously eroded. Markets, and especially informal markets, require bargaining, the simulation of preferences, and the suppression of information normally sent up to superiors.

---

[10] Cf. Sanford Dornbusch, "The Military Academy as an Assimilating Institution," *Social Forces*, 33 (1955), 316–21.

On the other hand the "old boys" will be scattered about the economy in such a manner as to make some informal cooperation mutually beneficial. Classmates from the training school and friends from earlier stages in one's career are likely to be in similar positions in the hierarchy, for example enterprise managers or sector supply officers. To the extent that a manager has a choice, he may tend to give preferential treatment to these old friends. Friendship as a form of empathy may ease the path to resolution of conflicts over specifications and delivery times. But there are two dangers in this sort of arrangement. One is that the leadership has no effective means of control over the criteria used to make such informal decisions, so that their social efficiency is not guaranteed. The other is that under pressure "old boy" ties may well be turned into informal exhange (market) arrangements.

The Use of New Information

Most of the discussion of planning and control in earlier chapters applied to the problem of getting increases in output by expanding or multiplying existing facilities. Growth without technological change falls within both the economic and organizational schemes used there to generate decisions. Nor does there seem to be any important differential impact of this problem on the two kinds of economic organization we have been considering. New factories, as well as old factories expanded in familiar ways, fit into the existing rules and roles, and may be handled within the same framework as the older organizations.

However, most growth in recent decades has been accompanied by considerable technological change. The new facility differs from the old in important ways, and because it is new all participants have less confidence a priori in its performance characteristics. This kind of growth has discernible—and apparently quite important—differential impact on different types of economic systems. We will begin with the problem of introducing an already known innovation into practical operation.

The difficulties in introducing change effectively are simply stated but not so easily resolved. They stem from inertia, and the greater opportunities for distortion of information by interested participants when the information is relatively uncertain. In a time of rapid change, inertia may be somewhat less of a problem simply because there is more experience with its effects. However, risk aversion and interest-oriented foot-dragging remain as powerful disincentives to the eager acceptance of innovations. A loose classification of innovations will help show likely differential impact vis-à-vis our alternative organizations.

Consider first minor modifications of existing production processes, where by minor is meant that the change is not very risky or expensive and can be made fairly rapidly. A firm operating in a market or under soviet conditions should have a strong incentive to make use of an innovation of this kind, since it directly rewards the decision maker through the normal pattern of material incentives. The monopolist or the soviet manager operating under a weak cost reduction incentive would only be interested if the innovation produced an output increase. But in general the large number of innovations of this kind that are more or less internal to the enterprise do not conflict with vested interests at the enterprise or higher level. One constraint that might become effective stems from the possibility that even minor modifications would become known by higher agencies and would be used as a basis for norm raising. Another stems from the possible need for quota adjustment if input mix is affected by the innovation. Organizationally speaking, if an innovation gets entangled in the bargaining process it is no longer minor.

The command society faces some special problems with respect to this kind of change. The more accurate information flows in the command society imply that there is a greater gain, in terms of the efficiency of planning and control, from standardization of production processes than in the soviet type of organization. For this reason there is likely to be greater control exercised from above on minor modifications, especially where physical facilities are to be modified. The need for approval of higher bodies means that fewer such changes are likely to be undertaken, but that they spread more quickly to other similar enterprises when they do occur. However, the mere fact of shifting the decision to a higher level would probably inhibit the initiative of the firm-level participants who in other systems are the major innovators of this kind. It may well be that for minor modifications a well-functioning soviet type of organization is more "dynamic" than the command society.[11]

The situation is quite different when the innovation is a new production process, one which would substantially alter procedures within existing firms or which calls for an entirely new type of plant. It appears to be exceptionally difficult to win acceptance of this type of innovation in a soviet-style organization. The chief difficulty is the greater uncertainty that surrounds all innovations which directly affect interests beyond the confines of the firm. For each activity a complex and costly bargaining process must also be admitted so as to establish the norms which determine relative valuations of this and other activities of participants. The branch staff probably has a more detailed knowledge of the engineering performance characteristics of a new process than members of the firm; it may also have exaggerated ideas as to the speed with which it can be installed and made to operate up to design. Officials of the firm fear the effects of possibly excessive new demands and the short-run costs of installation and operational mastery. This leads to a very strong and much complained of propensity to procrastinate.

To the extent that uncertainty is smaller and short-run production incentives are weaker in the command society, problems with new processes are less severe than in its hierarchic counterpart. On the other hand the strict hierarchy, with its limited

---

[11] The soviet firm's incentive would be weakest if the firm were very successful, in which case the ratchet effect would inhibit attempts to increase overfulfillment of targets.

delegation of competence, may have serious effects on the initiative of those lower down. The new process may be easily and accurately fitted into the planning and control scheme, but costs of getting to this stage could be higher than in the soviet system.

A change in the manner in which a good is produced is either an internal matter for the soviet-type firm or involves relations between the firm and higher levels of the hierarchy to which the firm is subservient. A change in the kind of goods produced, however, has wider effects, and poses a rather different problem to the system. In the first place a new good is by its nature not a standard one. Not only must potential users adjust to its properties, but there may be opportunities for minor alterations in the good's properties to enhance its usefulness to consumers, industrial or otherwise. But this means contract negotiations, raising the issues discussed earlier under the heading of goods produced to specification. The treatment of this class of goods is an especially inefficient area in the soviet type of organization.

As already noted, short-run pressures inhibit other than minor innovation at the firm level, a feeling with which branch authorities, under similar pressures, are likely to sympathize. These pressures operate for new goods as well as for new processes, and for precisely the same reasons. This also applies to information problems, though the chain of information flow is now lengthened to the consumer, whose information from the supplier or his branch agents is not wholly to be trusted.

When either a new good or a new process requires different inputs, the firm is faced with the problem of establishing informal relations with the new suppliers in order to increase its confidence that delivery schedules will be met. The uncertainties surrounding supply and its informal aspects are a further hindrance to prompt acceptance of qualitatively new tasks.

The problems of contractual relations and supply uncertainties are to some extent endemic to any hierarchic system, stemming as they do from the destruction of market incentives for achieving agreement between firms. The command society will not escape them, though improved planning should reduce the force of supply uncertainties. However, the problems of information distortions and the short-run nature of pressures would be much less important for the command society than under soviet conditions. For this reason the operational problems of introducing new and different goods are probably less serious in the former than in the latter.

Broader changes which involve innovations in a large number of firms or industries or the creation of new industries can be thought of as a combination of the kinds of changes considered above. Again inertia and uncertainty are the primary hindrances whose differential impact by organizational type is perhaps best explained as differences in the pattern of appropriability of gains which these organizational types create. Where indivisibilities are large and gains dispersed, the relative advantage of the more centralized decision is greatest. However, there is one additional factor which works to the disadvantage of the soviet organization. The use of multiple control organs means that to some extent an enterprise has a number of competing superiors whom it must make some effort to please. Unless a broad innovation does not create a diversity of interests among these bosses, the enterprise will be able to count on support for its own dilatory attitude from at least some of these superiors.

So much for innovation borrowing. It is also true that even primarily borrowing nations still must do some innovating on their own, both in adapting engineering designs to specific needs and in the less fixed aspects of response to daily problems, some of which always turn out to be unique. And then at some point the time comes when the frontiers of technology are reached in some industries, so that further progress requires the development and application of entirely new ideas. In what ways does the structure of economic organization facilitate or hinder this creative process? Unfortunately there are no simple answers to this most fundamental question; but perhaps a few speculations are not out of place, since probably many would make their judgment among economic systems primarily on the basis of the answer to this one question. One might well feel that among a set of alternative systems, each of which is capable of tolerably inefficient solution of other problems, the decision would go to that system which most promoted creativity, regardless of its relative inefficiency in other areas.

It is probably still natural to most of us to think of creativity as being a rather personal and individual process. In the United States about 40 percent of patents are awarded to individual researchers rather than groups, and the image of the lonely scholar or scientist remaking the world in his study or lab finds its "R and D" counterpart in the creative tinker to whom those patents are often awarded. Perhaps the main support for this view lies in the intuitive and somewhat mysterious nature of creativity even in rather mundane fields. The individual often is not aware of the logical processes that he used, and even has difficulty in describing the evidence which proved suggestive. So long as intuition and "personal knowledge" (that is, knowledge that before the fact of innovation the individual is unable to communicate) play a decisive role in creativity, it will be a very difficult thing to routinize or centralize.

Another great barrier to the effective organization of creativity lies in the lines of communication that are needed. An essential feature of most innovations is the bringing together of several disparate lines of thought or operations. These, being put together in a new way, are likely to represent the result of the existence in one decision unit of stocks of knowledge in unusual combinations. But unusual combinations are precisely what organization is designed to prevent; it serves rather to restrict and specialize the stock of information provided to each participant. Probably this factor is the major one in generating the appearance of stultification and plodding dullness that is all too common in the middle ranks of large organizations. And this is the part of a bureaucracy that would be directly concerned in the development of much industrial innovation.

On the other hand, a decentralized and particularly a market form of organization faces some problems of its own with respect to innovative activity. First there is the question of appropriability; does a unit (individual) which can hope to reap only a portion of the benefits of an innovation have adequate incentives to undertake to develop it? Then there is the related question of monopoly. Communication of the idea, once developed, makes appropriability less feasible, so that business secrets pose a dilemma for society, a balancing of the gains and costs of incentives to the innovators as well as to "society itself." And where monopoly does occur, there may be incentives to withhold the innovation from the market because of its effect on gains to the unit from its current activities.

Then there is the problem of scale. In a modern society much information relevant for innovation is inevitably specialized in a highly structured way. The number of recognized fields of specialization for scientists and engineers is growing rapidly, while many innovations require the knowledge of many of these fields to be brought to bear more or less simultaneously. A division of labor into teams and even hierarchies is the result, and casual observation suggests that the economies of scale for research are increasing in many areas. It might be true both that there are enough interesting projects to make it possible to keep *all* research at the individual level, while continuing to produce useful results, but also that the gains from effective organization of research will far outweigh the costs in terms of small-scale research foregone.

Finally there is apparent a certain hierarchizing even in the work of individual pure scientists. The importance of this informal hierarchy has perhaps been most strongly asserted by Thomas Kuhn;[12] it is based on the standardization of knowledge and outlook imposed on scientists during their training period, a standardization which helps sustain and reinforce a consensus as to

[12] *The Structure of Scientific Revolutions* (Chicago: University of Chicago Press, 1962).

what is useful research and what constitutes a solution to a problem. Access to research equipment as well as to the ears of fellow scientists depends on following rules which in effect are policed by the recognized leaders of a field and its principle trainers of new scientists.

Whatever the extent to which this is an accurate picture of interactions among scientists,[13] the case is likely to be somewhat stronger for the kind of research and development which would appropriately be carried out within an industrial hierarchy. For here the properties of the solution are likely to be far better known, and at times even the costs of development and of alternative solutions may be roughly known.[14] Such knowledge can be put to use to increase the efficiency of research so that possibly centralization may be appropriate in order to take account of the external effects.[15]

Even if all these factors favoring highly organized innovative activity are really operative, there remains the question as to whether the organizational structure appropriate to research is also appropriate to the operation of industry. For example, a useful organization for much innovative activity may be the task force which is formed to solve a specific problem and which tends to be reformed with many changes in membership with each new

---

[13] For a different view see Michael Polanyi, *Science, Faith and Society* (Oxford: Oxford University Press, 1946); also his *Personal Knowledge* (Chicago: University of Chicago Press, 1958).

[14] A special kind of technician problem is thus likely to arise for the scientist who goes to work in an industrial laboratory, as he is asked to adjust to a very different conception of what interesting problems are.

[15] One way in which external effects may appear is suggested by the discussion in Burton H. Klein, "The Decision Making Problem in Development," in National Bureau of Economic Research, *The Rate and Direction of Inventive Activity* (Princeton: Princeton University Press, 1962), pp. 477–97. Suppose that there are several possible solutions to a research and development problem. Each of them has a relatively small chance of panning out, but the chance of at least one of them working is much larger. If specialization of knowledge leads a different decision unit to consider each alternative, no development may be attempted, while a centralized decision unit will find that the expected gains far outweigh the expected costs when all possible solutions are taken into account. To put it another way, uncertainty may create external effects for choice-decentralized organizations.

task. The *ad hoc* scientific advisory committees to various government agencies, and especially those concerned with military procurement, which have proliferated in recent years, provide one kind of prototype. Another has a history in industry: the troubleshooter and his staff who develop a reputation for dealing effectively with tough problems and are shifted around to deal with them as they arise within a large organization.

Such task forces can be found within large scale industry in market economies. They might be fitted in to more structured hierarchies as well. However, one of their most useful properties is their exemption from standard rules of procedure. They tend to be disruptive of highly structured hierarchies, and of hierarchies whose structure is largely informal; the former because alternatives to standard routines are nonexistent, and the latter because it takes time to learn the informal rules of procedure in a new location in the hierarchy before a unit can function effectively.

These few speculations cannot be taken too seriously. They suggest that the looser market system, with its competing decision units and less regulated and formalized communications system, has some important advantages for the innovative process. These advantages appear greater for the earlier stages of innovation than for the later, and for direct innovation than for borrowing. For a system where the central government is involved directly in industrial operation and innovation, the use of markets for industrial exchange offers the flexibility that results from the availability of both choice- and authority-decentralized and centralized organizations to carry out the innovations. On the one hand, effective and broad communication is essential to the innovative process, and is likely to be most effective when lines of communication are well established and the participants habituated to them. But the creation of change usually requires a novel union of bits of information, which implies that flexibility and channel switching are of great importance. There is no clearly apparent organizational resolution of this dilemma.

Institutional Equilibrium and Stability

Toward the end of Chapter Four it was suggested that there is a rough and ready organizational equilibrium built into the soviet system, which is combined with a more or less cyclical process of limited organizational adjustment. Because of the high uncertainty level in the system, this equilibrium has proved to be rather stable in the face of the dramatic changes that accompany the processes of modernization.

A command society is a more rigid form of social organization, with only a limited range of environments within which it is capable of sustaining itself. Perhaps the property most sensitive to environmental change in the command society is the attitude of participants. However, simple infeasibility of the structure is another likely cause of failure, of transformation into another system. In a sense, the Chinese Great Leap may represent an instance of this. The infeasibility in this case stemmed, so to speak, from attempting to apply the techniques of the Jesuits to the environment of the Navy. That is, the Chinese had a relatively favorable environment in terms of the attitudes and commitments of party members and others to the ideals and ideology of the leadership, but they did not appreciate the technical aspects of planning and controlling an economy which possesses a significant industrial sector. The requirements of coordinative activity were grossly underestimated, with reliance apparently placed on the ability of the party cadres to make wise decisions. Perhaps the cadres had the commitment to do so, but they lacked the appropriate information. It remains unclear whether, even with a full appreciation of this problem and a willingness to devote resources to dealing with it, an acceptable technical solution is at hand even yet. By virtually ignoring coordination problems, the Chinese unfortunately did not succeed in testing the hypothesis that a solution which meets the minimum requirements of consistency with the command society can be found.[16]

What happens when an attempt is made to install a command society in an unfavorable environment, or when a successfully functioning command society is faced with a changed and inappropriate environment? Two possibilities among many are the subject of brief speculation. One such process might run as follows. Suppose a successfully functioning command society is faced by an environment which changes in one of two ways. The first is that the leadership finds (or at least feels) that external challenges to the system are fading, so that the ideology no longer serves to define effectively goals in whose service the leadership can manipulate the society. This may lead to the substitution of worldly, self-seeking attitudes on the part of the leadership. Before long the participants cannot fail to notice this change, which would tend to render ineffective the indoctrination, and to stimulate the permeation of worldly attitudes throughout the society. The effects on discipline would constitute a threat to the leadership, which might well be met by the substitution of coercion for the more subtle controls of the past. The decline of effective commitment plus coercion would create strong pressures for simulation on the part of the members, and particularly for the establishment of personal loyalties between superiors and inferiors as a form of security against arbitrary actions. All this might occur without destroying the solidarity of the elite corps toward outsiders, unless opportunities for transfer without serious penalty existed. The end result might be a brutal and oppressive regime both within and without, one in which succession involved a desperate conflict, but in which the organization was able to maintain indefinitely its authority against outsiders.

A second path might occur when the environment began

---

[16] For a description of party and economic organization in China, see Franz Schurmann, *Ideology and Organization in Communist China* (Berkeley: University of California Press, 1966).

changing in ways which tended to disrupt traditional modes of response. For example, if middle-level hierarchs began to find themselves in a position to make decisions which they felt served the goals of the society better than those actually made by the leadership, the former would be faced, even though they pre-served their commitment, with a serious role conflict. Should this type of situation persist, the evaluation of orders, simulation, and the undermining of the effective authority of the leadership would be a likely consequence. In such a situation the leader-ship might be unwilling to resort to extremes of coercion on members, because they recognized that the independent acts of the latter were often justified in terms of the society's goals. One possible response would be some devolution of authority. If they sought simultaneously to preserve the command function, they would merely lend further impetus to resistance lower in the hierarchy. Again the result might be the formal preservation of a command society, with the continued issuing of commands known to be inconsistent, but with the tacit if unwilling accept-ance of informal means of resolving these conflicts by the lower-level participants. The uncertainties faced by participants in such a system could lead to the rise of personal cliques as above, and to the transformation of commitment into at least partially self-seeking motives on the part of many participants. Depending on the environment, such a system might exhibit a certain stability, since movement back to a command society was infeasible and movement "forward" to a more explicit influence exchange system was unacceptable to the leadership since that would entail a further reduction in their power. Even though stable for organizational reasons, it might be extremely inefficient, combining many of the disadvantages of both systems.

As has been emphasized such organizational dynamics are highly speculative. If they seem to possess some plausibility, it is nevertheless very difficult to separate organizational from environmental factors. On the other hand, as has also been emphasized, it is only when some such models of organizational influences have been constructed that appropriate hypotheses can be constructed for testing the significance of the organizational factor.

In conclusion, the following has been claimed for the effectiveness of the command society as an organizational form for the economy:

(1) It should be restricted to the modern sectors so that appropriate routine responses can be built into the attitudes of the participants.

(2) Boundary problems do not seem serious except between labor and management. Flows of noncommand goods into and out of the system can be organized hierarchically.

(3) The mobility barrier within the factory may create problems, especially in full employment situations. Recruiting for the managers' corps from among workers is at best a partial melioration of this problem; since a relatively small number can be co-opted, an insufficient incentive is created to change worker attitudes substantially.

(4) In the Soviet Union and in parts of Eastern Europe the communist parties have functioned roughly as command societies, but the industrial hierarchies have not. Conflicts of interest and orientation between these two hierarchies have been serious, and have contributed to the apparent stability of the soviet form of industrial organization by, among other things, making both sides unwilling to discuss openly (perhaps even among themselves) certain technical and organizational problems of the economy.

(5) Plan making can be routinized and schemes found which provide support for command organization. However, there is no near prospect of producing an optimal plan in detail; therefore some choice-decentralization with respect to output decisions is inevitable.

(6) Short-run enterprise control is likely to be more effective under the command society than under soviet conditions, provided that product standardization is recognized as an important instrument for making feasible plans. The time span of control of the former is more appropriate to the range and complexity of the factory manager's decisions than is that of the soviet system.

(7) Innovational activity may be weak under both forms. Possibly

the command society's chief problem would be with small-scale innovations, because of the control need for standardization among units. Its chief advantage over the soviet form would probably lie in the greater acceptance of approved innovation among enterprise managers.

(8) As a command society, such an organization mixes strong emotional commitment with the orderly description and solution of problems. Both elements are really essential to the application of the system to an economy: each is a key ingredient in reducing the uncertainty level of all participants. Thus attempts to rely on only one of these elements, as apparently the Chinese relied on party commitment during the Great Leap, are not tests of the effectiveness of the command society when applied to the economy.

Part III

Decentralized
Socialism

CHAPTER SEVEN

Reforming the Classical Soviet System

Most of the problems with the soviet form of planning and control seem to be connected with the high uncertainty level at which the system operates. The planners are uncertain about goals and about the accuracy with which the plan itself reflects *any* specific goal; the intermediate organizations are uncertain how much enterprises under their control can be permitted to deviate from the plan, and of the real capabilities of these enterprises; the enterprises are uncertain as to the real expectations of higher organizations about their performance, and whether they will be supplied with the means to achieve any specified goal. These uncertainties are generally recognized by participants and others to be excessive, and to result in both very crude control of the system and some serious deviations from efficiency.

Reform proposals are rife in these societies today and not a few reforms have been tried out or are being prepared for practical application. This chapter is not designed to survey these schemes. Rather a small number of possible reorganizations are considered. They were selected in order to bring out several points about the requirements of a reform scheme for soviet conditions rather than for their practical prospects. We begin with two alternative enterprise reforms, follow with a comparison of branch and regional organization at the intermediate level, and conclude with a discussion of the interaction between hierarchy and market at the various levels of relative use of each.

Target Socialism

From Chapter Four it will be remembered that the equilibrium conditions for the output-input decisions of the classical soviet firm were of the form,

$$(1) \qquad [p_i(G_\pi + G_Q) + G_i] = -[p_j(G_\pi + G_Q) + G_j]\frac{\partial x_j}{\partial x_i}$$

This posed several difficulties both for the enterprise manager and for those responsible for controlling the firm's reactions and stimulating the firm to respond appropriately to plan changes. If the gross-output target played a large role in decision making, so that G_Q tended to dominate the parenthesized expressions, then assortment decisions would be strongly influenced by relative prices and so would be relatively insensitive to plan changes. The complexity of the bonus system could create difficulties in determining an optimal adjustment, and would pose especially difficult problems for those faced with specifying the enterprise criterion. The price of a good tended, *ceteris paribus*, to have a greater effect on the producer of the good than on its consumer. And finally, mistakes in previous periods tended to be corrected by adding to the number of control variables appearing in the criterion, so that past failures made future decisions even more complex.

Is there a revision of the criterion which would preserve the general features of hierarchic planning and control, with its emphasis on enterprise targets expressed in physical terms, while permitting a simpler and more easily managed set of decisions at both the enterprise and enterprise-control levels? Let us consider the implications of the following criterion:

$$(2) \qquad G = G(Q_1, Q_2, \ldots, Q_n)$$

where $Q_i = (x_i - \bar{x}_i)$, the amount by which the targeted output or input, $\bar{x}_i$, is overfulfilled or underfulfilled, is fully disaggregated so that there are no longer any aggregative indices in the criterion. We may call this approach "target socialism" in keeping with its emphasis on physical output targets.

Maximizing this criterion, subject to the constraint of the production function described in Chapter Four, gives as equilibrium conditions:

$$(3) \qquad \frac{1}{\lambda} = \frac{F_i}{G_i} \qquad \text{or} \qquad G_i = -G_j \frac{\partial x_j}{\partial x_i} \qquad \begin{array}{l} (i,j = 1, \ldots, n) \\ (i \neq j) \end{array}$$

But this is similar in form to the efficient equilibrium conditions achieved under appropriate conditions by competitive capitalism:

$$\frac{1}{\lambda} = \frac{F_i}{p_i} \qquad \text{or} \qquad p_i = -p_j \frac{\partial x_j}{\partial x_i}$$

Note that the G_i are differential production bonuses. They tell the manager, for some given level of production of commodity i, how much his bonus will be raised if he increases overfulfillment of the plan for that commodity by one unit. Alternatively, if i is an input, it tells how much the bonus decreases with an additional over- or underplan use of a unit of the good. By setting the differential output bonuses at the same values as the corresponding shadow prices derived from the national plan, the controllers will stimulate firms with the appropriate technology to exactly achieve the plan.

In this way the value and the physical aspects of the plan are fully integrated. However, the physical targets themselves may be formally meaningless. Even if enterprises were not informed of them, their incentive to produce those amounts would remain. One might argue that, given the zone of compliance that exists for most members of a hierarchy, the announcement of a set of targets would provide some direct stimulus to take them seriously, for example in cases in which the plan fails to describe reality with close accuracy so that the two kinds of plans are mutually inconsistent. Given the uncertainty as to the consequences of applying indirect stimuli such as prices, the use of output targets might increase the confidence of the planners that the plan will be fulfilled, as well as the confidence of the managers that those targets are indeed the ones desired by the planners.

Another weakness of the targets is that a change in the plan which is signaled to enterprises by changes in physical targets may provide no incentive for the enterprise to adjust.[1] Unless the G_i functions have the targets as arguments, the optimal enterprise adjustment is unchanged by alterations in these targets. However, again there are other aspects of plan change which may stimulate some response by the enterprises. In addition to the compliance effect there is the likelihood that a change in targets will be accompanied by a change in input allocations. But if the incentive system is unchanged, an inertial force is created which may make plan alteration quite hard to achieve.

However, in principle this problem may be dealt with quite easily in target socialism. The incentive scheme will be illustrated for the two-variable production function and a special case of the criterion. Suppose the criterion has the following form:

(4)

$$G = \alpha + p_1(x_1 - \bar{x}_2) + p_2(x_2 - \bar{x}_2) - k_{1/2}(x_1 - \bar{x}_1)^2 - k_{2/2}(x_2 - \bar{x}_2)^2$$

The effect of the last two terms is to tie the incentive scheme to the physical output targets, while preserving equality between corresponding shadow prices in the national plan—prices entering into enterprise calculations and differential output bonuses in the initial equilibrium position. Thus for the two-

---

[1] In general, the equilibrium G_i are functions of the Q_i. However, if G is a linear function of the Q_i, then $G_i = p_i$ and a change in $\bar{x}_i$ will have no effect on enterprise equilibrium. In this case target socialism is equivalent to market socialism, and price adjustment must be the instrument for finding equilibrium or the optimal plan.

variable production function the enterprise equilibrium condition is

$$[p_1 - k_1(x_1 - \bar{x}_1)]f' = -p_2 + k_2(x_2 - \bar{x}_2)$$

and the sign of the comparative static effect of a change in input target, $\bar{x}_2$, is

$$\frac{\partial x_2}{\partial \bar{x}_2} = \frac{k_2}{k_1[(f')^2 + 1] - f''[p_1 - k_1(x_1 - \bar{x}_1)]}$$

which is positive unless the equilibrium occurs at a point of substantial underfulfillment.

Note that for $(k_1 = k_2 = 0, \alpha = p_1\bar{x}_1 + p_2\bar{x}_2)$ G is simply a profits function, and the firm thus behaves as a profits maximizer. But enterprise controllers can now alter enterprise behavior in predictable directions without changing prices, by the direct method of changing output and input targets.

Figure 7.1 illustrates the scheme for the case of fixed inputs and two variable outputs. AB is the production possibilities curve and point C is the plan target. Plan shadow prices are represented by the slope of PP' and so a profit maximizing firm would choose C. Under target socialism the branch ministry has defined a criterion whose indifference curves are convex to the origin, such as W_1 (representing alternative pairs of values of x_1 and x_2 which yield a constant value of G in equation (4). This is defined so that its slope at C is the same as PP', so the target socialist chooses that point also.

During the plan period, stocks of x_1 begin decreasing and those of x_2 begin increasing, so the planners adjust the targets to point E. The adjustment being small, they will have used the plan prices in choosing this target from among other alternatives, in response to the change in constraints in the original plan. But the old prices remain in effect until the end of the plan period. Consequently the change in plan would not affect the behavior of the profit maximizing firm or of the market socialist firm. But the criterion of the target socialist firm has shifted, one of its new indifference curves being W_2, which is tangent to the price line passing through E. This shifts the firm's choice of outputs from C to D. Because the criterion had relatively small curvature, D, though in the right direction, represents substantially less than the targeted change. Had a criterion like W_3 been in use, a

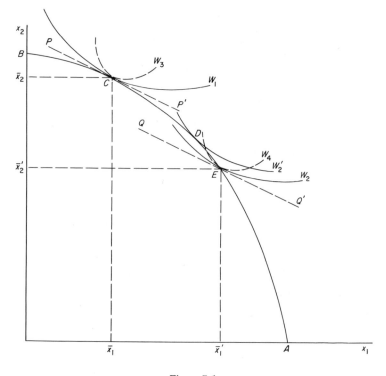

Figure 7.1

point closer to E would have been chosen. The choice of curvature would be based on an estimate of the fineness with which production can be controlled, and of course may vary widely from one industry or even one particular enterprise product to another. In practice the planners may not be able to choose targets on the production possibility surface. However, the secondary incentive system gives them a static incentive (i.e., ignoring things like the ratchet effect) to go to that surface and, except where failure by the planners is large scale, to go to a point on the surface near the target.

Several features of this scheme are worthy of comment:

(1) Making the plan and controlling the enterprises are separable processes, with the latter decentralizable to the branch. The planners must produce the shadow prices implicit in the plan specifications, but do not need to worry about price adjustments to fit the control scheme. The branch controllers can produce a control system which takes the plan as given and builds the incentive scheme around the given prices and output targets.

(2) The separation of control processes can be carried even farther. Questions of distributive justice can be dealt with at any level. Even the returns to the individual firm can be adjusted without affecting the location of the optimum parameters like α and k in the example.

(3) As described above, the incentive scheme encourages the firm to hit the plan targets. However in individual cases, it would not be difficult for the branch controllers to introduce an overfulfillment incentive within the general criterion format, which preserves at least some aspects of enterprise sensitivity to target changes.

(4) The interplan and intraplan procedures are quite distinct. During the plan period there would be no price changes, in principle at least. When data change, the planners would compute the new optimum targets, using the shadow prices given in the plan. Enterprise adjustment would be achieved by sending down these results in the form of target changes. On the other hand, in constructing a plan for the next period the planners would produce a new dual solution, in prices as well as in quantities. The new prices would be the base points for the next period incentive scheme. In most cases the form of the criteria would probably not change from period to period. In this way local adjustments of output and the local terms on which alternatives were offered would not be allowed to build systematic deviations from efficient solutions into the general plans.

(5) This scheme should improve assortment control considerably. Short-run control of assortment no longer relies heavily on prices, as

it does under the classical soviet system. Instead target adjustments can be made quite effective in preventing excessive dearth or super-fluity of individual items. The control of supply must be carried out at a level above the firm; nevertheless it appears possible to make it a relatively flexible and low-cost scheme. The fineness of control can be adjusted for individual goods by varying the curvature of the enter-prise criterion's indifference lines. And this adjustment can be carried out at a relatively low level in the hierarchy without efficiency cost.

(6) Some aggregation and disaggregation in plan making is inevit-able, and this inserts elements of uncertainty into the targets. How-ever, the stability of prices over the plan period eliminates at least this source of instability of aggregation. Also it seems likely that most temporally adjacent plans will require changes in only a moderate number of prices. Relative prices for groups of related products should remain constant, once a reasonably accurate measure of rela-tive scarcity has been achieved, with target change serving as the method of adjustment to imbalance.

(7) Such a scheme could only be applied to enterprise control if quite a good plan-making system were also installed. This means not only a plan in quantity terms but a set of related shadow prices—which the leadership was willing to trust as a reasonably accurate statement of optimal means to their ends, and which the enterprises found, by and large, to be feasible. Such schemes are available in principle, but there is really no present basis for assessing their prac-ticality. (See Chapter Three.)

(8) Maintaining balance by means of target changes requires prompt and flexible response to observed imbalance. There must not only be a good plan but a method of making quick adjustments to the plan during the period of its operation. The plan itself provides a vital instrument for this in the form of the shadow prices which measure the cost to the overall economic objective of given changes in constraints. The planning schemes of Chapter Three also provide simplified calculation routines for rebalancing after minor changes in the targets.

(9) Many of the incentives to distort reported information would persist in this scheme, which after all preserves the basic organizational features of the soviet system. However, the tying of value and quantity

plans together reduces considerably the scope for misreporting, since values are now, within limits, a useful measure of performance, and relative scarcities are known with greater confidence.

(10) Intraplan adjustment incentives, if followed precisely by managers, would not lead to wholly optimal adjustment to target changes. This can be seen by noting that in the comparative static adjustment, the equilibrium value of $\partial x_2/\partial \bar{x}_2$ is not necessarily unity. However the change is in the right direction, and can be made larger and stronger for individual cases by varying the curvature of the criterion indifference lines. Short-run maladjustments of this kind should not become serious if the plan period is fairly short so that major adjustments are carried out primarily by constructing a new plan rather than by adjusting the old one. Also these maladjustments should not carry over from one plan to the next.

(11) The scheme is also applicable to the command society as a criterion for choice-decentralized enterprise decisions. In this application, variable bonuses could not be paid out for achieving various levels of the criterion. Instead the scheme would serve as an enjoined secondary criterion for options not covered by direct command, as discussed in the preceding chapter.

In certain ways this scheme represents a choice-centralization with respect to the classical soviet organization. This is true in the sense that levels higher than the firm now make the primary production-level decision for a wider range of goods. The criterion, being more detailed, also in principle reduces the range of choice among officially acceptable alternatives open to the manager. On the other hand, if the scheme were successful the greater amount of accurate information available to the manager would give him more confidence in his estimates of alternatives—i.e., in estimating whether the leadership will in fact consider an alternative to manifest successful performance by the manager.

However, with respect to authority, there does not appear to be a significant change on the centralization–decentralization dimension. The enterprise criterion is still assigned the manager, and the criterion is interpreted by the manager in a generally choice-decentralized way, except over the range of the compliance effect. This latter might perhaps be enlarged in an informationally more efficient organization, so perhaps only in this sense is authority-related centralization increased.

Libermanism and a Decentralized Hierarchy

The recent ferment of discussion in the Eastbloc on the law of value and the expansion of the manager's range of independent decision making have led to a series of experiments in less centralized enterprise control. These experiments have taken a variety of forms in the various countries, but we will not attempt to follow their details. Some of the changes are related to adapting the system to what is interpreted as the needs of ideology, in particular the interpretation of Marxian value theory as having normative value for a socialist economy—a problem which is not relevant for our purposes. Others pertain to the appropriate criteria for enterprise adjustment, only some of which is relevant.

Instead of repeating this history and the competent evaluations already performed, we will take a simple and extreme view of the attempts to decentralize within the soviet hierarchic system and explore its consequences. Let us suppose that "Libermanism" means reducing the arguments of the enterprise criterion to two variables: gross output and profit. The enterprise equilibrium condition is simplified by dropping G_i from equation (1). For the case in which both goods are either inputs or outputs the simplified condition is:

$$p_i(G_\pi + G_Q) = -p_j(G_\pi + G_Q)\frac{\partial x_j}{\partial x_i}$$

or

$$p_i = -p_j\frac{\partial x_j}{\partial x_i}$$

Only in the case where one good, say the jth, is an input, and the other an output, will the adjustment be different from the competitive capitalist solution:[2]

$$p_i\left(\frac{G_Q}{G_\pi} + 1\right) = -p_j \frac{\partial x_j}{\partial x_i}$$

As is to be expected, in this case the equilibrium marginal product is smaller as a result of the term in parentheses, indicating *ceteris paribus* a relatively higher level of output.

The application of this extreme form of Libermanism would almost certainly require the abandonment of the supply system. It could only be preserved if the planners had nearly perfect information and processing ability. For only then could they determine an optimum with sufficient clarity to push enterprises to it by means of the indirect instrumentality of prices—and even then only under special technological conditions, such as the absence of constant returns in the vicinity of equilibrium.

The instruments of enterprise control would then be prices. This seems to imply that essentially market socialism has been adopted (except that firms are profit maximizers rather than followers of the Lange-Lerner rules). However, if it is added that prices must not move about with great frequency, this cannot be the case. Perhaps the idea is that the planners will perform the short-run chore of preserving the balance between price changes. But this means a return of the supply system, and a need for instruments that the planners can use in bringing about balance. Within this context there is a genuine dilemma: either market socialism or physical output targets, but not both.

This "Libermanite" loosening of the bonds would thus seem to be inconsistent with the aim of preserving the main features of the soviet type of hierarchy. Some preservation of both the supply system and specific output and input targets is essential if the short-run planning and control hierarchy is to survive.

[2] If Q refers to net output, the following equation applies only for values of j denoting labor inputs.

And for a system which did not have reliable scarcity ratios, the extent of reliance on prices as instruments would seem to be dangerous for a partially "relaxed" control system.

The introduction of an effective price system into the hierarchic decision scheme would require considerable reorganization, especially in order to make possible frequent price change in response to supply–demand imbalance, so as in turn to avoid too widespread recourse to specific quantity targets. But as has already been suggested, this creates instability in the aggregation–disaggregation procedure which uses these prices as weights, and so would increase the uncertainty level. We seem to be describing a process of return from Libermanism to the mixed soviet enterprise criterion.

In the final section we will return to this question. Suffice it to say here that there seems to be a basic incompatibility between the soviet type of planning system and the choice- (but not authority-) decentralized enterprise-control schemes currently in vogue in Eastbloc countries. Though the problem is widely recognized, proposed solutions which attempt to deal with the issue appear not to have seen the light of day.

Branch vs. Regional Control[3]

The main factors which are relevant for the choice of an intermediate, hierarchic economic planning and control organization may be briefly summarized:

(1) For political reasons the regional form has the advantage that some form of regional political organization is essential, while a branch political organization is not. *Ceteris paribus*, a regional form of economic organization is therefore simpler.

(2) In terms of the planning scheme, it has been suggested that the decision depends essentially on the distribution of zeroes in an overall national technology matrix disaggregated to the level of local

[3] The issues with respect to Soviet economic organization are very well summarized in Peter Wiles, *Political Economy of Communism* (Cambridge: Harvard University Press, 1962), Chap. 8. See esp. his summary table on p. 161.

production sites. The question then becomes whether these zeroes permit the division into a more self-contained set of regional or of branch intermediate organizations. This provides no clear basis for decision. A more developed economy is likely to be more interdependent with respect to both divisions than a less developed economy. And once the choice is made, organizational pressures are created which tend to make the units more self-contained than they would be otherwise.[4]

(3) Under the soviet type of organization and, indeed, under any planning scheme with current applicability, a key question for planning and control is the stability of the coefficients used at each level. A regional intermediate organization tends to put great emphasis on interregional flow coefficients which are notoriously unstable.

(4) Efficient information collection and processing depend in an important way on the stock of information possessed by each organization. In this a regional organization would seem to be at a considerable disadvantage as compared to branch organization. The branch stores a limited stock of technical data relating to a specialized technology, while the regional organization requires information of comparable quality with respect to a wide range of technology. This affects both the knowledge of alternatives and the confidence in which aggregate coefficients can be held.

(5) Under a regional system a primary task of the central planning bureau will be to coordinate interregional flows. This seems less directly related to the center's goals than the coordination of interbranch flows, unless regional autarky is in fact a central aim.[5]

Essentially the adoption of a regional system means a closer integration of transportation planning into the plan-making process. The soviet system has tended to place transportation

---

[4] Michael Keren, "Industrial vs. Regional Partitioning of Soviet Planning Organization: A Comparison," *Economics of Planning*, 4 (1964), 143–60. In terms of a formal planning scheme, the zeroes are not always a decisive consideration. For example, if the decomposition principle, described in Chap. Three above, is to be applied, the division into self-contained units is not necessary, though the speed of convergence of the scheme may be affected by the pattern of zeroes. Cf. George Dantzig, *Linear Programming and Extensions* (Princeton: Princeton University Press, 1963), pp. 466–69.

[5] Though presumably it *is* related in the case of international flows among Eastbloc countries.

planning near the end of the process, so that this interdependence is kept to a minimum. Despite oft-cited individual cases of extraordinarily inefficient hauling of goods around the country, it does not appear that this has been a fundamental source of inefficiency in the past.[6] And the detailed nature of transportation planning creates great difficulties if inserted too near the beginning of a planning process that starts with a high degree of aggregation and proceeds to disaggregate in stages. In soviet planning and control the advantage seems clearly to lie with branch organizations placed hierarchically between enterprise and center.[7]

Mixing Markets and Direct Controls

The classical soviet system makes extensive use of exchange under contract. Many flows of goods from one enterprise to another are matched by a flow of money or credit in the opposite direction and are the result of contractual agreements. And almost every flow of goods out of the enterprise is matched by an opposite flow of credit. The effect of the plan is sharply to limit the range of the parties who can enter into a given type of exchange, and to impose severe restrictions on the terms of the contract. In principle the plan should limit negotiation to relatively minor aspects of delivery schedules and product specification.

In practice, however, the range of alternatives open to enterprises is rather greater than this. In particular there is the system of informal exchanges mediated by the *tolkachi*, by which

[6] Alan Abouchar, *Spatial Planning in a Developing Country: A Programming Analysis of the Soviet Cement Industry*, Ph.D. dissertation (unpublished), Berkeley, 1965; Holland Hunter, *Soviet Transportation Policy* (Cambridge: Harvard University Press, 1957).

[7] Keren, *op. cit.*, has suggested that the introduction of a multistage planning scheme such as the decomposition program may shift the advantage from branch to regional level. His argument is essentially based on the distribution of zeroes in the technology matrix, so the comment of footnote 5 above applies to his argument. Also his conclusion is not based on consideration of the implications of aggregation on the choice, or of the question of the relation of the arguments of the national criterion to the planners' goals, or of the question of controlling implementation of the plan.

enterprises are able to adjust their input-mixes and reported outputs. The legal constraints on such operations have not been entirely effective in soviet-type economies. However, they have served to set limits to the exchanges. There is a suspicion that many such exchanges are tolerated *de facto* because they are felt to be useful for making minor corrections which result from bad planning. On this interpretation, the legal ban serves the function of limiting arbitrage on tradable goods. An alternative price system cannot be allowed to provide a substitute criterion for that imposed by the state.

To the extent that the informal exchanges do function in the manner described, one could not accept Granick's assertion that planning and the market are mutually inconsistent under soviet conditions.[8] In this case the plan dominates, and the exchanges serve as a secondary, more or less supporting, phenomenon. Of course they do not function perfectly in this regard—there is too much ignorance of alternatives, and the decision criteria imposed by soviet-type institutions are too defective for that. But it is not unreasonable to speculate that on balance the informal exchanges support rather than defeat the purposes of the planners.

However, there is another and more fundamental sense in which Granick's assertion about the incompatibility of market and plan may be true. Suppose that the informal market is allowed to develop further, into a system of open exchanges on markets in which prices are formed without direct state intervention. Now inconsistencies between plan and market are likely to be frequent. The free market changes the terms on which alternatives are offered enterprise managers, and can lead to substantial reallocations of rationed goods, with the consequence of substantial shifts in the national output mix. The plan and the state-imposed incentive system still set limits on tolerable deviations from the assigned targets. But the planners are now faced

[8] "An Organizational Model of Soviet Industrial Planning," *Journal of Political Economy*, 67 (1959), 123–24.

with the dilemma as to which set of goals to pursue: those from which the plan was derived, or those implicit in the market valuations. One might question whether the control system could be made effective against the incentives toward informal payments to individuals as well as to enterprises which such a mixture would create. The prognosis might be one of institutional instability: a tendency to move either back toward the classical soviet system or toward a system which accepted the market valuations as expressions of most social goals.

One other element in this mixed system which is worthy of comment is the advantage that appears to accrue to task-oriented rather than organization-oriented direct controls when these controls are imposed to a limited extent on a basically market economy. The American experience during World War II with the Controlled Materials Plan suggests that limited controls on a few commodities which are essential inputs to the priority products can be made to work reasonably well. Operating through a system of prime contractors who themselves controlled the allocation of scarce inputs among subcontractors, a system was created which made it possible to identify the final product for which each allocation was made. In this way a considerable amount of flexibility was built into the controls.[9]

In the soviet type of economy the controls are institutionalized through the branch hierarchies, which precludes this sort of shifting, task-oriented control hierarchy. As the number of controlled commodities increases, the effectiveness of a task-oriented control system no doubt decreases. Again this suggests that there is a broad range of mixture of direct control and market which is likely to produce unacceptable levels of inefficiency.[10]

---

[9] James Fesler, *et al.*, "Allocating Materials," in Lester Chandler and D. Wallace, eds., *Economic Mobilization and Stabilization* (New York: Holt, 1951), pp. 107–35.

[10] Cf. Gregory Grossman, "Notes for a Theory of the Command Economy," *Soviet Studies*, 15 (Oct., 1963), 119–23; Wiles, *op. cit.*, Chap. 1.

The above discussion was conducted in a vacuum in the sense that the mode of operation of the markets was not specified. As soviet-type systems continue to consider alternative forms of economic organization, several alternative market forms may be produced. In the chapters that follow we will consider one or two possibilities which were suggested by the Yugoslav experience with a highly original variant of market socialism.

CHAPTER EIGHT

Illyria:
Market Syndicalism[1]

The Yugoslavs have gone further than any other communist country in developing market exchange relations. Their approach, based on workers' management as an important aspect of enterprise decision making, is only one among many possible ways of organizing socialist market decision processes. It will be given primary attention here, partly because there is some experience with the system which can be used to suggest casually empirical analytic assumptions, and partly because the workers' council approach has considerable appeal elsewhere both in and beyond the communist bloc. That is, this form has a past and some prospect for a much greater future.

However, following the procedure used in the rest of this study, we will be dealing with Illyria, a place which bears some resemblance to Yugoslavia, but in which affairs are much simpler and behavior much more uniform. The present chapter deals with microeconomic aspects of resource allocation which are derived from a model of the enterprise. In the following chapter some aspects of public policy relating to maintaining stability, investment control, and the operation of the labor market are

[1] A slightly revised version of "The Firm in Illyria: Market Syndicalism," *American Economic Review*, 48 (1958), 566–89.

discussed. A third chapter considers the internal structure of the firm and some possible variations in organization.

The key features of productive organization in the Illyrian economy are two. First there is the operation of individual material self-interest as the dominant human motivation. This assumption is basic to the laissez-faire models of capitalism, but operates differently in the Illyrian environment because the workers are at the same time managers. They are interested in profits as well as wages.

The second key feature is the resort to markets as the means of allocating resources. There is no state plan of production and allocation which sets targets for each firm, at the same time providing the firm with its needed inputs. Instead the firm must purchase what it needs from other firms on the relevant markets at the going prices, and endeavor to sell its own output in a similar manner. The incentives of the worker-managers thus play a key role in the allocative process. They are the Illyrian equivalent of the soviet incentive criteria and the capitalist's profit incentive.

The state plays a special role in relation to the Illyrian productive apparatus because it owns the means of production. This may be interpreted as meaning that the state has acquired a right to a functional share in the income of the enterprise, by virtue of granting the enterprise the right to use the state's property. This interpretation need not be made, however. It may simply be assumed that the state in Illyria, as elsewhere, has a taxing power which it may use in the public interest. In addition it serves the usual watchdog functions of the capitalist state, refereeing disputes arising out of the market system and controlling fraudulent activities.

We shall begin with the problem of current allocation. That is, we assume that the state has already provided the means of production to each firm, and that the firm has no incentive at the moment to expand its capacity. What sort of current allocation decisions will our Illyrian firm make under these conditions?

The Competitive Firm

The Illyrian firm is paid for its product by purchasers, just as is its capitalist counterpart. It must pay for its purchases of inputs from other firms in a similar manner also. But other aspects of costs differ a bit from the capitalist situation.

In the first place there is the state, the owner of the means of production. For the moment we will assume that the state takes its putative functional share of the firm's income in the form of an interest charge on capital. Let us assume that a rational depreciation system permits state and firm to reach a valuation to be placed on the total capital in the form of plant and equipment which is in the hands of the firm. The tax then amounts to a percentage of this value—the state fixes the percentage—or a fixed amount to be paid over by the firm. Under certain assumptions the charge could be equal to the scarcity price or rent of capital. This will be the only tax paid by the firm.[2]

Secondly, there are the worker-managers. Activated by their own material self-interest, the workers will be interested in profits as well as wages. Their obligation to the state ceases with the payment of the fixed interest charge. Their obligation to other producers ceases when they have paid for goods obtained from them. Since there is no investment the remainder of the firm's revenue belongs to the workers. It is thus difficult to make a distinction between wages and profits, since the workers are residual recipients of the firm's income.

A distinction will however be made between wages and profits since it is useful for comparative purposes. The initial assumption is that the state fixes the contractual wage, which is to be treated on the firm's books as its labor cost.[3] The remainder, when all costs have been deducted, is profits. These are to be distributed to the workers in proportion to the accounting value

---

[2] The state also owns the land, but for the moment we shall assume that land is a free good.

[3] Alternative assumptions will be treated in the next two chapters.

of their work. The firm may operate at a loss, in which case wages paid out will be less than the contractual wage.

The mechanism of decision making is a simple one. The workers at a general election choose from among their members a council, which serves a function analogous to that of the board of directors of a corporation. It appoints a manager to operate the firm, gives him general instructions as to how to act, and checks periodically on his performance. On the job, all workers are under the manager's orders. They may not disobey these orders unless they violate the general instructions. Grievances are handled by the council as part of its responsibility both for maintaining the worker's security against arbitrary action by the manager and for maintaining the worker's income by judicious action in the market place. Workers are free to leave the job at any time. They may also be laid off. Hiring and firing is the ultimate responsibility of the workers' council, though it may decide to act merely as a board of appeal against the manager's decisions.

Finally, we assume that the firm is operating in purely competitive markets both for inputs and outputs. That is, our firm sells or buys too small a share of total output of any product for variations in its own level of activity to have a significant effect on price.

The One-Output–One-Variable-Input Case

A simple case which brings out the principal features of the model is that in which there is a single variable input and a single product. The variable input to the firm is labor, which is homogeneous—only one skill type of worker employed—and whose accounting cost per worker, w, is fixed by the state. Variations in output can be achieved only by varying the *number* of workers employed since hours of work also are fixed by the state.[4]

---

[4] Alternatively, hours of work are fixed by the workers' council by majority vote, in which case the work-leisure choice could be made differently in different firms.

Thus we have a production function which describes the technical conditions under which the firm may transform labor, x, into the salable product y:

(1) $$y = f(x)$$

Over the feasible range of output, the marginal product of labor will be assumed to be positive but declining as output increases.

The manager makes the decisions as to how much to produce. What is his criterion? The workers' council is interested in maximizing the incomes of the workers. Indeed, each member of the workers' council is interested in maximizing his own income. But in this case there is no conflict of interest among the workers, since each receives the same wage and the same share in profits.[5] The workers' council instructs the manager to produce up to the point at which the average income (wage plus profits share over the time period in question) per worker is a maximum. The manager, being himself a worker, is only too happy to oblige.

The manager's job now is to calculate the desired output and then to produce it. As a basis for his calculation he knows the firm's production function, the prices p and w—given by the market and the state respectively—and the criterion prescribed by the workers' council. He might proceed by considering

(2) $$U = py/x$$

the average receipts per worker, and

(3) $$K = w + R/x$$

the average costs per worker. The difference between U and K is average profits per worker, so maximizing this difference will satisfy the workers' council's criterion.[6]

[5] Conflicts might arise in case the criterion specified by the workers' council would lead to layoffs. But as long as these amounted to less than half the work force (and less than half of the members of the workers' council) a majority decision would still follow the criterion.

[6] Since wage cost per worker is fixed by the state, maximizing profits per worker is equivalent to maximizing the sum of wage per worker and profits per worker. We are also deliberately idealizing the decision process by which the manager determines his appropriate level of output.

Equilibrium for the Illyrian competitive firm is described graphically in Figure 8.1, where the values of U and K are plotted against x, the number of workers. The solution is not altered by making x rather than y the formal choice variable. U has its maximum value at the point at which marginal and

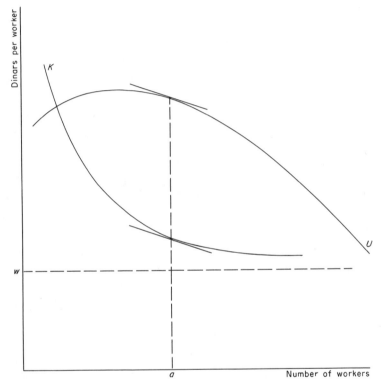

Figure 8.1

average product are equal, and declines as the number of workers is either increased or decreased from this value. The k-function is a rectangular hyperbola asymptotic to $x = 0$, $K = w$. Profits per worker reach a maximum when the difference between U and K is greatest, which is the value of x for which the slopes of U and K are equal. According to Figure 8.1 the equilibrium value of x is a.

Our equilibrium condition is that the slopes of U and K be equal, or alternatively that marginal per-worker revenue equals marginal cost per worker.[7] This is the Illyrian equivalent of the capitalist condition that price will equal marginal cost under rational management, or of the market socialist rule that managers act so as to set marginal cost equal to price. The Illyrian condition states that wages per worker (or, what amounts to the same thing, profits per worker) are maximized if the competitive firm chooses the output at which marginal per-worker revenue equals marginal cost per worker. This condition has more in common with the capitalist "rule" than with the Lange-Lerner rule. For the Illyrian rule represents the *result* of behavior of a specified kind (wage-maximizing behavior), as does the neoclassical rule (profit-maximizing behavior). In the market socialist economy of the Lange-Lerner type, however, the managers are directed by the state to act in a certain way, the rule not being connected explicitly with the motivations of the managers.

What is the meaning of this equilibrium? How does it compare with the equilibrium position of the traditional firm? We may consider first the effects of changes in the parameters on the Illyrian firm's behavior, and then contrast the equilibrium positions of Illyrian and capitalist firms under similar technological and market conditions.

[7] Marginal per-worker revenue, it will be noticed, is not the same thing as marginal revenue per worker. The former measures the change in average revenue per worker brought about by a small change in output, while the latter measures the average marginal revenue per worker. In symbols, marginal per-worker revenue is:

$$\frac{d(py/x)}{dy} = p \cdot \frac{x - yx'}{x^2}$$

(here and elsewhere in this chapter primes denote derivatives) while marginal revenue per worker is:

$$\frac{d(py)/dy}{x} = \frac{p}{x}$$

Referring to Figure 8.2, suppose that the firm is in equilibrium producing, under revenue and cost conditions represented by U_1 and K_1, an output corresponding to the level of employment a. The state now raises the interest rate, so that R is increased. This shifts the cost curve up to K_2. But at the output corresponding to a, curve K_2 is steeper than is U_1.[8] That is to

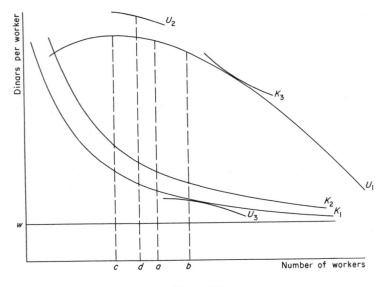

Figure 8.2

say, at employment level a the rate of decrease of average cost per worker is greater than the rate of decrease of average revenue per worker. Consequently it will be to the workers' advantage to raise output until average cost and average revenue per worker are decreasing at the same rate. In Figure 8.2 this is represented by employment level b where the slopes of U_1 and K_2 are equal. This result can be generalized into the theorem:

[8] Since $K = w + (R/x)$, $dK/dx = -R/x^2$. Therefore, if $R_2 > R_1$, $|dK_2/dx| > |dK_1/dx|$ at $x = a$.

A change in the fixed costs of the competitive Illyrian firm leads to a change in output in the same direction.

Further increases in R would lead to further increases in output. If K_3 were the relevant cost curve, the firm would be earning zero profits. Even if R were increased beyond this point, output would continue to increase, as the worker-managers strove to minimize losses. Under these circumstances the workers would be receiving less than the calculated wage w. So long as no better alternatives were available elsewhere, the workers would continue to work in the given firm despite this fact, under our assumptions.[9] Decreases in R of course have the opposite effect. At $R = 0$, the cost function becomes $K_4 = w$, and output would be at the level corresponding to the maximum value of U_1. A negative interest rate would convert K into a hyperbola asymptotic to the same lines as before, but located below w on Figure 8.2. Employment would be less than c and the competitive Illyrian firm would be in equilibrium with average costs falling.[10]

Price changes may be considered in a similar way. Suppose that an increase in demand for the industry's product leads to an increase in the market price p of our firm, which is currently in equilibrium at employment level a of Figure 8.2. This will shift U_1 upward to position U_2. But at the current employment level, U_2 will be steeper than K_1.[11] That is, at a the rate of decrease of average revenue per worker is greater than the rate of decrease of average cost per worker. Output and employment

---

[9] In the Yugoslavia of the mid-fifties wages up to 80 percent of the calculated wage were guaranteed by the government. If this were true of Illyria, then at outputs beyond that which yielded $0.8w$ to the workers the maximization criterion would cease to apply. Continued operation at such a level would eventually lead to bankruptcy.

[10] As in capitalism, this would only be true over the range in which marginal product was declining. Beyond that range the second-order condition for equilibrium would not be satisfied, so that if a solution existed it would not be a maximum. It may also be noted that over this range of values the supply curve would be positively sloped.

[11] $dU/dx = (p/x)[y' - (y/x)]$. Hence if $p_2 > p_1$, then $|dU_2/dx| > |dU_1/dx|$ at $x = a$.

will contract until these rates are again equal, as at employment level *d*. Our theorem is:

A change in price to the competitive Illyrian firm leads to a change in output in the opposite direction.

The lower limit to a price-induced output contraction is, roughly speaking, at employment level *c* where average and marginal product are equal. If falling price were to shift the revenue curve down to U_3 a zero-profits position would be reached. The remarks above regarding operations at a loss would apply equally if falling price rather than rising fixed costs were the cause of the losses.[12]

Under the usually hypothesized market and technological conditions, the Illyrian competitive firm possesses a negatively sloped supply curve. This does not mean however that Illyrian competitive markets are inherently unstable. For example, Figure 8.3 depicts the industry supply and demand curves in such a market. If demand were to shift from *DD* to *D'D'*, point *A* would no longer be an equilibrium position. If this is a "price-adjusting" market in the usual sense, the adjustment

---

[12] The workers' criterion, $S = w + \pi/R$, where π is profits. Then maximizing this subject to the constraint of equation (1), the effects of changes in p and R can perhaps be seen more clearly by considering the resulting equilibrium condition:

$$(4) \qquad \frac{dS}{dx} = \frac{p(xy' - y) + R}{x^2} = 0$$

or

$$(5) \qquad \frac{y}{x} - y' = \frac{R}{px}$$

Thus the right-hand term of (5) measures the difference between average and marginal product in equilibrium, which will be positive (decreasing average product) if R is positive. But the difference between average and marginal product is a monotonic increasing function of output, beyond the point of maximum average product (at which point the difference is nil). So, from equation (5), if R is increased, the difference between average and marginal product, and hence equilibrium output, will be increased. On the other hand, an increase in p means a decrease in the difference between average and marginal product, and hence a decrease in equilibrium output.

mechanism is such that the direction of price movement over time has the same sign as the amount of excess demand. In the diagram, excess demand is now positive so price increases, and eventually equilibrium is restored.

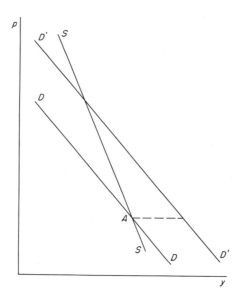

Figure 8.3

On the other hand, if the demand curve has a steeper slope than the supply curve, the adjusting mechanism described above will lead away from equilibrium and the market will be unstable. To be assured of stability this possibility must be avoided, which means that some further constraint must be imposed on the structure of the firm specified above.[13] The problem of instability is most likely to arise when product demand is relatively inelastic, or when marginal product is relatively large and declining slowly as output increases.

[13] See the Appendix to this chapter.

If the state changes the calculated wage w, there is no change in any of the variables relevant to the firm. The K function (see Figure 8.1) shifts vertically up or down as a result. The income of the workers is unchanged, though more income is in the form of profits (if w is reduced) and less in the form of wages.

The Illyrian equilibrium can now be contrasted with its capitalist counterpart. Consider two firms, one in Illyria, the other in a capitalist country. They have identical production functions and are operating in purely competitive markets. In addition, market prices are equal in both cases, as are fixed costs, and the Illyrian calculated wage w^I equals the going capitalist wage w^c. In Figure 8.4, the U and K functions describe the revenue and cost positions of the Illyrian firm under alternative levels of employment. The rates of change are also drawn in. At

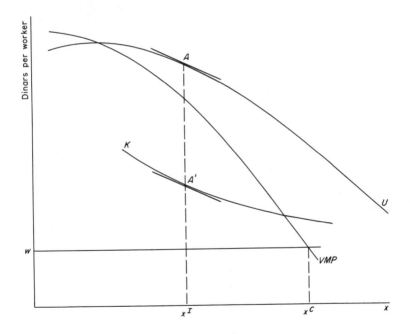

Figure 8.4

the intersection of the latter, the Illyrian firm is in equilibrium, producing the output corresponding to employment x^i.

In describing the equilibrium of the capitalist firm, it will first be noted that U also expresses the value of the average product of the capitalist firm under our assumptions, since $U = py/x$. The capitalist value-of-the-marginal-product function bears the usual relation to U, and the capitalist output is found at the point x^c where VMP equals the wage, since output y^c is a single-valued function of labor input.[14]

In the diagram the capitalist output exceeds that of the Illyrian firm. But this need not be the case. For example, by increasing w^c it would be possible to reduce the equilibrium output level of this firm to the Illyrian level or even below. Under our assumptions, a necessary and sufficient condition that the outputs of the two firms be equal is that the equilibrium marginal products be equal. The capitalist value of the marginal product is equal to w^c. In Illyria the value of the marginal product is equal to the "full" wage, i.e., the calculated wage plus the profits share to each worker.[15] Therefore the Illyrian full wage equals the capitalist wage, and equality of outputs implies zero profits.[16]

Thus the Illyrian firm is capable of producing, in the short run, at a level equal to or even greater than that of its capitalist counterpart. And the state can affect output decisions of the firm via its ability to alter the parameter R. If it is willing to use the fixed tax for capital use as an instrument of policy in attaining desired levels of output, and consequently is willing to make discriminatory charges on this basis, it may create an environment in which it is in the material interests of the worker-managers to produce at the competitive capitalist output, or at

[14] We are assuming that the capitalist firm too can vary only the number of workers employed and not the hours of work.

[15] From footnote 12, $S = (py - R)/x = py'$ in equilibrium.

[16] We assumed at the start that $w^I = w^C$. Since the value of w^I really does not make any difference, a more significant statement would be: equality of outputs implies equal wages.

some other preferred rate. Alternatively, if the industry were in long-run equilibrium in both countries and demand, labor force, etc., conditions were identical, both firms would produce the same output.

Finally, the case of constant average product y/x may be noted. In capitalism this means one of three things: (1) if $VMP > w$ the firm produces at capacity; (2) if $VMP < w$ the firm produces nothing; and (3) if $VMP = w$ output is indeterminate. In the Illyrian case this means that U is a horizontal line. The maximum positive, or minimum negative, difference between U and K consequently is at infinity whatever the position of U on the diagram. The Illyrian firm always produces at capacity when average product is constant, regardless of the level of w.

The Case of Two Variable Inputs

In Illyria a single class of inputs, labor, is singled out for special treatment. The distinctive features of Illyrian behavior stem entirely from this fact. By extending our previous model to include the use by the firm of a variable nonlabor input, the special position of labor in the firm can be brought out more clearly. The production function will now have the two arguments,

$$(6) \qquad\qquad y = f(x, z)$$

If the usual assumptions of positive marginal products and diminishing returns to the factors are made, the equilibrium condition for labor use will correspond to that in the previous section, i.e., the value of the marginal product of labor will be equal to the full wage. For the nonlabor input however, the value of the marginal product will be equal to the price v of the input.[17] The workers react to changes in nonlabor inputs in the same manner as do capitalists: they will increase their use of the

---

[17] See the Appendix to this chapter for derivations in the two-variable-input case.

factor as long as it contributes more to revenue than to cost. On the other hand, they seem to use a different criterion in evaluating labor use. An additional laborer must contribute more to revenue per worker than to cost per worker in order for him to be employed. In fact, *only* the latter criterion is being employed in the model. It simply happens that the capitalist and Illyrian criteria lead to the same behavior with regard to nonlabor inputs. Whenever one of these factors contributes more to revenue than to cost it also contributes more to revenue per worker than to cost per worker. As a result the equilibrium conditions are the same. However, the two criteria do not lead to the same behavior when it comes to labor use. Because each laborer gets a share of the profits, it does not follow that an additional worker who contributes more to revenue than to cost will necessarily also contribute more to revenue per worker than to cost per worker. As a result, the equilibrium conditions for labor use are not the same in the two regimes.

An analysis of the effects of changes in the parameters R and p leads to less clear results in the two-input case than it did in the previous section: In the case of a change in fixed costs, the analysis may be illustrated by means of the factor-allocation diagrams of Figure 8.5. The curves in 8.5A are drawn on the assumption of a fixed input of factor z, and those in 8.5B on the assumption of a fixed level of employment. From an initial position of equilibrium in which x_1 of x and z_1 of z are being used, fixed cost is increased. This shifts K_1 upward to K_2, increasing labor input from x_1 to x_2, and consequently tending to increase output. However, there is now an additional effect which must be taken into account: namely the effect of the increase in labor use on the marginal product of the nonlabor input. If the latter is unaffected or increases, shifting VMP_1 upward to VMP_2, the increase in output is either unaffected or magnified. However, if VMP is reduced by the increased labor use, the amount of z used decreases, and the output effect of the increase in fixed cost is indeterminate by means of qualitative analysis alone. The latter, however, is a rather unlikely eventuality, since in the short run more labor will generally not decrease the usefulness of the other variable factors, and conversely. Consequently a change in fixed cost in the multifactor case will also tend to lead to a change in output in the same direction.

A more serious indeterminacy appears in the analysis of price changes. Without a good deal more information, it is not possible to state the effect on output of a change in price. The possibility

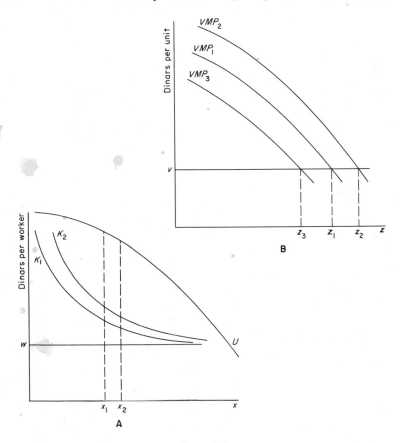

Figure 8.5

of a positively inclined supply curve emerges clearly however, and some presumption that the danger of instability, resulting from a negatively inclined and relatively elastic supply curve, has diminished. Whether or not a negatively sloped supply curve will result in the multifactor case depends on the importance of labor in the bill of inputs.[18]

Similarly, changes in the parameter v, the supply price of the nonlabor input z, have indeterminate effects on output. This is also true in the case of analysis of the capitalist firm with the same amount of information, though information sufficient to remove the indeterminacy in one case may not be sufficient in the other.

The statements made earlier comparing competitive capitalism with competition in Illyria generally apply in the somewhat more complicated two-variable-input case. We will consider here the problem of comparative factor allocation. As before, our two firms have identical production functions and are operating under identical market conditions so that:

$$p^I = p^C$$

$$w^I = w^C$$

$$v^I = v^C$$

$$R^I = R^C$$

the superscripts, as before, standing for "Illyria" and "Capitalism" respectively.

The situation is described in Figure 8.6 in which isoquants Q_i which are identical for both firms are drawn. Let us assume first that the capitalist firm is producing output Q_1. BB is the factor-cost line based on the values of w and v, so that the capitalist firm is in equilibrium at a factor mix represented by point N. Let us assume further that the capitalist firm is earning a profit

[18] Cf. equation (2) in the Appendix to this chapter.

at this level of operation. At the same output the Illyrian firm would be earning a profit too. But it would not be in equilibrium at point *N*. This is because *BB* is not the relevant factor-cost line for the Illyrian firm. In Illyria the value of the marginal product of labor is equated to the *full* wage, which includes the profit share. Consequently *BA*, representing a larger wage "cost," is the relevant factor-cost line for the Illyrian allocation decision.

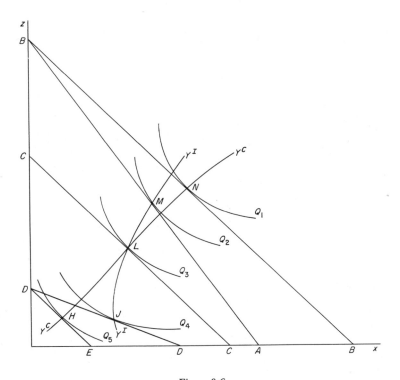

Figure 8.6

The Illyrian firm is in equilibrium then at point *M*, producing less output and using less labor than its capitalist counterpart.

Suppose now that market price falls to the zero-profits point. Capitalist output and factor mix contract along Y^C, say to point *L*.

Illyrian output and factor mix contract along Y^I, but also to point L, since the zero-profits full wage is equal to w. If price should fall further, so that both firms are incurring losses, the full wage will then be less than w. For example, under conditions which would lead the capitalist firm to produce at H, the Illyrian firm would produce at J. The Illyrian firm would produce more than the capitalist firm and would use more labor, so as to spread the losses around among as many of the worker-managers as possible.

The Y^I line, like Y^C, is positively sloped in the diagram, indicating that supply responds positively to an increase in price. It is perfectly possible for Y^I to have a negative slope under suitable cost and technological conditions, but it will still intersect Y^C at the zero-profits point.[19]

The slopes of the two supply curves can also be compared. When labor is the only input, the supply curves have opposite signs, but in the multiple-input case this need not be true. Both may have positive slopes. In Note 2 of the Appendix to this chapter it is shown that under assumptions sufficiently strong to ensure that the capitalist supply curve is positively sloped, the Illyrian supply curve will be either negatively sloped or steeper than its capitalist counterpart, for each level of output. One situation is shown in Figure 8.7, where the two supply curves intersect at the capitalist zero-profits point.

As a final aspect of the multiple-input case, we may consider a firm which is highly automated so that labor does not enter significantly into the short-run production function as a variable input. In this case, factor use and output are determined by the usual equilibrium conditions of capitalism. That is, with a fixed

[19] Figure 8.6 may also be used to contrast other comparative static changes. For example, an increase in w will increase the slope of BB without affecting that of BA. This will tend to move the capitalist equilibrium position at N closer to the Illyrian at M. An increase in R, on the other hand, will tend to make BA less steep without affecting the slope of BB. This will tend to move the Illyrian equilibrium position at M closer to the capitalist at N. When the equilibria coincide, in either case profits will be zero.

labor force, any addition to profits is also an addition to profits per worker. Such a firm would behave in exactly the same way as its capitalist counterpart, equating marginal cost to price and the marginal value products to the fixed input prices.

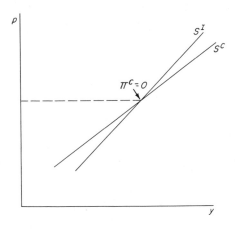

Figure 8.7

Market Imperfections: Monopoly

A comparison of output levels under competitive and monopolized market conditions in Illyria can be made using Figure 8.8. Labor again is the only variable input, and technology and demand conditions are assumed identical for the two situations. The output generated by employing b workers is the equilibrium output for each of the identical competitive firms. Is this output level optimal from the point of view of the monopolist? The cost function, K, will not change in the monopoly case. However, U, the average-revenue-per-worker schedule, will be different—reflecting the monopolist's ability to anticipate the price effects of altering his output rate. The effect of lowering price on intramarginal units is to make U steeper at the output rate determined by using b workers in each firm. Thus, to equate the slopes of K and U, the monopolist will move back toward a lower rate of output in each plant. This is true so long as the competitive equilibrium occurs at a point of decreasing average product and the demand curve is downward sloping.[20] A similar conclusion holds for the multiple input case. An Illyrian monopolist will tend to produce less than his competitive counterpart.

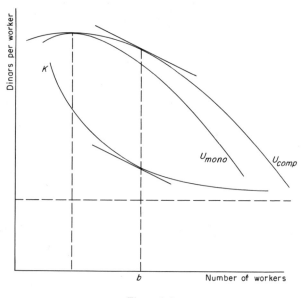

Figure 8.8

The Illyrian monopolist's behavior in response to changes in the capital charge, in fixed costs generally, or in price is similar in direction to that of Illyrian competition. If the demand curve is negatively sloped and not concave to the origin, a parallel rightward shift in demand will lead to a decrease in output if average product is declining. And for the same kind of demand

[20] It also assumes that the monopolistic firm faces no problems of obtaining a consensus among workers in different plants. This point is discussed in Chap. Ten.

and declining average product, an increase in the capital levy will lead to an increase in output.[21]

By an argument similar to those in the previous sections another comparative statement can be made:

Given the possibility of operating at a profit, the Illyrian monopolist will produce less and charge a higher price than his capitalist counterpart.[22]

---

[21] The assumptions are as above, except that p is now a variable. Assume

$$p = g(y, \alpha)$$

where $\partial p / \partial y < 0$ and α, a shift parameter, is defined so that $\partial p / \partial \alpha > 0$, and further that $\partial p / \partial y$ remains invariant under the shift. Solving for the first-order condition for a maximum:

$$y'(p + p'y) = (py - R)/x, \qquad \text{where } p' = \frac{\partial p}{\partial y}$$

This equilibrium condition may be differentiated with respect to R and α respectively, and solved:

$$\frac{\partial y}{\partial R} = - \frac{x}{2p'x + p''xy - x''(py - R)}$$

and

$$\frac{\partial y}{\partial \alpha} = - \frac{(\partial p / \partial \alpha)(x'y - x) - xy \dfrac{\partial^2 p}{\partial y \, \partial \alpha}}{2p'x + p''xy - x''(py - R)}$$

Knowledge of signs tells us that, as long as the demand curve is linear or convex to the origin, a change in R leads to a change in y in the same direction. With a similar demand curve, an upward shift in demand of the hypothesized kind will lead to a decrease in output if the firm is operating beyond the point of maximum average product, but an increase in output if average product is still increasing.

[22] Evsey Domar in a recent paper, "The Soviet collective farm as a producer cooperative," *American Economic Review*, Vol. 56, September, 1966, 734–57, has developed the comparative static analysis discussed in this appendix using a generalized production function. This gives a much more detailed picture of enterprise reactions under the assumed conditions, but does not change the general picture given by the results. Contrary to his assertion, no result of mine is reversed by his analysis, as the reader may see by comparing note 2 below (and especially equation 20) with his appendix note 3 (pp. 753–56) and especially paragraph (c) (i) (p. 755). For a discussion of his altered assumption about the supply of labor see Chap. Ten below.

APPENDIX TO CHAPTER EIGHT

(1) The Condition for Stability in a Single Competitive Illyrian Market Assuming One-Output–One-Variable-Input

From equations (2) and (3) in the text

(1)
$$S = \frac{py}{x} - w - \frac{\dot{R}}{x}$$

so that

(2)
$$\frac{dS}{dy} = \frac{p(x - yx') + Rx'}{x^2} = 0$$

where $x' \equiv dx/dy$. The equilibrium conditions

$$S' = px - pyx' + Rx' = 0$$

may be differentiated with respect to the parameter p:

$$\left. \frac{\partial S'}{\partial p} \right|_R = \left. \frac{dS'}{dy} \frac{\partial y}{\partial p} \right|_R + \left. \frac{\partial S'}{\partial p} \right|_{y, R} \equiv 0$$

$$= (-pyx'' + Rx'')(\partial y/\partial p) + (x - yx') \equiv 0$$

or the slope of the firm's supply function:

(3)
$$\frac{\partial y}{\partial p} = \frac{yx' - x}{x''(R - py)}$$

But $(R - py) = -pxy'$, since the equilibrium is preserved along the supply function. So for supply elasticity,

(4)
$$\eta_s \equiv \frac{p}{y} \frac{\partial y}{\partial p} = \frac{x'}{xx''}\left(\frac{x}{y} - x'\right) < 0$$

except over the relatively unimportant range in which average product is equal to or less than marginal product. Note that

$$x'' \equiv \frac{d^2x}{dy^2} = \frac{y''}{(-y')^3} > 0, \qquad \text{where } y'' \equiv \frac{d^2y}{dx^2}$$

We are assuming a price-adjusting market, in which the existence of excess supply or demand leads to price increases over time in the case of excess demand, and of decreases in the case of excess supply. Such a market will be stable when the supply curve is negatively sloped provided $\eta_D > \eta_s$. If we assume that production functions of all firms are identical, elasticity is invariant under the summation from firm to industry supply function. Thinking then in terms of industry demand and firm supply conditions, we have:

$$(5) \qquad \eta_D > \eta_s = \frac{x'}{xx''}\left(\frac{x}{y} - x'\right)$$

as a necessary and sufficient condition for stability.

(2) The Two-Variable-Input Case

$$(6) \qquad S = \frac{1}{x}[py - (wx + vz + R)]$$

and

$$(7) \qquad \begin{array}{c} y = f(x, z), \qquad y_x > 0, \qquad y_z > 0, \\ y_{xx} < 0, \qquad y_{zz} < 0, \qquad \text{and} \qquad y_{xx}y_{zz} - y_{xz}^2 > 0 \end{array}$$

Applying the first-order conditions for a maximum,

$$(8) \qquad \partial S/\partial x = (1/x^2)[p(xy_x - y) + vz + R] = 0$$

and

$$(9) \qquad \partial S/\partial z = (1/x)(py_z - v) = 0$$

or

$$(10) \qquad py_x = \frac{py - (vz + R)}{x}$$

and

$$(11) \qquad py_z = v$$

Further differentiation of (6) and (7) gives, at the equilibrium position at which (8) and (9) are satisfied,

(12) $$\partial^2 S/\partial x^2 = p y_{xx}/x < 0$$

(13) $$\partial^2 S/\partial z^2 = p y_{zz}/x < 0$$

(14) $$\partial^2 S/\partial x\, \partial z = p y_{xz}/x$$

and

(15) $$\frac{\partial^2 S}{\partial x^2}\frac{\partial^2 S}{\partial z^2} - \left(\frac{\partial^2 S}{\partial x\, \partial z}\right)^2 = \frac{p^2}{x^2}\left(y_{xx}y_{zz} - y_{xz}^2\right) > 0$$

Therefore equations (8) and (9) determine a maximum. Both the latter equations can be differentiated with respect to R and p and solved for:

(16) $$\frac{\partial x}{\partial R} = \frac{\begin{vmatrix} -1 & (p x y_{xz}) \\ 0 & (p y_{zz}) \end{vmatrix}}{p^2 x \begin{vmatrix} y_{xx} & y_{xz} \\ y_{xz} & y_{zz} \end{vmatrix}} > 0$$

(17) $$\frac{\partial z}{\partial R} = \frac{\begin{vmatrix} (p x y_{xx}) & -1 \\ (p y_{xz}) & 0 \end{vmatrix}}{p^2 x \begin{vmatrix} y_{xx} & y_{xz} \\ y_{xz} & y_{zz} \end{vmatrix}} \gtreqless 0$$

(18)
$$\frac{\partial x}{\partial p} = \frac{\begin{vmatrix} (y - x y_x) & (p x y_{xz}) \\ (-y_z) & (p y_{zz}) \end{vmatrix}}{p^2 x \begin{vmatrix} y_{xx} & y_{xz} \\ y_{xz} & y_{zz} \end{vmatrix}} \gtreqless 0$$

$$\frac{\partial z}{\partial p} = \frac{\begin{vmatrix} (p x y_{xx}) & (y - x y_x) \\ (p y_{xz}) & (-y_z) \end{vmatrix}}{p^2 x \begin{vmatrix} y_{xx} & y_{xz} \\ y_{xz} & y_{zz} \end{vmatrix}} \gtreqless 0$$

The slope of the supply function at the equilibrium point,

(19) $$\frac{\partial y}{\partial p} = y_x \frac{\partial x}{\partial p} + y_z \frac{\partial z}{\partial p}$$

so that

(20)

$$\frac{\partial y^I}{\partial p} = \frac{y_x(y_z y_{xz} - y_x y_{zz} + (y/x)y_{zz}) + y_z(-y_z y_{xx} + y_{xz} y_x - (y/x)y_{xz})}{p(y_{xx} y_{zz} - y_{xz}^2)}$$

A similar analysis for the capitalist firm gives the following expression for the slope of the supply curve:

(21)

$$\frac{\partial y^C}{\partial p} = \frac{y_x(y_z y_{xz} - y_x y_{zz}) + y_z(-y_z y_{xx} + y_{xz} y_x)}{p(y_{xx} y_{zz} - y_{xz}^2)}$$

The two expressions differ only in the addition of a final term within each set of parentheses in the numerator of (20). Note also that (21) is positively sloped for nonnegative values of y_{xz}. This difference

$$\frac{\dfrac{y_x y_{zz} y}{x} - \dfrac{y_z y_{xz} y}{x}}{p(y_{xx} y_{zz} - y_{xz}^2)}$$

is negative for nonnegative values of y_{xz}. Hence for any given value of y, equation (20) will be less than equation (21), which is to say the Illyrian supply curve will either be negatively sloped or will be steeper than its capitalist counterpart.

CHAPTER NINE

The
Illyrian Environment

The use of the special enterprise decision criterion, which is the basis of the model considered in the preceding chapter, has a number of implications for other aspects of economic behavior than product-market equilibria and stability. The labor market, investment, government stability policy, and oligopoly behavior are all affected to a greater or lesser degree. In this chapter some of these effects are discussed. For the most part the discussion is looser and more speculative than in Chapter Eight. The aim here is to suggest in general terms the environmental consequences of using workers' management rather than to present explicit propositions, which would tend to be rather sensitive to relatively minor changes in assumptions. In effect we are returning to the level of abstraction adopted in earlier chapters.

Decentralized Investment

In the short-run comparisons it was shown that a competitive Illyrian industry will yield the same equilibrium as the corresponding competitive capitalist industry, provided profits are zero in the latter. This suggests that Illyrian enterprise decision patterns may be capable of sustaining a long-run competitive equilibrium.

In turning to long-run adjustment let us first consider the optimal industry adjustment, which in capitalism is characterized by zero profits and occurs at the minimum point of the long-run average cost curve. This point is optimal in the sense that if all firms in the industry were using this scale of plant, the required output would be produced at the lowest possible cost, in terms of resources valued at equilibrium prices.

We may think of the choice involved in terms of Figure 8.6 in which units of labor and units of capital are plotted, together with isoquants and price lines for the two factors. Given the relative factor prices as depicted and given that the long-run equilibrium price in effect is expected to remain so, a capitalist entrepreneur must choose his scale of plant and the proper input mix. Suppose point *L* to be the correct point, then any other choice by the capitalist will result in losses to the firm in the long run.

Under our assumptions, the capitalist will be content with the optimal, factor mix, for example, *L*. Will the Illyrian entrepreneur? In part the answer has already been given in the last chapter. The present situation does not differ formally from that involving allocation of two variable factors in the short run. The only difference is that profits in the two systems are both zero. As was seen, under these circumstances the Illyrian firm chooses the same allocation as the capitalist. Both firms will operate at the minimum average cost point.

This point does not have the same comparative static properties in Illyria as it does in capitalism, however. The difference lies in the way the two firms respond to a change in price. Suppose after arriving at long-run equilibrium, product price suddenly rises in response to an increase in demand. The capitalist firm will respond by increasing its output along its marginal cost curve. The Illyrian firm will not expand its output along the same curve, however. Its response will be less "flexible" in the sense that it will either reduce output or will increase it by less than will the capitalist firm for a given price change.

In the case of a price reduction, the capitalist firm will cease operations, since there is no longer any position at which it can earn profits. (This is in the long run, of course; in the short run it need cover only variable cost.) The Illyrian firm, however, may not cease operations. Its action depends on the labor market. If workers are available who are willing to work for less than the contract wage (they might be hired at the contract wage but would receive less in their pay envelopes), the firm may well continue operations in both the long and the short run despite the accounting losses.

The latter result does not mean that the optimal outcome cannot be obtained in Illyria, however. If labor is rationally allocated, workers in fact will not be willing, nor will they be forced, to work at less than the contract wage. This is, in Illyria as in capitalism under our assumptions, precisely the wage which will clear the labor market when all firms are producing at the optimal point.[1]

We now consider the investment decision with respect to capital intensity. Assume for the moment that there is no plowing back of profits. Firms which invest always borrow to do so, and may borrow freely at the market rate of interest. We will also assume that the cost of obtaining a given piece of capital equipment is the same in Illyria and in capitalism. The choice then is whether or not to add the new unit of capital. Will capitalist and Illyrian firms react in the same way?

The answer may be given by reference to Figure 9.1. The axes depict net profits (in the Illyrian case profits per worker) this year (year 0) and next (year 1). At point P both firms choose to make no investment, and next year are in the same profit position as they were this year. The curves depict alternative intertemporal profit combinations open to the firm under

---

[1] The competitive optimum is often interpreted as being, not a zero-profits point, but a normal-profits point, i.e., a rate of return on capital at which capitalists are just willing to do their economic bit to sustain the equilibrium. On this interpretation the identity between Illyria and capitalism can be preserved, provided the state sets the capital charge just high enough to equal the sum of debt service cost plus normal return under capitalism.

various assumptions as to technology. The possibilities can be shown by comparing the curves pair by pair. The assumption of identical technologies facing each firm is maintained, but this time we are considering how the behavior of both firms is altered when the technology is changed in various ways.

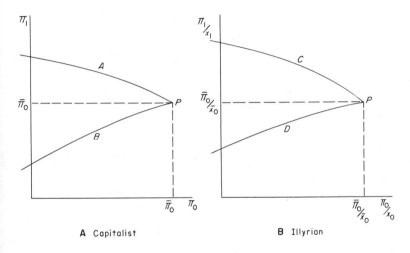

Figure 9.1

Assume first that curves A and C represent the feasible alternatives. The technology is such that by carrying out investment, both profits and profits per worker can be increased over present levels. Clearly both firms will wish to invest under such conditions. But if A and D depict the technology, then the Illyrian firm will not invest since, though profits increase, the investment is relatively labor intensive, increasing employment to the point at which profits per worker can only decline. With B and C describing the technology the situation is reversed. The capitalist firm will not invest because profits fall as a result, but in a very capital-intensive process, labor requirements may fall even more rapidly, thereby increasing profits per worker for the remaining workers. The Illyrian firm does invest in this case.

Our conclusion then is that the Illyrian firm will have a tendency to invest in more capital-intensive processes than its capitalist counterpart, even to the point of occasionally investing under conditions in which profits (but not profits per worker) are expected to fall as a result. This tendency is irrational, in the social sense that its results in a classical competitive environment do not lead to pareto optimality as does the corresponding activity by the capitalist firm. The general tendency might be justified along lines of the existence of external diseconomies which lead individuals to undervalue labor in their planning under capitalism. Such a position does not seem justifiable, however. Decentralized investment decisions by existing firms will not lead to the optimal combination of resources.[2]

The peculiar separation of ownership and use of capital in Illyria necessarily provides some distinctive aspects to the production and exchange of capital goods. The second-hand market for capital equipment is a case in point. The state must require the user to pay the interest charge on all capital presently under the given firm's control; but it would be unwise to prevent the firm from selling any equipment it could no longer use. The state must continue the interest charge with the purchaser because otherwise no one would use new equipment, but would immediately sell it and buy other equipment to avoid the charge. This means that the prospective purchaser must deduct the interest charge from the stream of services the equipment is expected to render as a part of the calculation of the present value of the equipment to him. The seller, on the other hand, will deduct the same amount from the services expected to be rendered by the equipment in calculating its present value to himself. The deduction on both sides leaves the relative net prices offered and asked unchanged in Illyria and capitalism. It is as if all equipment in capitalism were purchased with funds

---

[2] There will be differences in the results in the two situations because of other differences in the capital market—especially if Illyrian firms are forbidden to make debt issues. Also we are ignoring the effects of these differences on speculators.

obtained by bond issues secured by the equipment purchased, and sale of the good always involved transfer of the debt to the purchaser. Though the calculations would be different, the allocative results need not be different in the two systems.[3]

A problem still remains, however, and that is whether the state must place any limits on the sale of capital. The danger could arise from a situation like the following. Suppose that during a boom period, with full employment of labor and capital, the workers in a firm decide to sell large portions of their capital equipment. Under such conditions they could command a good price, and the gain from such action could be distributed as a wage supplement. Workers need not fear for the future of the firm, because it would be easy to resign and take a job at another firm. It might even pay some of them to sell the equipment to another firm and then go to work for the purchasing firm, since they would have concentrated the capital gain from the economic situation into a few hands. Such activity might be economically disruptive, but "rational" from the point of view of the worker-managers, who are not affected much by reductions in the net worth of their own firm so long as alternative employment is available.

Should this occur frequently, some form of control would be essential. Probably the simplest requirement would be that firms could use gains from the sale of capital only for the purchase of new capital or the maintenance of old.[4] Such a requirement would add little to governmental administrative cost, since such sales would already have to be reported in order to levy the capital charge properly. The allocative consequences probably would not be serious.

[3] Provided the effects on risk patterns in the two economies are ignored, which is admittedly a large proviso.

[4] In Yugoslavia there has been a rule stating that proceeds from the sale of capital equipment cannot be counted as income by the firm. The incentive to sell is elimination of the depreciation and capital charges tied to the article. The rule suggested in the text keeps the seller interested in the sales price and, in a growing economy, need not have much effect on efficient allocation.

The handling of depreciation also is complicated by the pattern of ownership. The state as owner has an interest in the maintenance of existing equipment. It cannot trust the workers' self-interest to maintain a given capital stock at initial value because the workers can move to other firms. In addition, there would be a tendency to depreciate capital in the accounting sense as swiftly as possible in order to reduce the size of the capital charge.

Under such circumstances, the state must require maintenance of capital, which implies setting the initial valuation of capital as well as the depreciation rates. In addition, it must require minimum allocations to a depreciation fund, to prevent the state's capital stock from being transferred to the workers in the form of wages as it is used up. This is one area in which the state cannot decentralize because of the nature of the institutions in Illyria.[5]

By maintaining a certain excess labor supply, the state could reduce most of these tendencies on the part of worker-managers, but at the possible cost of inefficient layoff policies. That is, in a labor surplus situation the workers' councils may be reluctant to lay off their colleagues, which of course violates our behavioral assumption of Chapter Eight.

If investment by firms themselves is likely to be in socially undesirable directions, reasonable success in decentralized investment may still be obtained if most investment turns out to be made by new investors. We have seen that they will invest in a way that is consistent with equilibrium, provided the economy is near long-run equilibrium, though if they expect to earn profits, their technology too will tend to involve relatively less labor use than their capitalist counterparts.

Decentralized investment is thus seen to be potentially a

---

[5] This does not mean that the state must decide how depreciation funds are to be used in detail. Probably no more than the requirement that they be used for maintenance, repair, and replacement somewhere in the economy would be sufficient. But the actions of firms would have to be checked to ensure compliance.

weak link in Illyria. Because of its ownership of the means of production, the state is obliged to engage in some regulation of capital markets, in particular in treating sales of produced capital and depreciation control. In addition, such decentralized decision making as would be carried on under these conditions is likely to be overly capital-using, thus foregoing opportunities for increasing the social product which would exist under other institutional arrangements. A successful and reasonably rational investment program requires either modification of the institutions of decentralized decision making, or direct decision making by the state—on a more substantial scale than would be required by considerations of efficiency under competitive capitalism.[6] However, whether these misallocations would be substantial remains an open question.

Entry and Exit of Firms

Where will the promoters be found to enter a profitable industry under Illyrian conditions? There are several possibilities. We have already seen that existing firms will have an incentive to expand operations under certain circumstances, though not always in the same direction as would be indicated under capitalist conditions.

Would individuals ever be in a position to act as promoters? The constraining factor for individual promotion is the prohibition of individual equity holdings. The promoter could not expect to be given any substantial reward out of profits, because of the combination of profit sharing and nationalization which are fundamental features of the system. Workers' management also means that the promoter must lose control of the firm as soon as operations are begun. Only if a group of promoters were large enough or persuasive enough to dominate the workers could their authority be maintained. The result would certainly

---

[6] Considerations of uncertainty and the determinants of profit expectations which are vital to the investment decision are ignored in the above discussion.

not be workers' management and so would violate Illyrian principles. These facts would seem to eliminate this classical form of entrepreneurship, except for the smallest undertakings where private property rights might be allowed.

There is another side to this coin, however. The state needs savings, and also would like to find some method of making decentralized investment decisions for some fraction of capital formation, if only to save information processing at the center. Furthermore, there seems to be nothing in Illyrian principles as so far described which would prevent private and enterprise debt, as opposed to equity issues. Is there a difference in principle between putting money in an interest-bearing bank account and buying bonds? Probably not, so long as there is effective control of the bond issues. The problem is whether exploitation is involved in paying interest; but a negative attitude on this point is derived from traditional socialist ideology and especially Marxism, not from any principles of industrial democracy. If interest is paid by banks, why not on private and enterprise bond issues?

One could envision private promoters playing an important role in Illyrian investment decisions, provided debt issues bearing a risk premium were permitted. The promoter would search out an opportunity, would sell his idea to the state, and in return would be permitted to buy some share in the initial capitalization. An interest rate on such bonds could be set by the state, say at twice the rate on savings accounts, to provide for incentives and also to permit the indigent promoter to borrow funds for this purpose. The promoter's risk would be that the enterprise would be unable to pay interest on this debt. Limits to size of issue might easily be set, and resort to further issues by firms during the course of normal operations forbidden. A consequence would be lower returns to the workers in the firm, and to the government's tax receipts from the firm. The gain would be in the strengthening of decentralized search incentives, and especially in the use of knowledge of particular industries which is bound to be possessed by many officials, technicians, and even workers in the industry.

Having gone this far, why not go a step farther and permit profit sharing by promoters? This would associate the promoter more directly with the risks of innovation, and need not entail giving him a voice in management. Again there appears to be no ideological bar from the point of view of industrial democracy, and there seems to be some prospect of more effective use of the knowledge already built into the economy.[7]

A further step, which would permit the promoter to participate in the management of the new firm, *would* overstep the bounds of Illyrian principles, however desirable it might seem. If the promoter has special knowledge he might be hired by the firm, thereby automatically granting him a share in the profits. If his skill is organizational rather than technical the problem is quite different. To become manager he would have to convince the workers that he was the logical man for a managerial post. He could not, however, simply be appointed manager by virtue of his status as promoter. Illyria might miss the opportunity to take advantage of externalities of commitment.

One would expect that despite the two primary ways in which decentralized investment may occur—expansion of existing firms with the approval of the existing labor force of the firm, and private promotion of new firms (government units could do this too)—centralized investment by the state might still be a most important investment process. Since decisions in this area would be rather similar to those in more centralized economies we will not discuss them here.

The effect of the state's entry into an industry is worth a comment or two. We have seen that for given factor-supply prices a firm sets a rate of output which tends to vary little with changes in product demand. Consequently, in the market for

---

[7] The advantage is similar to that of coinsurance in situations where risk-shifting affects incentives. See for example Kenneth Arrow, "Uncertainty and the Economics of Medical Care," *American Economic Review*, 53 (Dec., 1963), 941–73.

a homogeneous product the new firm will immediately move to this output rate, with the effect of shifting down the demand curves facing other firms in the industry. That is, the effect of entry is, roughly, to increase industry output by the "own" rate of the new firm without affecting very much the output of other firms in the industry.[8] Market price declines accordingly, and wages per worker in the old firms decline, very roughly, in proportion.

The state thus has a powerful weapon in its hands to counteract the effects of monopoly or in general of undesirably high wages in an industry. As such a tool it is discriminatory because of variable gestation periods from industry to industry. But because of its strong and unequivocal effects, the threat of entry could be a powerful weapon indeed.

When will a firm leave an industry? Circumstances are somewhat different in Illyria both because of state ownership of the plant and because there is no simple dividing line between profits and losses. One might say that a firm is operating at a loss if it is unable to pay the contract wage, but what meaning does this have? Certainly not that in the long run it will not continue to operate under these financial conditions, which is the significance the dividing line has under capitalism.[9] As yet we have provided no rule for fixing the contract wage, and have seen that changing it has no effect on Illyrian behavior or even on the income of the workers (unless there is a tax tied specifically to profits or wages under this definition).

There is one method of exit which is unique to Illyria. Suppose there is full employment, with workers in nearly all industries earning at least the contract wage. Then a firm whose market position does not permit payment of the contract wage will be unable to attract workers, assuming of course that

---

[8] Of course the Illyrian form requires that the new state-sponsored firm adopt its own system of worker management as soon as it begins operation. The new industry equilibrium would be at lower price and higher output.

[9] The distinction is not so much in the degree of flexibility in the two situations, but with the market on which the relevant decisions are made. It is the labor market that is relevant for the Illyrian enterprise's to-be-or-not-to-be decision.

workers do have information about the full wage being earned in various firms. If some excess demand for workers should develop, workers in the marginal firm will shift to more profitable firms and, like the old soldier, the marginal firm will gradually fade away until, for lack of workers, it is forced to close.[10] Such a firm has no way of avoiding exit. The full wage is determined by market conditions so that the marginal firm cannot offer higher wages to the workers who are leaving (unless of course the firm is subsidized). Indeed as workers leave, and the firm's output deviates still more from the optimal rate, the full wages of the remaining workers will fall still further with respect to rates in other firms. While this is going on, a peculiar effect is felt within the industry. As the marginal firm's output falls, so does total supply. This tends to force up product price. The higher product price may help the marginal firm vis-à-vis producers in other industries, but not in its own industry, where the higher price is received by all firms. However, to the extent that supply curves are negatively sloped, these firms will begin laying off workers and this will reduce the number of opportunities available to workers in the marginal firm who are thinking of quitting. As we have seen, this latter effect, if it exists at all, would probably be very weak.

To put it another way, the bankruptcy signal comes in a unique way under Illyrian conditions. Instead of the owners of the firm finding their profits turned to losses, the workers in the firm find their effective wages declining until opportunities look better elsewhere. Depending on the formal level of the contract wage and the state of the labor market, this may occur even though the firm is nominally operating at a profit. The effect may be felt over a period of time as workers leave individually and in small groups, and replacements become steadily harder (though perhaps never impossible) to find.[11]

---

[10] This can happen even if there is no net excess demand, but one firm is earning higher profits per worker than another.

[11] A firm might retain workers by shifting profits investment to additional wages. However, this merely postpones the problem, since too little investment means higher cost in the long run.

Another and more conventional form of bankruptcy would occur if the firm were unable to meet its fixed obligations to the state or to private debt holders. Up to now we have been assuming that the workers would bear the full brunt of any fall in net revenue. However, it seems unlikely that a socialist state would stand idly by while workers in an industry were reduced to starvation in order to meet these fixed obligations, a situation which could very well happen if there were an excess labor supply in the market. One likely response would be for the state to fix some minimum wage rate, and provide loans or even grants to firms which were unable to pay wages at this level. Then exit would come when the state decided it was no longer willing to subsidize a firm in this way. An effective bankruptcy procedure would permit the exit decision to be made after a survey of the assets and prospects of firms in more than temporary difficulties. Some exit procedure is essential, both to correct errors made by planners and private investors, and as a means of adjusting the production sector to the changing relative scarcities that are a concomitant of economic growth. Something like this approach has been adopted in Yugoslavia.

Oligopoly

Price and output decision making under capitalist oligopoly conditions is not well understood, so it would be pointless to attempt a detailed analysis for the Illyrian case. However, a few differences in tendencies emerge from what has already been said. These will be listed briefly here.

(1) The incentive to collude in order to increase profits per worker exists in Illyria, and in general is satisfied by higher prices and lower output than under competition.

(2) Monopoly is less satisfactory under Illyrian conditions because the equilibrium price is higher than under capitalist monopoly.

(3) Individual firms in an oligopolistic market have an incentive to prevent reduction in their market share similar to that under capitalism. However, the incentive to increase one's market share

will frequently be weaker than under capitalism because of the more limited range of circumstances under which profits per worker increase significantly with output.

(4) In response to technological or other environmental change (such as a rightward shift in the demand curve) the Illyrian firm does not have the capitalist incentive to increase the *industry's* output, under a wide range of circumstances. However, an exception to this could occur in the case of technical change which leads to a more capital-intensive plant. In this case the investment incentive may be stronger in Illyria, and this may more than compensate the output-restrictive behavior reflected by the competitive supply function.

(5) Since profits are shared among the workers in an enterprise, the effects of concentration on income distribution are likely to be quite different in Illyria than under capitalism. High profit rates contribute much less to increasing the skewness of the distribution in the former case.

These comments suggest that, whatever the truth of assertions that capitalist oligopoly tends to be progressive, the Illyrian oligopoly will be somewhat less so except with respect to income distribution. However, the variety of possible oligopoly situations is so great that this conclusion must remain somewhat dubious.

The Labor Market

Labor policy is the key problem in all socialist writing. Reformist thinking has tended to focus its criticism on the results of using market mechanism in allocating and remunerating the nation's labor force. This central interest has often been expressed within a labor theory of value, so that the relative desirability of any two goods is measured by the amount of labor "embodied" in them. The inability of such a theory to explain adequately the formation of market prices is well known and widely accepted, even among Marxists. But whatever theory he uses, the socialist will be particularly interested in the way any given institutional pattern influences the allocation of labor.

There have already been some signs of peculiar operation in the Illyrian labor market. The "old soldier" bankruptcy process of the last section is a case in point. The problem is that there is no simple way in which a firm can offer higher wages in order to retain workers. Every firm is subject in its wage policy to a basic constraint imposed by the wage and profit allocation rules. The only way a firm can bid workers away from other firms is by operating successfully, by earning profits high enough that the full wage is higher than elsewhere. And if the new workers are essential to successful operation, the firm can offer them only prospects, not a firm commitment to higher wages.

There is some flexibility of course. If the firm itself can set wage differentials, this would probably be done by fixing the contract wage to each class of workers and making profits shares proportional to contract wages earned in the relevant period. Then a key engineer could be offered a higher contract wage by the low-profit firm. The wage however would have to be high enough to compensate for the relatively low profit rate of the firm, unless the engineer had high expectations that the firm's profits would rise in the future. If the workers themselves, or an elected committee of workers, formulated such offers, they would take into account the cost to themselves. For a single engineer of special competence, this cost might be insignificant. But for a wage category covering a number of positions in the firm, things would be quite different.

To the extent that firms are inflexible in their wage offers, changes in labor market conditions may not generate effective signals for adjustment by the participants. This problem appears to be most serious when there is unemployment. If after firms have completed their adjustment to market conditions, there is excess supply of labor, a lowering of contract wage rates will have no effect on the market. All that will happen is that already employed workers will receive a larger share of their unchanged full wage in the form of profit shares. There is no material incentive for firms to hire the unemployed workers, and no way in which the unemployed in any numbers can make themselves more attractive to the firms as prospective workers.

As will be discussed below, the usual macroeconomic instruments can be an effective means of increasing output and employment. In addition, investment policy may be oriented toward full employment effectively, since as a consequence of supply inelasticity, each new firm has a virtually fixed "own" rate of output which is relatively independent of product price.[12] In Illyria the market mechanism cannot be relied upon to create full employment; the state must assume responsibility here, even under conditions of flexible prices and favorable real balance effects.

The state can in principle find an overall full employment policy, as will be indicated below. (See the section on Macroeconomics.) However, this does not ensure full employment for each wage category. Existing industrial societies, including the Soviet Union though possibly excepting Communist China, use some sort of quasi-market mechanism to adjust relative wage rates. Though there are many frictions in these markets, there are strong tendencies, on both supply and demand sides of the market, to adjust as usual to changing relative scarcities. In Illyria however, this kind of adjustment can be blocked if full reliance is placed on the setting of wage differentials within the firm. It will often not be true that upgrading a wage category to get more productive workers will pay off in terms of the full wages of the present work force. If this is a serious problem a different sort of labor market organization may become necessary.

A promising possibility is that the state fix the contract wages for the various types of labor in accordance with the market socialist price rule. Organizationally this would not be quite so simple as is claimed by market socialists, but it would seem that

---

[12] This exaggerates the rigidity, especially for firms in which labor is a relatively unimportant variable input. However, it serves to concentrate attention on a problem that will recur frequently.

the problem could be handled adequately in the following manner. Through a system of labor exchanges, the wage board would keep tabs on the state of supply and demand for labor of various skill types. A job classification table would assign each available position and each available worker to a wage class. Within each wage class, workers and positions would be assigned to groups for which similar qualifications were required. Firms would be free to hire workers at the contract wage specified by the wage board for the appropriate job group. The wage board itself would be instructed to raise the wages of a group to the next higher classification when excess demand developed, and to lower wages to the next lower classification when there was excess supply.[13] Given a successful aggregate full employment policy by the state, the wage board would thus provide some market incentives to adjust to changing market conditions. Wage differentials would provide information to workers and students as to the nature of job alternatives. The same would apply to firms, who would now be adjusting to parametric or given wage rates. If in addition, firms were required to allocate profit shares in proportion to earned contract wages, the problem of setting differential wages would in principle be completely removed from the decision-making competence of the firm itself.

Unfortunately this would not be the end of the problem. One important difficulty would occur in countries facing a long-run excess supply of unskilled labor. This would be the case in most developing countries, but is not necessarily peculiar to early stages of development, as witness the United States during recent years. The rule applied strictly could easily take the contract wage to zero, and almost certainly would reduce it below subsistence standards. Presumably a socialist state would not submit to anything like this state of affairs, and would be

---

[13] Equity would surely require that wage changes apply to already employed workers. Efficiency considerations would point in the same direction unless discrimination were perfect.

forced to set some minimum wage for all workers. Since unemployment compensation would also be a matter of essential social policy, the minimum wage would presumably be set at a level sufficient to motivate the unemployed to accept offers of work.

A second difficulty has to do with the identification of excess supply and demand. Labor varies not only in skill but in location, and its mobility may be weak in the short run. Excess supply itself may discourage entry quite apart from wage differentials. As a consequence, the timing of wage changes is difficult to specify and should vary from one trade to another. Equally swift reaction to changes in the markets for physicians and for lathe operators would have quite different consequences. An element of judgment on the part of the wage board would be hard to avoid, and this in turn would lay the board open to political pressures.

Then too who would make the classification of positions? The participants have a strong and often mutually incompatible interest in the outcome, and outsiders are ignorant. How important relatively are the intensity of work, the extent and nature of the training prerequisite, the pleasantness of surroundings? An effective system would probably require some measure of control over job shifts within firms, to prevent unwarranted upgrading.

On the other hand, it should be remembered that establishing wage differentials takes a good deal of effort in all industrial societies. Negotiation on this issue is one of the more important aspects of union-management relations in the United States, while in the Soviet Union job classification for norm-setting purposes also involves a major effort.

It has already been noted that this approach would eliminate an important source of intrafirm conflict. If the firm can control neither the method of profit sharing nor the contract wage, each worker in the firm finds that the only way his regular full wage will increase is with an increase in profits per worker. He would be indifferent to changes in the relative numbers of workers of different skill types, except insofar as they affected his own full wage; and all workers would gain or lose together as a result of any given change. If intrafirm conflict were to become a really serious flaw in the operation of Illyrian firms, this kind of bureaucratic wage-differential determination might be the preferred alternative.[14]

The labor market problems would be minimized if there were full employment, or perhaps better, slightly overfull employment. Then workers would have ready-to-hand alternatives both to low profits and to "unfair" contract wage changes by the firm. And worker groups contemplating discriminatory wage setting would be given pause by the knowledge that loss of those workers to other firms might be the result, which would surely mean lower full wages for those remaining.

Unions

Concentration of economic power through collusive association can also occur on the labor market, and may in fact originate on either side of the market.

Firms, controlled by already employed workers, might attempt to hire additional workers along a curve marginal to the supply curve, taking account of the rents to be gained or lost; or workers, forming unions, might attempt to bargain for more from prospective worker-employers. The reverse of course

---

[14] Another solution to labor market adjustment which is consistent with Illyrian forms of organization was proposed some seventy-five years ago by an Austrian economist, Theodor Hertzka, in his utopian novel, *Freeland* (Chicago: Appleton, 1891 [first published in Vienna, 1889]). His idea was to require firms to accept for employment all workers who offered themselves. Workers would presumably seek out the firms whose profits per worker were highest, thus serving as a general equalizing force against interfirm wage differentials. The great advantage of this rule is that at a single stroke it eliminates all unemployment. Hertzka was an egalitarian and felt that most workers in any given firm should get the same wages, exceptions being made only for exceptionally productive workers or scarce skills, where a bonus would prevent them from being lured away. For such a system to work, there would not only have to be effective social sanctions against loafing but also a technology in which labor was highly substitutable in the short run.

might occur too: if employed workers controlled the unions they would be in a position to attempt to negotiate new employment at lower wages; or if the unemployed workers controlled the unions they might be able to force higher wages for new employees, or, more likely, higher employment than the already employed would desire.

Bargaining of this kind would very likely have a harmful effect on allocative efficiency. On the other hand, the fact that similar things happen under capitalism should be sufficient warning against the assumption that such a system could not work at all. The question is, could behavior of this kind be avoided or mitigated?

If we follow our previous assumption that the state fixes differential wages, the answer is yes. Under such circumstances, there would be nothing to bargain about except levels of employment. Provided the wage scales were enforced, and also that the unemployed did not control the unions,[15] hiring could be carried out on the basis of maximum profits per worker without intervention by the unions.

Indeed, unions would seem to have lost most of their *raison-d'être* under Illyrian conditions. With wages fixed in absolute level by conditions on the product market, and with differential wages set by the state, the unions' primary function would have been eliminated. And with the workers' council in control of work rules and safety conditions, union defense of worker rights within the factory would become redundant. Probably some informational activities might persist, but these too would be eliminated if industrial associations were formed. By making workers into managers, the strictly labor aspects of union activities become anachronistic.

The situation would be quite different if differential wages were set freely by workers. Unions would probably be organized

---

[15] A reasonable assumption, if we presume that a socialist state would take effective measures to prevent large scale unemployment. See Chap. Eight for a discussion of employment policy.

along craft rather than industrial lines. Strikes over differential wage rates could become a commonplace, and the usual problems with jurisdictional disputes would arise. Unions could then become a strongly divisive force among workers. It seems that if unions became powerful, they would either have to be subject to stringent controls or one of the more centralized wage-setting schemes discussed earlier would have to be adopted. However, with workers' councils already in the field and serving as a potentially effective substitute, difficulties with unions might well never arise.

Macroeconomics

An efficient Illyrian government will have to undertake an extensive program of investment, picking up inadequacies of the market, externalities, which are more extensive than in the competitive capitalist case. Not only will the traditional investment and public consumption activities associated with interdependence have to be provided by government or under government control, but corrections to the nonoptimal investment incentives of market participants will also have to be made. In addition, as was seen in the last section, the government will assume responsibility for keeping employment at an appropriate level.

One or two special aspects of the Illyrian government's control problem will be discussed in this section, using a simple aggregative model of a closed economy. This model will show for a simple case the direction of effect and power of two major instruments of macroeconomic policy. Since the results are counterintuitive for Illyria, and rather different from standard models as well, a "control" model will be presented first. It will show that for an aggregative model similar to the Illyrian one, except for one assumption about aggregate supply, the results are conventional. Thus the peculiar features of the Illyrian results do stem from the "Illyrian" assumption and not from other aspects of the model.

The tenor of the control model may be suggested by calling it, somewhat facetiously, Swedish. Its Swedish features are the assumption that there is a national wage bargain struck for each planning period, and that the determination of the investment ratio is removed from direct market influence. We assume competitive capitalist markets, so that the demand for labor is determined by

$$(1) \qquad\qquad w = p^0 y'^0$$

where w is the money wage rate, p^0 is the equilibrium price of the national product, and y'^0 is the equilibrium value of marginal physical product. The national wage policy serves to set the money wage rate:

$$(2) \qquad\qquad w = \bar{w}$$

It is assumed that labor supply is sufficient at the going wage, so that the equilibrium will lie on the demand curve for labor. There is no money illusion but there may be excess supply of labor in equilibrium. National product, y, is determined by a single-input production function:

$$(3) \qquad\qquad y = y(x)$$

where

$$y' > 0, \qquad y'' < 0$$

and where x is employment, and y' and y'', the first and second derivatives of the production function, are functions of x. Finally we have an equilibrium condition for the money market,

$$(4) \qquad\qquad Mk = p^0 y^0$$

where k, the reciprocal of the income velocity, is assumed fixed by existing institutional arrangements, and M, the supply of money in money terms, is an instrument of state policy.[16]

By substituting the fixed value of the money wage rate into equation (1) there remains a system of three equations in the

[16] The superscript zeros, indicating equilibrium values, will be dropped in what follows, except where there is a possibility of ambiguity.

three unknowns, p, y, and x and the two parameters M and w. Assuming the government can control these parameters, we may consider the effect of changing them on equilibrium values of the variables.

First, it is easy to see that all three variables must move in the same direction as M. For example, equation (4) says that the product py must increase when M increases. Equation (3) says that y and x must vary in the same direction. And equation (1) says that equilibrium price and marginal product vary in opposite directions which, from the shape of the production function, means that x and p must vary together. Hence from equation (4) the three variables move in the same direction with changes in M.

Second, when the parameter w varies, it remains true that y and x move in the same direction, but from equation (4) y and p must move in opposite directions. From equation (1) it is seen that p must not decrease when w increases. For then y' would have to increase, implying a decrease in y which is excluded by the money market condition. Therefore an increase in the money wage rate tends *ceteris paribus* to increase prices and reduce output.

This is one of that variety of macroeconomic models in which rigidity of money wages makes monetary policy directly effective in influencing levels of output and employment. This in turn suggests that the economy is operating within striking distance of full employment. There are two features of it which seem a little unusual. Both are the result of an attempt at maximum simplification. On the one hand, there is no explicit treatment of investment, while on the other, there appears to be no distinction between monetary and fiscal policy. The first is justified by our assumption that, in effect, the state controls all investment through nationalization of the saving process. Since the aim of the model is to show the effect of government policies on the market economy, the process of determination of investment composition—being a decision internal to the government

—should not play an endogenous role in the model. The share of the product going to nonconsumption is determined, however, when the government fixes values for the two parameters under its control. The distinction between monetary and fiscal policy, though vital to the Keynesian debate, is not important in contrasting Illyrian and "Swedish" macroeconomics, and so its consequences have been consolidated into a single monetary-fiscal parameter, M.[17]

We may turn now to comparisons with the Illyrian macro-model. The difference between the assumptions of the two models comes wholly in the labor market, as a result of the production-equilibrium condition. The amount of labor hired and its full wage, including profits bonus, must in Illyria be consistent with the equilibrium condition for the single-argument production function:

$$(5) \qquad\qquad py'x = py - R$$

The return to a single-input production function is justified here, as in the control model, because the planning period is too short for the stock of capital to vary, and production too inflexible in the short run for substitutions among inputs to affect significantly aggregative outcomes. Again, the supply of labor is assumed at least equal to equilibrium demand.

Equations (2) through (4) remain as in the previous model. However, we may as well omit equation (2) since, for reasons given in previous sections, the contract wage has no effect on outcomes, provided information is available to the public on profits achieved by individual firms. The instruments available for state manipulation of the economy are the supply of money, M, and the capital charge, R. Note that, as in the control model, the interest rate (which influences R) plays no direct role either in determining money market equilibria or in fixing the demand for investment. As before, the demand for investment operates

---

[17] Since the effects of a change in k are the same as M in both models, it has been ignored.

in the background, fixing the state's policy toward its instruments. R is a fixed charge per time period on the production sector which is an instrument of state policy; that is—directly at least—it is independent of both output rates and profit levels, and so is a parameter of the model.[18]

[18] The formal comparative statics for the Illyrian case follow. Differentiating (4), (5), and (3) totally with respect to M in the order specified we have

$$
\begin{bmatrix}
p & 0 & y \\
p & (-py' - pxy') & (y - y'x) \\
1 & -y' & 0
\end{bmatrix}
\begin{bmatrix}
\dfrac{\partial y}{\partial M} \\[2mm]
\dfrac{\partial x}{\partial M} \\[2mm]
\dfrac{\partial p}{\partial M}
\end{bmatrix}
\equiv
\begin{bmatrix}
k \\
0 \\
0
\end{bmatrix}
$$

The determinant of the 3×3 coefficient matrix,

$$D = py'(y - y'x) + pyxy''$$

is indeterminate in sign with the given information. Let us assume for the moment that the marginal product is declining slowly so that y'' is close to zero. Then D is positive and, solving (2), we have

$$\frac{\partial y}{\partial M} = \frac{ky'(y - y'x)}{D} > 0$$

$$\frac{\partial x}{\partial M} = \frac{k(y - y'x)}{D} > 0$$

$$\frac{\partial p}{\partial M} = \frac{kpxy''}{D} < 0$$

Output moves in the same direction as the supply of money, but p decreases when M increases.

Following the same procedure to evaluate variations in R, and remembering that D is the same for this problem, we have

$$\frac{\partial y}{\partial R} = \frac{-y'y}{D} < 0$$

$$\frac{\partial x}{\partial R} = \frac{-y}{D} < 0$$

$$\frac{\partial p}{\partial R} = \frac{py'}{D} > 0$$

That is, an increase in the capital charge tends to reduce output and increase the price level.

The effects of changes in R and M can be seen by concentrating attention on (1) and (5):

(1) $$Mk = py$$

(5) $$R/p = y - y'x$$

and noting that

$$\frac{d(y - y'x)}{dx} = -y''x$$

which is positive. Assume that the economy is far enough from full employment that marginal product is declining very slowly, so that y'' is close to zero. Then $(y - y'x)$ will increase much less rapidly than y, though it moves in the same direction.

If R increases, p and y must move in opposite directions from (1); similarly, from (5) p and $(y - y'x)$ move in opposite directions. But since R has increased, an increase in y which compensates the decrease in p in (1) will not induce a sufficient change in $(y - y'x)$ in (5) to more than compensate the decrease in p. Therefore the reverse must happen, so our conclusion is that a change in R leads to a change in p in the same direction, and of y in the opposite direction. The macroeconomic impact of R in Illyria is the same as that of $\bar{w}$ in the Swedish case.

If M increases, it follows from (5) that p and $(y - y'x)$ (and hence y) must again move in opposite directions. But y must change relatively more than p if (5) is to remain in balance. Hence a change in M leads to a change in equilibrium y in the same direction, and a change in p in the opposite direction. Naturally, in both models the production function assures that equilibrium employment always moves in the same direction as output.

The output decrease in response to an increase in R appears to conflict with the results obtained in the previous chapter where, for competitive firm and industry, output tended to move in the same direction as the capital charge. There is no conflict, however; the environment has changed from the micro to the macro level. As a result, price has become a variable, and it is this interaction between the price and output variables at the macroeconomic level which leads to the reversal in response. Because of the slowly declining marginal product, the price level must bear the major burden of adjustment to the changing capital charge. The same sort of thing is happening when M changes. Thus the anomalous microeconomic behavior with respect to output response is converted to anomalous price response at the macroeconomic level. This can be brought out more strikingly by comparing the two models. Note first that for the same values of M and k, and identical production functions, it is possible to choose $\bar{w}$ for the control model and R for the Illyrian model in such a way that both economies produce the same output. If they are set so that

$$\frac{w}{p^S} = \frac{p^I y^I - R}{p^I x} \qquad \text{(all equilibrium values)}$$

then equilibrium marginal products and prices in the two economies will be the same. Consider now an increase in M. The multiplier will be larger for Illyria than for the control model. As a consequence of the decline in price in Illyria, a given change in M will induce a more than proportionate change in y [see equation (1)]. In the control model, price and output move in the same direction. Hence a change in M induces a less than proportionate change in output. So M is a more powerful instrument under Illyrian than under "Swedish" conditions.

Another striking feature of the Illyrian case can be seen by watching the behavior of the two models as full employment is approached. This can be signaled in the model structure by assuming an increasingly rapid decline in marginal product (increasing absolute value of y'') which reflects the developing supply bottlenecks. In the control model, an increase in M is now increasingly reflected in changes in the price level rather than in output, since the latter are increasingly hard to come by.[19] But in Illyria a more substantial change occurs. When marginal product declines rapidly enough the effects of parameter changes are reversed! Further increases in M now begin to induce reductions in output, and increases in R to induce increases in output. No such shift in sign occurs in the control model.[20]

In a "Swedish" environment the money wage rate, even though formally an instrument under state control, probably cannot be manipulated independently of M. At least a simultaneous variation of both w and M in opposite directions, aimed at mitigating the price effects of a given output policy, would be resisted, in one case (money wage decrease with increase in M) by labor and in the other by management. This problem, however, cannot be derived from the model, and at present we are not concerned with the impact of power or influence on outcomes. At any rate, formally R and w are nearly equivalent in their impact on outcomes. The signs of their effects are the same, and their magnitudes appear to be rather similar. We might also note that the magnitude of the output effect of changing R appears to be even greater than that of changing M, in the Illyrian case. Comparing the numerators of the employment multipliers, we see that $k(y - y'x)$ is larger in absolute value

---

[19] The comparative static results for the control model, derived in the same way as in footnote 18 above are:

$$\frac{\partial p^0}{\partial M} = \frac{kpy''}{pyy'' - p(y')^2} > 0 \qquad \frac{\partial p^0}{\partial R} = \frac{-py'}{pyy'' - p(y')^2} > 0$$

$$\frac{\partial y^0}{\partial M} = \frac{-k(y')^2}{pyy'' - p(y')^2} > 0 \qquad \frac{\partial y^0}{\partial R} = \frac{yy'}{pyy'' - p(y')^2} < 0$$

$$\frac{\partial x^0}{\partial M} = \frac{-ky'}{pyy'' - p(y')^2} > 0 \qquad \frac{\partial x^0}{\partial R} = \frac{y}{pyy'' - p(y')^2} < 0$$

[20] In the Illyrian model the denominators of the comparative static solutions are sensitive to the magnitude as well as the sign of y''. In the control model only the sign, not the magnitude, of y'' affects the qualitative results.

than y, for k less than 1. However, the price effect of changing R will also be greater, as can be seen from equation (5).[21]

Our Illyrian macroeconomics have been developed in terms of specific and highly aggregative models which tend to emphasize supply-side determination of equilibrium. The results might be quite different if different models were chosen; all that can really be said in defense is that the basic structure of the model, aside from the production sector, yields roughly the expected Keynesian results for the control model. It should also be noted that the model is too aggregative to show how an Illyrian policy maker might use macroeconomic instruments to influence the real investment ratio. In both the above models, $y'x$ gives the equilibrium level of private consumption, so that $y - y'x$ shows the part of total product assigned to public consumption and investment. These magnitudes are determined uniquely by the level of output, so that no sectoral reallocation is possible once the level of output has been chosen.

The Government's Instruments

As a socialist economy, Illyria has a well-defined set of economic objectives which are determined by the political process. The state will naturally assume the responsibility for achieving these. This in turn requires that the aims be made specific enough to be converted into concrete guides to action. In brief, a plan is required.

Problems of finding an optimal development plan will not be discussed. For Illyria the problems are not strikingly different from those faced by development planners everywhere. However,

---

[21] Note that the widespread existence of constant returns to scale in the short run would not affect the appropriate qualitative conclusions derived above. The Illyrian competitive firm will not operate in the area of constant returns, but will move out to the point at which productivity begins to fall. And that is the point at which the present analysis begins. Note also that constant returns do not have any effect on the supply rigidity either. The tendency for Illyrian firms to have an "own" rate of output which is relatively inflexible in the face of changes in market conditions is quite general.

Illyrians do have one important advantage in comparison with soviet planners: the market yields a set of relative valuations of goods which can be a very useful guide to the selection of the best among alternative plans. The problem that requires some further discussion at the moment is how, given a good plan, the Illyrian authorities can go about converting it into action over the short run.

The plan itself will presumably contain a desired level of national product, and will specify the share going to consumption. For marketed consumer goods there is little reason to go into further detail, since the decentralized Illyrian market environment will itself determine relative prices and outputs. Public goods and most investment fall into a different category, however. Here the state must make detailed plans as to what projects are to be carried out in the given time period. For example, for an investment project under the centralized program, the state must see that the proper technology is chosen and then obtain the resources, many of which come from the market economy, with which to execute the project. A similar problem of production and distribution arises in the case of collective consumption.

Obviously the state will have dealings on a large scale with the market sector of the economy. This raises the question of finance, as well as that of maintaining some resonable degree of stability in the market sector while carrying out its own programs. The problem is similar in kind though larger in scale than that under capitalism. To what extent will Illyrian financial institutions differ from capitalist ones?

It seems clear that nationalized banks will play an important role in Illyria. They are needed to make both short-term and investment loans to firms, and presumably consumer loans as well. They may also serve as holders of both demand and savings deposits of enterprises and households. The portfolios of banks would contain a variety of debt instruments comparable to those of a capitalist bank. A scarcity charge would also have to be placed on loaned funds, for direct rationing would seem inconsistent with the market decentralization. The government might even sell bonds to the banks, or borrow in some other form. The major portfolio difference would be the absence of equity issues.

As for other financial institutions, there seems to be no reason why insurance companies could not exist, organized on worker-management principles and operating to provide insurance against actuarialized risk at a profit. The question as to how their assets would be distributed is a little less clear than in the case of banks. If debt can be bought and sold, insurance companies are not at a great disadvantage because of the absence of equity issues. If not, their only alternative is interest-bearing deposits at the banks.

The nationalization of land would preclude the development of real estate companies. However, effective use of the market mechanism would require that some provision for transfer of land among users be made. In this area substantial government regulation is unavoidable, but reasonably successful allocation would be difficult if the prospect for windfall gains were completely excluded. At any rate, speculation in land would certainly be excluded by preventing those who are not prospective users from acquiring property rights.

What sort of impact on the market sector will the government be able to have in this environment? Assuming that the banks are operated "in the public interest" rather than under worker management, the question again is one of the nature and effectiveness of the indirect instruments under state control. One typical problem faced by the instrument wielders would be inflation control. The investment budget requires a shift of resources from consumption to investment without raising the price level significantly. As we have seen, the basic Keynesian instruments of monetary and fiscal policy are at hand, and it appears from the earlier analysis that they are quite sensitive in their impact on the level of output, and can be used to vary output without seriously disturbing the overall price level.

In terms of the model in the previous section, it is possible to maintain a neutral money policy by operating simultaneously with the two instruments M and R. From equations (4) and (5)

$$p = \frac{R}{y - y'x} = \frac{Mk}{y}$$

in which equilibrium values of price, output, and marginal product appear. By decreasing M and R proportionately, the above equations show that no effect on output results; instead p decreases in the same proportion. Appropriate variations in R and M may be used then to obtain some combination of output and price effects.

The effect of shifting resources out of consumption is a question that the previous model cannot be used to answer, however. As compared with the capitalist situation there are two difficulties: the peculiar supply response of individual industries, and the fact that there is no separation between profit takers and labor. Policies designed to move an industry along its supply curve will be of little or even of negative effect, and policies designed to stimulate investment via profits inflation will also have the opposite effect from that desired.

For the purpose of influencing the behavior of individual firms and industries, the state has three primary indirect instruments: money supply, excise taxes (positive and negative), and interest rates. If the state and some decision units from the market sector are competing for the output of, say, the construction industry, the state can get what it wants by outbidding its competitors. Buyers of nonlabor services react as do private decision units on this score; so a higher price, even if it reduces gross output of the industry, can have the effect of eliminating a sufficient portion of the competing buyers. The extra profits that the industry would then earn can be siphoned off by raising discriminatorily the interest charge on capital or even on short-term loans. Another possible defense against windfall profits—which inflate consumer demand and eventually destroy the

state's competitive advantage in bidding—would be an enterprise income tax, which of course need not be discriminatory to
be effective.

Much of this difficulty could be avoided if the enterprises
used windfall gains to carry out investment projects approved in
the plan. As we have seen, this may often occur but such action
cannot be relied on, especially since the worker-managers have
an alternative use of these funds as wage bonuses. The state also
cannot be sure that the workers will choose the right projects,
from the point of view of the plan, and the state is presumably
reluctant to extend direct controls to the decentralized investment process. Therefore, some unintended investment will
probably occur, which is, from the point of view of the state's
investment objectives, similar in its effects to an equivalent
increase in consumer demand. Unplanned investment projects
compete for the resources needed for planned investments.

A successful policy of redistributing resources into planned
investments then requires a reduction in both wage and average
profit levels per worker. It does not appear that the broad macro-
instruments of money supply (nondiscriminatory), interest rates,
and debt manipulation will be very successful in making such
shifts. Even the enterprise income tax (i.e., a tax on value added,
on profits plus wages) does not appear to be an exception. As the
supply relation suggests, its primary impact would probably be
on prices rather than output.

Instead the state is compelled to resort to discriminatory use
of instruments to achieve real redistribution. Excise taxes, high
capital charges, and heavier income tax rates, possibly combined
with credit rationing, would be needed to restrict output in
consumer goods industries, while their opposites were applied to
industries producing investment goods.

The above is based on the assumption that the investment
ratio implicit in existing technology and institutions is not that
arrived at in the plan. One might hope that once a proper
structure of capital had been achieved, such indirect manipula-

tions would become less needed, and macropolicy would be used primarily to counteract exogenous shifts—for example in world market conditions—and as an instrument of relatively nondiscriminatory anti-inflation policy. Except under such circumstances there would not seem to be available any relatively neutral instruments for resource redistribution.

Finally, there is likely to be a temptation for the government to resort to price control. The short-run inelasticity of supply and the possible conservatism of oligopolies point in this direction. The temptation would be especially strong when the government was competing for scarce resources for the completion of its own projects under oligopoly conditions. The threat of entry, that is, the threat that the government would see that a new factory was built in the industry if prices were not kept in line, is another possible response which falls short of formal price control, and which could often be effective. Another situation in which price control would be tempting is in the case of sharp divergences in interenterprise pay scales for the same kind of work. When such a situation becomes generally known it could induce "political" strikes, that is, strikes aimed at changing government policy. Subsidies to the low-wage factories and price control for the high-wage factories are possible though not particularly desirable responses.

CHAPTER TEN

Illyrian Stability

Some attention has already been given to the question of Illyria's institutional stability. For example, the possibility of trade unions playing a role in wage decisions and organizational response to imperfect market conditions were discussed in the last chapter. This discussion continues in the present chapter, beginning with the impact of internal decision making within the firm, and ending with a brief discussion of the prospects for some alternative institutional adjustments.

Inside the Firm

So far little consideration has been given to the way in which the firm's decision making is to be organized. It has simply been assumed that there is some decision-making process which would always produce decisions in the worker's interests. If there were genuine consensus among all the firm's workers there would be no problem: a delegate with some technical competence would be named and he, representing the "general will" of the workers, would make reliable decisions. However, we have seen that there are some areas of conflict, and we may suspect that workers will not always be effective managers, both because of lack of initiative and because, as a council, they would not know how to control themselves as a work force. What are the prospects for effective decision making within the firm?

Before looking at some organizational alternatives, it will be useful to run through the kinds of decisions to be made by the firm and the extent to which there is harmony or conflict of interests among the workers. This should make a bit clearer just what the firm's social-decisions process will have to do.

First, consider a firm with a bare minimum of decisions to make. If the state fixes both the contract wage of all workers and makes profit sharing proportional to earned contract wages, there will be no conflict among a firm's workers over either wage differentials or the appropriate levels of employment of the various skill types. This will be true regardless of the technology of the firm—whether it is single or multiproduct, whether several plants produce in accord with mutually independent production functions, or whether there are joint products. The reason is that *each* worker's individual interest is to see that for each skill type, workers should be employed just to the point at which their individual contribution provides an addition to overall profits per worker. Output and relative employment levels are the things to be decided by the firm, and the workers will have no difficulty in agreeing on the decisions if they can agree on the facts.[1]

An exception to the above might occur when layoffs are contemplated. The workers who felt threatened by the impending layoff would no longer have an incentive to maximize profits per worker. But even here, a full employment policy successfully followed by the state should eliminate any such considerations. This is because the threatened worker would have to balance the presumably moderate costs of being laid off against, not the wage he had been receiving, but the lower full wage accruing to workers in a firm which is operating inefficiently. In most cases the number of threatened workers would be a small fraction of total employment, so that, even though the threatened workers

---

[1] We are assuming a reasonable degree of cultural homogeneity and a predominance of worldly attitudes among the workers.

opposed their own layoff, efficiency would still be in the interest of a potentially dominant group.

For a competitive firm, price policy would be determined by the market, and hours of work would be fixed by the state on our minimum decision-making assumption. There would still remain two important types of decisions: the question of the share of profits to go to investment rather than wage bonus, and the conditions of work. Conflicts on the first decision would hinge partly around the time horizons of workers, which might vary with skill levels and seniority, partly around the differing degrees of social consciousness of the workers and their personal commitments to the given firm and town. The question of working conditions would be a matter of the work-leisure choice, which would include variations in optimal labor intensity among workers. This latter is a potentially divisive issue, in that any individual worker's interest lies to some extent in the most comfortable conditions for himself but the most productive conditions for others.

It is conceivable that all these questions might be resolved at periodic mass meetings of the work force. Such a decision process would be very unwieldy if the number of men was large, and would make quite inefficient use of the knowledge available to the firm. It seems more likely that a manager would be elected by the workers to perform the coordination tasks and prepare reports for mass consideration. Of course the manager might be a committee rather than a single person. And in the larger firms a legislature might be interposed between the masses and the executive, to provide still further concentration of collecting and processing of knowledge. In what follows we will consider some of the problems which might arise, while moving at times away from the minimal-decision assumption.

The Manager

There are two primary questions relating to management of the Illyrian firms: will the manager do as he is told, and will he be obeyed?

Taking the first question first, we may say that there is no problem so long as workers and managers get the same reward. A competent manager will be acting in his own as well as the workers' self-interest with every "rational" decision he makes, and there is no reason to suppose that difficulties would arise. But in a modern factory no such situation exists. There is not only a wide variety of skills, receiving pay at rates which may give the highest paid worker three or more times the wage rate obtained by the unskilled, but there is also the dichotomy between blue and white collar. The office and technical staff are often paid on a different basis, perform a rather different kind of work, in particular a kind that brings them into close contact with the managerial staff, and tend to differ from production workers in many social characteristics. In such an environment it is by no means clear that the manager will respond willingly to the instructions of the workers' council (legislature).

The possibilities are legion. Perhaps most serious is that of an informal alliance between manager and staff against the work force in the shop. It is a reasonable prospect because of the likelihood of similar backgrounds and propinquity on the job. It is dangerous because it could provide this group with a virtual monopoly of knowledge on technical and financial matters, or at least a monopoly of interpreting skills. Under such circumstances the wage and perquisite structure might come to reflect the power of a group rather than its productivity. Featherbedding and discriminatory hiring and firing would also become possible. In such a case the main advantages which worker control would seem to offer could hardly be realized.

Of course the market sets some limits to a firm's ability to engage in this sort of discrimination. But there is reason to believe that these limits are rather wide. In the short run the response of the labor market, especially to localized excess supply, is often sluggish. This provides the supply-side opportunity. On the demand side the existence of elements of imperfect competition provides some financial slack which may be allocated to favored groups without reducing the full wage to other workers below the rate at which they will seek other employment. In a developing economy the unskilled peasant boy is perhaps the ideal candidate for this kind of victimization. For the more developed economy perhaps the older semi-skilled worker qualifies best.

One possible instrument for controlling this situation was suggested previously: state fixing of the contract wage. This made no difference in the homogeneous labor models developed in Chapter Eight, but introduction of skill differentials would mean that relative shares in profits would be fixed *de facto* by the state instead of within the plant. The problem is that this throws a large burden on the state, which would now be engaged in direct control of a large number of prices. Much of the advantage of decentralization would be lost. In addition, control over many aspects of the labor exchange could not be brought under central control except at tremendous administrative cost. However, the perquisites and fringe benefits associated with employment would inevitably remain, to a considerable extent, under control of the firm.

Probably this problem can be prevented from becoming serious only if the workers can be given the power to control effectively the manager's decisions, and if continuous thought is given to preserving as wide a range of common interests among the parties as possible. The first of these implies control of the manager's appointment, and probably at least veto power in hiring and firing of all staff. If anyone else holds the responsibility for appointing and dismissing the manager, the latter's ties to the firm will be weakened and his own interests and those of the workers will tend to diverge.

The problem of expanding the harmony of interests of participants is very complex. Basically it is a matter of avoiding as far as possible situations in which decisions must be made which involve one man's gain and another man's loss (both being employees of the firm; a loss to outsiders is of course quite another matter). These situations cannot be wholly avoided; for

example up- or downgrading of jobs in response to changing
technology or organizational improvements is inevitable and
often divisive. In such cases the workers' council can serve as a
body sanctioning the manager's decision by approval, but the
basic problem cannot be avoided. Still more sensitive would be
changes within the salaried staff. So long as a white collar
coalition is a threat, such issues would almost inevitably generate
conflict.

More positively, the manager's incentives must be similar in
kind to those of workers if he is to be motivated toward mutually
beneficial decisions. As a sharer in the profits the manager would
have this motivation, provided significant variations in profits are
a possibility and are involved in his usual decisions. However, no
system can wholly remove sources of conflict between leader and
led. Looked at generally it would seem that many sources of
conflict between management under state-run or capitalist
industry would be mitigated by placing the manager under a
system of worker control, simply because of the increased harmony of interests. It is very frequently the manager's allegiance
to others—stockholders or the state—which generates conflicts
with workers.[2]

The answer to our second question—will the manager be
obeyed?—is more difficult. There is a circularity in the line of
authority in the Illyrian firm, with the manager controlling the
workers, and the workers in turn—either directly or through the
workers' council—controlling the manager. How could any discipline be maintained under such conditions?

Most of the writers on the subject in the past have answered
simply, "It can't." As Peter Wiles put it, in an article addressed to
Poles who had just introduced workers' councils in their industrial plants, there is a certain "tension" that must be maintained
between worker and manager if the former is to do his job

---

[2] Plus the workers' ignorance of the effects of alternative decisions. An effective
body of representatives of the workers could be in a position to collect such information.

properly.[3] The arguments are similar to those against democrat-ization of military hierarchies: one-man decision making, it is claimed, is the only efficient way to make this particular set of decisions. Of course political democracy consists precisely in the control of the controllers by the controlled. The degree of indi-rectness in the process would perhaps not be less in the large firm than in local government in a democracy. As for the smaller groups, consensus leadership, in which the leader controls his peers without the support of strong, formalized sanctions, is hardly a rare phenomenon. The assertion that such a form of social organization is, in general, infeasible can hardly be sus-tained.

More serious is the objection that, though by no means infeasible, such a system of control would be inefficient. The argument is that under such leadership, discipline would be lax. In modern factory production, attention to detail and fairly intense concentration on the job are essential. Under lax discipline the quality as well as the quantity of work would be low in compari-son with other forms of organization.

There is no ready answer to such an argument. One aspect of the problem concerns the harmony-of-interests thesis. An order given by a manager to a worker to stop malingering is plainly dis-harmonious in its consequences. Obedience is desired by the manager, but hardly by the worker. In particular, even his material interests are not necessarily in harmony with obedience. The increase in his profit share resulting from an increase in his own productivity will, *ceteris paribus*, be insignificant in all firms of any size. And if labor possesses disutility, increasing his own output involves a cost to him. By the criterion of economic rationality, the worker is justified in continuing to gold-brick.

However, this is not an apt description of the situation, since it ignores the social environment within which the order is given. Or at least it deals only with one side of this environment.

[3] Peter Wiles, "O samorzadzie robotniczym inaczej," *Diskusja o polskim modelu gospodarczym* (Warsaw: Książke i Wiedza, 1957), pp. 182–91.

Actually, the manager too would benefit insignificantly, in terms of his own income, from an increase in the productivity of a single worker. However, the response of the worker would be of considerable importance to him in terms of whether he is able to sustain his authority in the shop. The worker's response, if not affected significantly by considerations of personal gain, would be influenced by the reactions of his fellow workers. If they approved flaunting the manager's authority he would be tempted to try it. If they disapproved, such tendencies might be inhibited.

This brings the problem down to a question of the attitudes of the workers as a group. And at this point we must leave it. One can say that without the boss-worker tension there will be mass indifference to achieving competitive quality standards among workers and managers alike. One can say that the general introduction of worker control would provide for a spontaneous interest in effectiveness of plant operation, for only under this system would the worker have a genuine day-to-day stake in successful management. One might point to the previous remarks about general harmony of interests. Nothing, however, can be proved.

One final point may be in order. A rational economic system must equate not only marginal rates of substitution among the usual goods and services purchased by an individual, but also marginal rates of substitution between these goods and leisure. Leisure itself is a complex good depending in part on the number of hours of nonwork, the kinds of nonwork available, and their cost, but also on the intensity of work. In no existing industrial system is there much opportunity to carry out adjustments of work intensity by means of markets. The system of worker control provides a partial mechanism if workers are given some control over the conditions of work. Perhaps arguments that worker control cannot work are translatable into marginal language as saying very nearly the opposite: namely, that such a system would provide greater rationality in adjusting the work-leisure desires of individuals. That is to say, in factory labor the dissatisfaction generated by deviations from the individual optimal intensities of labor under existing conditions is greater than the deviations generated by a tendency of workers to reduce that intensity when they are their own managers. If indeed productivity is lower, it is a sign of closer concordance with the conditions for pareto optimality.

The Workers' Council

The question of the ability of the workers to get compliance from the manager was discussed above. A similar problem arises with regard to the ability of the workers to give any effective orders at all: we refer to the possible analog of the managerial revolution. Is it possible for the elected manager to control the workers as he often does the capitalist board of directors?

The answer is that the situation is sufficiently different to make such a result dubious. The capitalist problem arises because of the rationality of wide dispersion of ownership among equity holders under modern capitalism. Under such conditions, even large stockholders in a firm are often not in a position to give enough time to the firm's affairs to exercise effective control. The manager takes over essentially by default, so long as he is reasonably successful in providing dividends and "growth."

Such a dispersion of interests would of course not occur among a firm's workers. They are being influenced daily by managerial decisions. They can hardly avoid taking an interest in these decisions. At least this is true for some types of decisions, particularly those relating to work rules and wages.

The danger that the workers might not try to exercise effective control over managerial decisions is perhaps most acute with regard to financial matters. There is the problem of knowledge, and the fact that such matters are not a part of the daily business of the vast majority of the workers in a firm. There might be a strong tendency to leave these questions entirely in the manager's hands, especially if, as in the capitalist case, he seems to be generating reasonably satisfactory results.

This suggests that harmony of interests can be not only a support but also a threat to the system of control, for it may lead to apathy on the part of the controllers. The consequence, managerial control, might still look more like the strict Illyrian situation than modern capitalism, but it would not be workers' control.

The ability of the typical manager appointed by a group of workers may also be questioned. The workers' interest is similar to that of a board of directors, in that both want a man capable of realizing profits on their firm's operation; but the workers' council in addition wants him to have certain attributes essential to his peculiar position in the Illyrian firm. There is the danger that the workers will elect a man who is popular more often than one who is competent.

This is another aspect of the argument that democracy is inefficient. To meet this problem, some controls over decision making by the workers could perhaps be instituted—without being administratively costly or destroying any fundamental aspect of worker control. Minimum technical requirements of training and/or experience might be required as a condition for the franchise, thus providing a floor of skills to all participants in the managerial system. Essentially this problem is one of knowledge, and probably is most acute in large firms which use a complex technology. It is certainly conceivable that electoral choice by workers is inefficient under such circumstances. Appointment by a group outside the firm would render the relations between workers and director a bit ambiguous, however. In large factories, some sort of representative body would presumably have to substitute for the labor force in practical decision making.

There remains the question of the effectiveness of the workers as a decision-making body. Will the majority decisions of such a body tend to deviate from the decisions which are optimal with respect to the material interests of the factory labor force? Ignoring for the moment such questions as whether a consistent standard of evaluation *can* be developed where the actors have varying tastes, we can say that conformity of their decisions to some such optimum depends (1) on their getting adequate knowledge on which to base their decision, and (2) on their acting in the interests of the workers as a whole rather than serving their own individual or group interests.

The question of knowledge besets any organization of any size. The only peculiar feature of the Illyrian case is that workers probably are less well educated and less experienced in many aspects of economic decision making than would be their opposite numbers, the capitalist board of directors or the relevant officials of a Soviet ministry. Unless they could obtain and trust in the cooperation of some of the technical staff, their decisions might go awry from lack of proper information. Experience would help, and so would preparation during the course of formal education. But plainly such a system of control would be of questionable efficiency in situations where the workers are poorly educated or where there is both a large number of unskilled workers and a complex technology. Diseconomies of organization would be rather large under such circumstances. The system of worker control would be at its best where complex factory production is not a new phenomenon.

The problem of cliques has already been mentioned. In the case of the workers' council, a certain minimum circulation of the elite can be ensured by setting limits to reelection to office. This of course will be at some cost in terms of efficiency of decision making, since even in a well-developed factory system the number of workers capable of handling decision-making problems would in all likelihood be rather small.

Whether workers would actually be represented by their elected delegates in larger plants is a large question which cannot be adequately dealt with here. Circulation of membership among a reasonably large fraction of the workers, as is practiced in Yugoslavia, is perhaps a useful device for enhancing "representativeness," provided the competence and influence of the council is not seriously threatened by such action.

One key to providing representativeness lies in the election system. We will mention here only the question of whether issues or personalities should or would dominate the elections. Keeping issues to the fore would probably require a two-party system, and this might not be attainable under factory conditions, except perhaps in the largest factories. Nor would it seem to be an efficient procedure, as it would tend to solidify groups and to magnify the conflict among interest groups, thus reducing the scope of harmonious decision making within the firm. In many ways the question as to whether issues should be to the fore in elections is simply the question of effectiveness of control by the controllers.

Institutional Stability

In this section the stability of Illyria with respect to four alternatives is considered: (1) the adoption of alternative hiring and firing practices by enterprise workers; (2) the substitution of managerial authority for worker authority in enterprise decision making; (3) the use of regional governments as investment promoters; and (4) the return to a hierarchic form of short-run economic control.

Three alternative employment situations may be briefly considered.[4] In the first, membership in the enterprise is fixed in the short run and so is the amount of labor supplied by each member. Such a firm will behave as a profit maximizer in order to maximize the incomes of the membership, subject to the constraint on labor consumed. The comparative statics will be that of a profit maximizing firm too—except that if labor is at all important as a technically variable input, responses will tend to be quite output-inelastic.

A second situation is one in which the membership is fixed but the members may vary their supply of labor to the firm. Suppose

---

[4] These situations are analyzed in detail in Evsey Domar, "The Soviet collective farm as a producer cooperative," *op. cit.*, though their relevance is assessed for the context of soviet-type collective farms rather than Illyria.

that all workers in the firm have the same marginal valuation of an hour less work, and that in the initial equilibrium this valuation is just equal to the full wage. The state now increases the capital charge, so that if hours of work offered per worker did not change the enterprise would hire additional workers. But the new full wage per worker will be lower than the old so that each member will wish to offer less labor to the firm. The latter effect counters the former and if strong enough could change the direction of enterprise adjustment.

In the third situation discrimination in hiring is permitted. As a consequence, full-fledged members will be willing to hire additional workers more readily than before, since, given that the firm is profitable, an additional worker adds less to cost than he did before. In fact an additional worker now has the same status as a material input in relative valuations, so that further enterprise adjustment is in accord with profit maximizing rules.

In each of the above examples enterprise adjustment violates the Illyrian rules. Changes in the direction of comparative static adjustment are especially disturbing, because they mean that the instruments in the hands of the state have become uncertain in their impact. They suggest that Illyria may be both economically and institutionally unstable.

In assessing their importance, the main point is that there are two respects in which Illyrian organization is attractive. The first is that a pareto optimal equilibrium can be sustained by Illyrian organization, given appropriate and apparently not overwhelmingly difficult action by the state with respect to macroeconomic policy. The second is that the organization provides a strong measure of industrial democracy. A leadership committed to these goals will thus have an incentive to protect enterprises from forces which are inconsistent with the achievement of the goals.

What instruments are available to it for this purpose? It may regulate working hours, if necessary by restricting overtime work as well as by fixing the standard work day or work week. It may forbid simultaneous membership in more than one enterprise. It may adopt a full employment policy, so as to reduce the unattractiveness of layoffs as a policy for a worker-managed enterprise. It may require that all workers be treated symmetrically with respect to wage bonuses. It may require periodic reports on policies and performance of enterprises. And so forth. There seems to be no dearth of instruments, each of whose effect should be to reduce the impact of these tendencies on enterprise decisions. Given the desire to implement Illyrian policy, these problems do not seem to pose a serious threat to organizational stability.[5]

A more serious threat to Illyrian stability would seem to be the possibility of returning to profit maximization by enhancing the authority of the manager. It has already been suggested that this would probably not occur as the result of a spontaneous process of power accretion within a large number of firms. More likely it would come from a shift to this position as the result of deliberate state policy. Should the peculiarities of the Illyrian adjustments tend to generate unacceptable outcomes, this response would be a likely choice by the state, since it does not require drastic alteration of the economic system and preserves the advantages of the market and of choice-decentralization. Even profit sharing could be preserved, provided the manager were given primary responsibility for the employment decision.[6] A profit-sharing manager would act more or less as a profit maximizer. However, his interests would no longer coincide with those of the rest of the members of the enterprise on as wide a range of

[5] Leaving aside the question of possible externalities, most of these regulations restrict the freedom of action of the worker-managers, and so may inhibit the achievement of pareto optimality. However most of them may be unnecessary. A reluctance to hire and fire may be overcome by convincing workers that the state will manipulate its own instruments effectively, so as to insure that the market signals do measure social costs and benefits with reasonable accuracy. Opportunities for alternative productive uses of time by members of a profitable enterprise are likely to be limited, so that this, the second of the above situations, need not be particularly important. Regulation of discriminatory practices may well be necessary, though it is not clear from the present vantage point just how detailed such regulations would have to be.

[6] Even this much might not be withdrawn from the area of worker competence. The rule might be that the manager decides on the number of people to be hired and fired while the workers decide on the names.

decisions, so that conflict within the firm might occur on a larger scale. This, plus the loss of an important element of industrial democracy, would be the opportunity cost of obtaining a more conventional economic response mechanism.

Another area in which the state might wish to counteract Illyrian outcomes is that of decentralized investment. Following the ideology of the commune, local governments might be given the status of investment promoters, perhaps with the incentive that the local tax base varied directly with the level of productive activity in the commune. An appropriately designed tax could lead communes toward investment in profitable projects out of their own funds or by borrowing. This kind of regionalism is much more attractive than that described in Chapter Seven because of the existence of the market which provides both alternative sources of information flows with respect to project alternatives, and the incentives provided by competition. Two main dangers to this approach would seem to be (1) the possibility of creating local monopolies, and (2) the concentration of future development in the already developed communes, whose current tax base would support a larger scale of investment activity. This kind of investment organization could be introduced as a supplementary process without affecting short-run Illyrian adjustment processes. Given that it was not accompanied by authority-centralization of communes with respect to enterprises, this policy does not seem to be institutionally destabilizing.

Like the classical soviet system, Illyria appears to be relatively stable with respect to pressures toward greater choice-centralization. The natural response to failures of the Illyrian markets is much more likely to be price control than output control, for reasons already outlined. And when output controls might be contemplated, they are likely to be *ad hoc* responses to particular problems; for example, exchange rationing to limit imported inputs of specified kinds. This sort of control is more likely to be task-oriented than based on branch hierarchies, so that the appropriate interest groups that push the organizational form toward something like the soviet organization are not so likely to develop in a piecemeal way. Also there is the limit to the extent to which such controls can be added in bits without seriously disrupting market adjustments. There is likely to be a large jump between the piecemeal-controlled Illyrian economy and a fully hierarchic decision process for producer goods, which is best expressed by the need for a supply plan in the latter case. And until the latter is created, the primary vested interest favoring such an organization does not exist, while organizations who oppose it are in the field and presumably have even acquired some measure of authority-decentralization. That is, in the Illyrian case choice-decentralization tends to create a certain amount of authority-decentralization of enterprises, so that it tends to become harder to reverse the process the longer the Illyrian organization is used.

CHAPTER ELEVEN

Conclusion

This book has consisted primarily of a comparison of some properties of various socialist economies. It has described these economies at a level as abstract as that of the socialist controversy, except that organization is specified in somewhat greater detail, and only the organization of production has been treated.

Attention has been concentrated on three main types of socialist economy, though variants of each type have been considered. The specification of two of these was suggested very roughly by the Soviet and Yugoslav cases. The third, a sort of party-run economy, was suggested by tendencies which exist in the Soviet and East European socialist states but which appear to be especially strong in China. Deviations of the models from reality are substantial, and are particularly large and speculative in the "party" case. In each instance some idealization was attempted, in the sense that certain possibly corrigible elements of the systems' malfunctioning were ignored. This was done partly to concentrate attention on what were felt to be the most important aspects of each system, and also to eliminate certain factors that are not essential parts of the organizational form itself, such as some applications of Marxian teaching to socialist economic policy.

This chapter presents a condensed overview of the conclusions. Each of the three basic forms is described briefly, and then some conclusions about them and comparisons between them are offered. The reader is reminded that in Chapter One such terms as "externalities," "centralization," and "organizational stability" are given specialized meanings.

Before describing the three basic forms, a word about the socialist controversy is in order. This discussion was deficient in terms of its own formulation of the problem in two main respects. The first is the incompleteness of the description of the price system's operation under socialist conditions, particularly the absence of a demonstration that price adjustment in disequilibrium converges to an optimal equilibrium. The second is the absence of any serious attempt to describe a socialist economy's incentive system and its implications for economic outcomes. In recent years both of these defects have been partially remedied, the former by mathematical economists and the latter by students of existing socialist economies.

The three organizations are:

(1) Classical soviet organization. This is relatively secularized as a society, with personal ambitions and material incentives dominating economic choice below the top leadership. Its hierarchic organization consists of the leadership which supplies the general criterion by which broadly described alternatives are evaluated; the planners, who test feasibility of alternatives, elaborate details of the criterion, make and adjust plans of varying time spans, and control the operation of ministries; the ministries, who aggregate and disaggregate plan data, arrange details of exchanges of goods and services, and control the operation of enterprises; and enterprises, which are the primary units of production and distribution.

(2) The command society. An ideal type which has as its most important intermediate activity the production of compliant zealots, that is, of administrators with a deep commitment to the aims of the regime and who are trained intensively to be not only technically competent but also obedient. The hierarchy of this organization has a structure which is similar to that of the classical soviet case.

(3) Illyria. A secularized, materialistically motivated economy. It is a special form of market socialism in which factories are managed by the workers. The leadership and planners plan and control the general lines of economic activity using primarily indirect instruments, except for some portion of capital formation where direct control is exercised.

Among the main conclusions and comparisons in the preceding chapters are the following:

(1) As compared to markets, hierarchies change the conditions under which economic decisions are made dramatically. In hierarchies arbitrage is very sharply restricted, incentive manipulation is centrally organized, and incentives may be very different from that of the profit maximizing businessman of traditional market theory.

(2) Different kinds of hierarchies may be used for economic decisions. The command society represents an extreme case of authority-centralization. It is also more choice-centralized than the classical soviet system with respect to output decisions.

(3) The most striking feature of the classical soviet organization is the very high uncertainty level at almost all points in the system. It is probable that at each level in which important decisions are made, there is less relevant information available to soviet officials than to the appropriate members of either of the other two basic forms. A consequence of this high uncertainty level is that fine adjustments in the economy are quite difficult to make. Paradoxically, there is also a tendency over the short run for the economic organization to become more complex rather than less, in response to the limited control capability. This generalized uncertainty is perhaps the principal externality of the soviet economic system.

(4) Though there are normative, optimizing elements in the soviet plan-making system, the high uncertainty level means that the operational plan is more nearly a control device than a picture of the optimal economic outcome.

(5) The soviet enterprise-control system is extremely complex. This serves to increase the uncertainty level, and makes indirect control of enterprise behavior quite ineffective. For example, the control scheme makes relative prices a dominant factor in enterprise

product assortment decisions, but price adjusters are not primarily concerned with enterprise assortment adjustment.

(6) The soviet system is relatively stable with respect to organizational change, except for a tendency toward a cyclical organizational response to information flows about performance. For example, secondary control organizations tend to proliferate in the leadership's effort to improve its information about performance. A point is reached, however, beyond which additional organizations reduce the leadership's knowledge of performance, thus creating pressure for return to a simpler set of organizations.

(7) The command society can function effectively if the environment is sufficiently stable that performance routines can be developed and applied without frequent and large scale changes, and if vertical communication up and down the hierarchy can be substituted widely for horizontal communication between members at comparable levels in the hierarchy. The environment of the economy bears a considerable resemblance to that of the interwar Navy with respect to these and other relevant properties. However, the industrial sector of a modern economy tends to be more complex, to change at least as rapidly, and to require relatively more horizontal contacts.

(8) The command society produces a lower level of uncertainty and a more sensitive planning routine and plan adjustment process than the soviet system. Consequently its plan will tend to be more nearly a picture of the optimum.

(9) There is a relatively high risk of infeasibility with respect to the command society as applied to an economy. And even if successfully established, it is subject to a strong prospect of organizational instability with respect to certain kinds of environmental or organizational change, such as the development of efficient, diverse, multiproduct production processes, or a reduction in the indoctrination effort.

(10) Hierarchic economies will tend to concentrate on a relatively narrow range of goals in response to organizational economies of scale. The command society will not put as much pressure on participants as the soviet system, and may have to pay a price for this in terms of inertia. Incentives of enterprise managers will be oriented toward longer-run considerations than under the soviet system, and prices will be more fully integrated into the enterprise-control system.

(11) Illyria is capable of sustaining a long-run pareto optimal pattern of resource allocation with a relatively modest measure of direct control by the state, primarily over investment policy. Decentralized investment criteria tend to favor capital-intensive projects.

(12) In comparable environments, competitive Illyrian industries will produce at the capitalist competitive optimum only if profits are zero in the latter. If profits are earned, Illyrian industries will tend to produce less, if losses, more. Comparative statics are peculiar, with supply curves being less elastic in Illyria, and in some cases negatively sloped.

(13) Market imperfections are a major externality in Illyria. Monopoly price will be higher than competitive price; indeed it will be higher than the corresponding capitalist monopoly price. Oligopoly industries will perhaps tend to respond to market signals by increasing output less frequently and by less than capitalist counterparts. However, state control of most of the capital stock gives the Illyrian leadership an unusually powerful leverage against unwanted market structures: reorganization of enterprises. In principle Illyria should be able to avoid nontechnological market imperfections.

(14) Indirect macroeconomic control of the Illyrian economy can be effective. In fact the multiplier may be larger under comparable conditions than under capitalism. However there is a danger of unstable reactions in the vicinity of full employment.

(15) Of the three basic forms, the command society may be capable of the most flexible responses in the short run. The highly choice-decentralized Illyrian firm should respond quickly to market signals but is inclined to adjust by means of prices rather than outputs. The soviet organization is especially unresponsive within the limits of the operational plan time span. Given feasibility, the command society's plan-adjustment routine may produce reasonably quick and accurate responses throughout the economy to changes in data. However, with respect to interplan adjustment, the soviet system appears in a somewhat more favorable light, particularly when large reallocations in the service of narrowly conceived goals are contemplated.

(16) Intraenterprise relations are least prone to conflict in Illyria, most in the command society. There is broad harmony of interests within the Illyrian firm under most conditions, while in the command

society the indoctrination of the managerial group tends to accentuate the interest conflicts with workers which are built into the organizational form.

(17) Reorganization of the classical soviet system without eliminating hierarchic control of the economy requires simultaneous adjustment of planning and control procedures if it is to yield significant results. A choice-centralizing alternative, target socialism, may be more attractive in terms of efficiency than a Libermanism which attempts to restrict price flexibility.

(18) Illyria is relatively stable with respect to many kinds of choice-centralizing reorganization, but may be unstable with respect to certain alternative forms of socialist market organization.

(19) The Illyrian market provides effective incentives for resolving interfirm conflicts of interest, at a relatively modest organizational cost. Both hierarchies provide less effective incentives, which leads to higher organizational costs of resolution, as a higher proportion of conflicts must be resolved at inefficiently high levels of the hierarchy.

(20) The command society is oriented toward systematic and widely applied innovation, at the cost of less small-scale innovation and piecemeal borrowing, because of the strong need for maximizing the similarity of comparable activities throughout the organization. The soviet system creates incentives unfavorable to application of innovations, except in high-priority sectors and with respect to minor innovations which can be independently adopted by an enterprise at relatively low risk. Illyria should be reasonably effective at piecemeal innovating and borrowing, though the choice-decentralized incentives to introducing large-scale innovation may be weak.

Index

A

Abouchar, Alan, 178n
Adjustment, *see* Market adjustment
Aggregation, and command economies, 145-149
and plan making, 59-60
and target socialism, 172
Allocative problem of socialist economy, Barone's version, 18
Illyrian version, 183
original formulations, 16-17
Almon, Clopper, 55n, 57n
Arbitrage in markets and hierarchies, 70-71
Arrow, Kenneth, 35, 217n
Authority centralization, 7-8, 9, 10, 173-174, 256-257

B

Bain, Joe S., 6n

Balassa, Bela, 87n
Bargaining, in command economy, 136-139
in market and command societies compared, 117-118
Barnard, Chester, 66n, 105, 110
Barone, Enrico, 15, 18-21, 22, 23, 24, 25, 27, 31
Baudin, Louis, 108
Bauer, Raymond, 66n, 130n
Benster, C., 60n
Bergson, Abram, 14, 30, 36, 37, 39n
Berliner, Joseph, 66n, 85n, 88n,
Bichowsky, F. R., 109
Birman, I., 98n
Blau, Peter, 106n
Bornstein, Morris, 86n
Bourke-White, Margaret, 108
Brucker, Joseph, 108
Brutzkus, Boris, 16
Brzezinski, Zbigniew, 130n
Bukharin, Nikolai, 21
Bureaucracy, *see* Organisation; Hierarchic organization

267